'Fraudsters'

By the same author

Close quarters
They never looked inside
The doors open
Smallbone deceased
Death has deep roots
Death in captivity
Fear to tread
Sky high
Be shot for sixpence
Blood and judgement
After the fine weather
The dust and the heat
The Etruscan net
The body of a girl
The ninety-second tiger
The crack in the teacup
The night of the twelfth
The empty house
Death of a favourite girl
The final throw
The black seraphim
The long journey home
Flash point
Trouble

Stories

Game without rules
Stay of execution
Petrella at Q
Mr Calder and Mr Behrens

MICHAEL GILBERT

'FRAUDSTERS'
Six against the law

Constable · London

First published in Great Britain 1986
by Constable and Company Limited
10 Orange Street London WC2H 7EG
Copyright © 1987 by Michael Gilbert
Set in Linotron Plantin 11 pt by
Rowland Phototypesetting Ltd
Bury St Edmunds, Suffolk
Printed in Great Britain by
St Edmundsbury Press Ltd
Bury St Edmunds, Suffolk

British Library CIP data
Gilbert, Michael, *1912–*
"Fraudsters": six against the law.
1. Swindlers and swindling–Biography
I. Title
364.1'63'0922   HV6245

ISBN 0 09 468050 7

CONTENTS

Introduction	9
WHITAKER WRIGHT – 1845–1904 – The Squire of Lea Park	17
HORATIO BOTTOMLEY – 1860–1933 – The Swindler as Lawyer	46
IVAR KREUGER – 1880–1932 – Internationalist	78
CLARENCE HATRY – 1888–1965 – The Swindler as Victim	106
LEOPOLD HARRIS – *fl.* 1920–1933 – War in the City	135
JOHN STONEHOUSE – b. 1925 – Death of an Idealist	160
Sources	193
Index	195

ILLUSTRATIONS

between pages 96 and 97

Whitaker Wright and his solicitor, Mr Lewis, in court (*BBC Hulton*)
Horatio Bottomley (*The Mansell Collection*)
Bottomley leaving the dock (*Illustrated London News*)
Ivar Kreuger (*Illustrated London News*)
Directors of the Kreuger company (*Illustrated London News*)
Leopold Harris (*The Times*)
Capsoni, whose evidence caused a sensation in Harris's trial (*BBC Hulton*)
Clarence Hatry (*BBC Hulton*)
Stockbrokers stay late because of the Hatry case (*BBC Hulton*)
Hatry's case hits the headlines (*BBC Hulton*)
John Stonehouse (*BBC Hulton*)

INTRODUCTION

(i)

THIS book is about six men who came into conflict with the Law. Four of them, Horatio Bottomley, Clarence Hatry, Leopold Harris and John Stonehouse were tried at the Old Bailey. The trial of Whitaker Wright was moved, with unexpected results, to the Royal Courts of Justice in the Strand. The defence of Ivar Kreuger was reserved for an altogether higher tribunal. If I refer to them here generically as swindlers, I realise that this is an inaccurate description in the case of Hatry and Stonehouse and an inadequate one in the case of Kreuger.

Should it be asked why, after a writing life-time largely devoted to real and fictional murderers, I should turn now to swindlers, the answer is simple. I find them more agreeable as characters and a great deal more interesting as performers. Nor is this a last-minute switch of opinion. Many years ago I wrote, consecutively, a life of Dr Crippen and of Arthur Orton. Crippen's proved a sordid and uninteresting study. Such drama as it exhibited was concerned with his flight and not with his crime. Orton, on the other hand, was one of the most intriguing men I have ever encountered. But whilst everyone remembers the little doctor, who now recalls the Tichborne claimant?

So far as likeableness goes, it is a walk-over for the swindlers. Tennyson Jesse may insist that 'everyone loves a good murder', but how can we love the murderer? Read the roll. Frederick Seddon who poisoned Miss Barrow and sat up all night watching her die. George Joseph Smith who drowned three wives and economised on their burial. Desiré Landru who strangled pet dogs as well as women. Haigh with his acid bath and Heath with his whip. In this horrible profession the women keep pace with the men. Madeleine Smith and Mrs Maybrick with their arsenic. Mrs Dyer, the baby farmer. Kate Webster with her meat saw and carving knife.

Now look, by way of contrast, at the leading swindlers. There is Ernest Terah Hooley, to whom a chapter would certainly have been devoted had his activities not paralleled so closely those of Bottomley (at one time they were even swapping victims). When Hooley was brought to book in connection with the affairs of the Cotton Mills Company, Norman Birkett, who was defending one of the other directors, wrote to his wife: 'Hooley is a charming man and I like him very much. He smiled now and then with quite a *radiant* smile. I can well understand how he got his money from susceptible people.' When Whitaker Wright was buried, the villagers came with bunches of violets and laid them on his grave. And when Lord Kylsant had served out his term of imprisonment, for irregularities in connection with the accounts of the Royal Mail Company, his tenants demonstrated *their* views by meeting his train at the station and drawing his car to his house under an arch of welcome.

(ii)

The six men considered here, though disparate characters, had important points in common. They none of them came from wealthy or established backgrounds – three of them, Bottomley, Wright and Stonehouse from humble families. All of them made their way to the top of their chosen tree by guts and enterprise. The point of greatest interest is to isolate the moment when they stepped off the high path they were treading and took the first fatal step towards criminality. With murderers no such analysis is generally needed. Murders are committed in a fit of rage, or as a matter of cold convenience. Not so the swindler. He has further to fall. What prompts him to the edge of the cliff?

We know too little of the early life of Leopold Harris to speak with any certainty. In the other cases the picture is clearer.

Whitaker Wright said, in his own defence, that what drove him to manipulate the balance sheets of his companies was the underhand attack on his dearest project, the Lake View Mine. The attack was fuelled by a dishonest report from engineers who had been bribed, he alleged, by his competitors. He would not sit down under this. He counter-attacked and took the steps which led to disaster.

With Bottomley we have to look back a long way. After a deprived childhood he is working as office-boy-cum-clerk in a City solicitors' office. Here he finds that the only real money coming into the office is the result of an ingenious swindle by the senior clerk. From the moment that he grasped this interesting fact he never looked back.

Discrepant accounts have been given of Ivar Kreuger's decision to step from the stance of tough and sometimes unpleasant business man on to the path of outright criminality. The Swedish psychologist, Dr Bjerre, asserts that it was the ease with which he found he could extract money from Americans that tipped the balance. (It is an argument sometimes put forward to Judges, that shopkeepers who do not guard their wares create petty larcenists.)

In the other two cases there is no obscurity. The protagonists have given us chapter and verse. John Stonehouse decided, early in 1970, that the Labour Party, which he had supported and which had raised him to ministerial rank, was not going to win the forthcoming election. It would be out of power for a period. Very well. During that time he would devote his undoubted abilities to the field of finance. He could then return to the political scene with some solid capital behind him. What came of that decision we shall see.

The case of Clarence Hatry is even clearer. Until that fatal Sunday meeting at his house in June 1929 he had trodden the path of rectitude with care and sometimes to his own disadvantage. At that moment he stepped off it – and into the abyss.

(iii)

The subject matter of this book is fraud. When considering it, it should be borne in mind that it is an offence of comparatively recent growth. Murder and robbery, the forcible taking of the life or the property of another, have been recognised as anti-social from the earliest times and punished accordingly. With fraud the essential difference is that no physical force is involved. Only the force of persuasion. Until the middle of the seventeenth century the view of authority of this form of cheating might have been summed up in the robust maxim that 'a fool and his money are soon parted'. The legislature saw no reason to protect fools.

What elevated fraud to the Statute Book was the growth of London as a centre of world commerce in the eighteenth century and the arrival, in the nineteenth century, of the limited liability company. The joint effect was a realisation that honesty was a vendible commodity.

The so-called 'invisible earnings' of the City of London are no more than the money which foreigners are prepared to invest in its banks, its insurance market and its public companies. Their willingness to do so will depend, in part, on the production of sound balance sheets and profitable trading accounts, but equally upon less tangible causes. When Ivar Kreuger went to the American investor for funds he found that the main factor which attracted money in his direction was the reputation of the Swedish business man for probity. And when Mr Justice Avory was castigating Clarence Hatry (preparatory to sentencing him to the maximum permissible term of imprisonment) he said that the intolerable aspect of his frauds was that they 'disfigured the commercial reputation of the country', and implied that this justified his exceptional severity. When you consider the matter analytically this seems odd. A burglar may be imprisoned for his crime, but he does not get an extra year or so added on because he is 'disfiguring the reputation of this country for honesty'.

In saying this I am not palliating the offence of fraud. But I am suggesting that the modern attitude to it is symptomatic of the British weakness for taking a good thing too far. Instead of 'a fool and his money are soon parted' the modern tendency is to protect a man with money, by every conceivable means, from losing any part of it. It is the same paternalistic outlook that forces children to drink milk and their parents to wear seat belts. One of its most dangerous manifestations is an Act of Parliament of 1958 called 'The Prevention of Fraud (Investments) Act'. This was the statute that nearly brought Stonehouse to grief in the affairs of the Bangladesh Trust. It will be considered in detail at the appropriate point. Sufficient to say here that if a man writes to a number of his friends suggesting that they invest money in some company, he has committed an offence for which he can be gaoled. Curiously, the main class of people who are unconstrained by this Act are stockbrokers. Recent events in the City of London seem to raise the question, *'Quis custodiet ipsos custodes?'*

INTRODUCTION

(iv)

A final point. These six cases demonstrate that if you should, unhappily, become involved in fraudulent activity you are going to need more than your fair share of luck. The first piece of luck is not to be found out at all. But if you are discovered and brought to trial, then two additional strokes of luck are needed.

It is essential to be brought to book at the right time. If it is a period of general prosperity, then your sins will be regarded with the sort of vague public tolerance which seems to be currently accorded to insider dealings on the Stock Exchange and other financial jiggery-pokery. If, on the other hand, it is a time of financial crisis you will receive no tolerance at all. Indeed, you will probably be blamed for the crisis – as Clarence Hatry found out in 1930.

An equally important stroke of luck is to appear in front of the right judge. Ideally, law should be dispassionate and even-handed. It would be a bold man who would maintain that it is invariably so.

In two of the trials, of Harris and of Stonehouse, the judge was demonstrably impartial. Bottomley was not unfairly treated, but he was unlucky. His style of advocacy depended on shrewd cross-examination, punctuated by flashes of wit and on his unquestionable eloquence. It was a simple chance that he should have finished his closing speech as the court rose on Friday afternoon. It had been said that a week is a long time in politics. It is equally true that two days is a long hiatus in legal argument and feeling. By Monday morning the effect of Bottomley's eloquence was beginning to fade.

The jury then had to listen to the judge. This was Clavell Salter, a man of strict propriety, with no sense of humour, known when at the Bar as 'Dry Salter'. It is not suggested that he was unfair. From Bottomley's point of view it was almost worse. He was dull. By the time the jury had listened to him for the whole of the morning and part of the afternoon Bottomley's eloquence and wit not only seemed irrelevant, they had been forgotten.

In the other two cases the picture is darker.

The judge selected to try Whitaker Wright was Mr Justice Bigham. He was an experienced commercial lawyer and his conduct of civil cases earned general approval. In the criminal courts he was less acclaimed. His biographer says that he was 'learned, industrious and full of confidence', but adds that he was 'inclined to the failings of those whose minds work quickly, disliking tedious arguments and full of robust common sense, often taking short cuts'. The robust short cut which he took in the Whitaker Wright trial was that he pre-judged the issue. His exchanges with the defending counsel became a subject of much unfavourable comment. His partiality was not well received by his listeners. It must be rare for a judge, at the conclusion of a case, to have made himself so unpopular that he needs police protection.

But it was in the case of Clarence Hatry that the personality of the judge was most apparent. I have dealt at some length with Mr Justice Avory hereafter and will not anticipate what I have to say later except to state a personal opinion: that Horace Avory was an excellent advocate who should not have been elevated to the Bench. A barrister, particularly in defence, is entitled to pull out all the stops on behalf of his client. When he reaches the Bench he must abandon his personal feelings and rely solely on the evidence and the law. This Avory seemed unable to do. As his biographer admitted, 'He seemed unable to hate the sin without conveying a detestation of the sinner.'

Further, he regarded himself as being charged with the welfare of the State. This is an idea which becomes particularly potent in the case of a Lord Chief Justice. His appointment is judicial, but his eminence is almost bound to give a social, if not a political colour to his views. It is clear, for instance, that Lord Goddard looked on violent young delinquents as a threat to the established order. Of his predecessor, Lord Hewart, Lord Devlin has written recently, 'He has been called the worst Chief Justice since Scroggs and Jeffreys . . . I should say that, comparatively speaking, he was the worst Chief Justice ever.'

The comparison with Jeffreys is interesting. He too was reputed to be a sound lawyer. The ferocious extent to which he regarded himself as being charged with the welfare of James II's State will be remembered.

With which few words on the offenders, on the nature of their offence and on the judges who tried them, I leave you to a consideration of six men who, is a perverted way, made history between 1890 and the present day.

In the three years which have passed since I undertook this book, I have received assistance from a great number of people. If, in mentioning some of the main ones, I omit others, I can only offer my apologies.

My thanks to Sir Raymond and Lady Brown who not only produced a bushel of information about Whitaker Wright and his connection with Witley Park and introduced me to that notable eccentric, the Reverend Randle Fielden, but also showed me round the estate and took me under the lake to the famous underwater apartments. Also to Theresa Garolfo of Wappinger Fall, New York, for researching the American Press.

To Julian Symons, an acknowledged expert on Horatio Bottomley, for help which included the production of a rare volume by Carter and Bell which he rightly described as 'the master key to Bottomley'.

To the authors and publishers of books from which I have quoted, listed on page 193.

To Mr J. W. T. Crocker, the present senior partner in the firm of William Charles Crocker, solicitors, of Farringdon Street in the City of London, for entrusting to me the massive (and historic) brief which his firm prepared for Roland Oliver, QC, who led for the Crown in the case of R. vs. Leopold Harris and Others.

To Michael Pearson of Kingston, Surrey, author of *The Millionaire Mentality*, for reading and commenting on my account of Clarence Hatry.

To the Deputy Director of Public Prosecutions for finding for me a copy of John Stonehouse's book *My Trial* after the British Museum Library had denied that it existed.

And last, but not least, to the London Library for its unrivalled supply of reference books and newspapers.

WHITAKER WRIGHT

The Squire of Lea Park

WHITAKER WRIGHT was born on 9 February 1845, one of a large family of solid, middle-class, chapel-going, Bible-reading Cheshire folk. If he had been born fifty years earlier he might never have extracted himself from this background; but the second half of the nineteenth century was a period full of promise for an intelligent ambitious boy.

Nothing is recorded about his schooling except that his studies included inorganic chemistry; but they were wide enough to allow him, when he crossed the Atlantic in 1866 in search of his fortune, to set up as a professional assayer with a bent towards all forms of mining enterprise.

The capital he took with him was precisely £100; worth, in those far-off days, $500. What followed was, later, recounted by Wright to a representative of the *New York Times*:

'How did I get my start? Why, I went West, and as I made a little money I saved it and bought a few shares in a mine that looked as if it would be profitable. It was only a few dollars at first, but all the time I was adding to my investments. I bought a mining claim outright for $500 and sold a half interest in it for enough to pay me back my original investment and provide a working capital. The mine proved profitable, and a little later I sold out my remaining half interest for a good profit. Then I did the same thing with other properties, and kept on doing it until I was dealing in amounts that made a profit worthwhile.'

This sounds like a chapter from Samuel Smiles's *Self-Help*. One doubts, though, whether it was really quite as simple as that. In his early mining enterprises Wright demonstrated an inner toughness of fibre which was never to desert him. He believed in seeing with his own eyes and working with his own hands.

Years later, in circumstances which will be recorded, he became the friend and the client of Sir Richard Muir, who had a unique opportunity of learning at first hand something about this period of Whitaker's career. What follows is from Sir Richard's *Memoirs*, published in 1927:

> It was a rough and adventurous life. Once, while prospecting in Idaho, near the Snake River, where the Indians were on the war path, an Indian and his wife pitched their tents near his hut and he paid them a call. He gave the woman a plug of tobacco, an act which probably saved his life, for shortly afterwards a war party of Indians came to his shanty to kill him, but the squaw who had received the tobacco induced them to leave. They proceeded down the river, and massacred three of Whitaker Wright's men.

Wright once said, 'after the first ten thousand dollars, the rest was easy.' The word 'easy' clearly means different things in different contexts.

1872 was the start of the great mining boom at Leadville, Colorado, on the upper reaches of the South Platte River, between the aptly named towns of Fair Play and Climax. By this time Wright had capital. He purchased a mining property for a million dollars. The man who sold it to him offered to throw in, for a fairly nominal sum, the property next to it. Confident, by now, in his ability to judge a mining prospect Wright turned him down. It was a mistake. His own property turned out to be worthless. It was the adjoining property that contained the rich seam.

This is probably the origin of the comment in the *Dictionary of National Biography* (which awards Wright the honour of four and a half columns) that, at Leadville, 'he made and lost two fortunes'.

By 1876 Wright concluded it was time to settle down. He moved to Philadelphia, went through the legal process of becoming a naturalised American, and married an American girl, whose father had been killed in the Civil War serving under General Grant. He also raised a family. There is an apparent discrepancy here. Muir, who was in a position to learn the details from Wright himself, says 'Three children were born and died in the city, and he erected a tomb to their memory in the local cemetery which stands to this day.'

This sounds convincing. On the other hand, the *New York Times*, reporting after Wright's death, simply says 'he settled in Philadelphia where he was married and his three children were born.'

What is clear is that there were three children: a son (also named Whitaker) and two daughters, all of whom survived their father, and are mentioned as having been present at his funeral. It is not impossible to reconcile the two accounts. It was an age of large families, and there may have been three earlier children who died in infancy. When Harold Frederic, correspondent of the *New York Times*, later wrote a play, *The Market Place*, which was clearly based on Whitaker Wright (thinly concealed under the pseudonym of 'Stornmont Thorpe') he awarded him a nineteen-year-old son, just out of Eton, and two daughters, the elder of whom is seventeen, and both of whom are strikingly beautiful. These discrepancies and hints are mentioned only as an example of the obscurity which surrounds, even now, the American chapter in Whitaker Wright's life.

Philadelphia was the culmination of the first part of that chapter. It was from Philadelphia that he set up and promoted 'The Sierra Grande Silver Mine Company', and 'The Colorado Coal and Iron Company', both financially successful ventures. He became president of the Philadelphia Mining Exchange and a member of the Stock Exchange of New York. Numbering among his friends such eminent men as A. J. Cassalt, President of the Pennsylvania Railroad, and the financier Charles M. Schwab, domestically happy and prospering in business, it might have been supposed that he would settle down to a life of increasing wealth and respectability and leave behind him a name as one of the most successful tycoons of that exciting era.

The next decade has an element of mystery about it. Muir says 'from 1879 to 1889 when he returned to England his life is veiled in obscurity and little is known about him but it is certain he left Philadelphia because of some trouble with his companies.' The *Dictionary of National Biography* identifies this as the failure of the Gunnison Iron and Coal Company but this was clearly only one of a number of difficulties. When Wright finally decided to return to his native country in search of new worlds to conquer, he was certainly no longer a millionaire, in pounds or in dollars; but he was solvent. He opened a modest office in Copthall Avenue, not far from the Stock Exchange.

What did he look like, this tubby pirate, preparing to board that rich craft, the City of London?

He weighed sixteen stone, had a huge head with a receding forehead and small, near-sighted eyes behind gold pince-nez spectacles. His neck swelled out over the high old-fashioned collar which he affected. His receding chin was later concealed behind a beard modelled on the one worn by the Prince of Wales. He kept his portly figure immaculately clothed in frock coats cut after the American manner. Twenty-three years in the States had not deprived him of a North Country accent; which he made no attempt to conceal, considering that it was useful as inspiring confidence in people he did business with. And the business which he was now engaged in needed a full measure of confidence all round.

His earlier ventures had been companies which acquired coal mines, tin mines and, predominantly, gold mines. The companies which he now formed were of a different type. They were 'promoting companies'. The money which the shareholders subscribed was used in the business of acquiring other mining companies or options on mining properties, and, when the appropriate moment arrived, disposing of them. This was a long remove from the man who had superintended his own diggings on the Snake River with a shovel in one hand and a gun in the other; but a similar degree of forethought and nerve was a necessary ingredient in the operation.

It was an astonishing epoch. The biographer of Sir George Lewis, most famous of Victorian solicitors, later to be Wright's friend and legal adviser, records: 'This was high noon for an Empire. God was smiling, and on England most of all. Naturally this euphoric, expansive mood affected the financial climate. It was a quintessential bull market and it made the City of London a Tom Tiddlers ground for company promoters.'

The pages of the *Financial Times* are a porthole through which one can glimpse the prospects which entranced the fortune hunters of the nineties. There is hardly a number which does not carry the prospectus of some attractive new venture: 'The Ivanhoe Gold Corporation', 'The Bonanza Gold Field', 'Mimosa Gold Mines', 'Burbank Southern Gold Fields' (two of its newly discovered lodes were 'Golden Secret' and

'Last Shot'). From such alluring prospects which was the investor to choose? A young lady palmist offered advice and was, no doubt, as useful as anyone else. Lake View Consols advanced. Westralians were strong. Auxiliary Associated Gold Mines receded. It was all a fascinating game.

But it was a game which needed good judgement. The explorer, Harry de Windt, describing his journey to the Klondyke Gold Fields at this time, warned 'Let the gold seekers take their time and make prudent preparations.' It was advice which should have been heeded by men who intended to journey no further afield than the dangerous and fascinating square mile around Threadneedle Street and the Royal Exchange.

In none of the cases discussed in this book is it more necessary to appreciate what was happening in England at the time, politically and socially as well as economically; for without this effort of recall it will be impossible to understand the forces that contributed to Whitaker Wright's success and which, when he seemed to be on the brink of disaster, very nearly saved him.

Politically it was the calm before the storm, but the storm clouds were already gathering. Two decades of Tory dominance were closing. A *Punch* cartoon shows the red Indians on the war path, Harcourt and Morley, Rosebery and Asquith waving their tomahawks with the young Lloyd-George helping them to stick on their feathers and their war paint. Lord Salisbury and Arthur Balfour are peering apprehensively from their tepee.

The old order was threatened, but it had not yet been destroyed.

> The rich man in his castle
> The poor man at his gate
> He made them high and lowly
> And ordered their estate.

This verse of the hymn, which our more self-conscious age omits, was still being sung in the churches of the nineties. 'The tenantry bobbed in the villages', says John Betjeman, 'but money could now buy a position equal to that of good birth. An economist might say that the world was cracking. But most of those who sat back in their carriages saw nothing wrong with the horses.'

By the time the last years of the century had run out, with the old Queen still on her throne and the Prince of Wales waiting with increasing impatience in the wings, Wright had obtained a position of real eminence in the City of London. His modest office in Copthall Avenue had been exchanged for a palatial headquarters in Lothbury. In 1897 the *Financial Times* produced a pictorial supplement entitled 'Men of Millions'. It included Whitaker Wright, along with fellow captains of industry, Barney Barnato, Ernest Terah Hooley, Colonel North, Woolf Joel and Horatio Bottomley. In fact rather an inauspicious quintet of fellow financiers. Two of them were destined for prison, one was murdered and one committed suicide.

If one has to look for the real reason for Wright's success it was surely that he became identified in the public mind as a reliable guide through the maze of mining enterprises which were shooting up on every side. He was the man who had been there and done it himself. The practical man. The man who knew his way around. Writing forty years later, and viewing him in the perspective of time, Rufus Isaacs' son and biographer says 'Whitaker Wright was a far greater public figure than any of his successors in the art of juggling with the assets of a group of associated companies.'

We now have to look at some of these companies.

In 1894 he floated 'The West Australian Exploration and Finance Corporation' and, in the following year, 'The London and Globe Finance Corporation' ('the Old Globe') out of which Wright reserved for himself, in each case, 50,000 Founder's Shares. When the two companies were amalgamated with 'The New Globe', he took, in exchange for his founder's shares, a block of 605,000 shares in this company, which was to be the headstone of his financial empire. 'The New Globe' floated, in turn, 'Lake View Consols' (the name was nicely calculated to inspire confidence in the Forsytes of the day) and the Ivanhoe and other mining properties.

These were all known as 'Westralians'. In 1892 Wright moved across to the North American continent with the formulation of 'The British American Corporation' (Brit/Am) to take over certain options in properties recently acquired by New Globe in British Columbia.

New Globe and Brit-Am now co-operated in the flotation of a handful of further Canadian companies; 'East and West Leroy', 'Columbia Kootenay', 'Rossland Great Western', 'Caledonia Copper', 'Loddon

Valley', and the 'Nickel Corporation'; all solid-sounding enterprises with the name that counted behind them: the name of Whitaker Wright. The shares in all of them reached satisfactory premiums, none more so than Lake View Consols whose shares rose, on the strength of a rich strike of ore, from £9 to £28.

In 1898 a further important company was set up, number three in ranking order. This was 'The Standard Exploration Company' (Standard). In spite of its name it indulged in no exploration activities. Its object was to bring together, under one umbrella, a number of smaller companies in the field of mining and exploration.

Standard was a public company. Its shares were quoted and dealt with on the Stock Exchange. It is worth devoting a little attention to it, since it was a prototype Whitaker Wright creation and demonstrates the way in which he worked.

Its share capital was £500,000 divided into £1 shares. Of these 286,000 were subscribed by the public, and the balance of 214,000 by New Globe. Of this money only £80,000 was actually spent on developing the mining properties which it had brought together. The balance was available for stock and share transactions by Wright. And was, in fact, so used by him *at his total discretion*. It is true that there was a Board of Directors. It had been carefully composed. The companies being taken over were represented by Lord Donoughmore, who unfortunately died shortly after being appointed; by a Mr Spensley, who rarely attended meetings; and a Mr Maclery, who will be met hereafter. The other three members were Lord Henry Edward Pelham-Clinton, Lieutenant-General the Honourable S. J. Gough-Calthorpe – and Whitaker Wright. All three of them were also members of the Board of New Globe, along with Lord Lock and Sir William Robertson, under the chairmanship of Frederick Hamilton-Temple, first Marquis of Dufferin and Ava, formerly Viceroy of India and Governor-General of Canada. The other companies had on their Boards different permutations and combinations of those distinguished ornaments of the late Victorian scene. And all of the companies had one thing in common. They were run totally and exclusively by Whitaker Wright.

This may seem an odd state of affairs to a modern reader, familiar with the responsibility and duty of care which successive Companies Acts have laid upon directors. It was achieved in two ways.

In the articles of the companies (documents which set out the 'house rules') it was specifically laid down that the running of the companies was to be left in the hands of the Managing Director; who was, in every case, Whitaker Wright. His fellow directors were chosen not only for their impressive names and backgrounds, but on account of their almost total ignorance of financial matters. In later proceedings they were disarmingly frank about this.

> *General Gough-Calthorpe*: I don't suppose I would have understood what was happening even if it had been explained to me. It was a matter of City Finance.
> *The Official Receiver*: But you were a director of a Company engaged in City Finance. Had you any idea of your duty?
> *General Gough-Calthorpe*: As far as I could ascertain it was to sign my name many thousands of times on share certificates.

When there are directors such as these, a heavier burden than usual falls on the auditor who has to protect the interests of the shareholders, supporting them, if necessary, against the Board. The auditor in a Whitaker Wright company seems to have taken a more broad-minded view.

> *Mr Worters*: In the majority of transactions we were only asked to confirm them.
> *Rufus Isaacs*: What were you there for, then?
> *Mr Worters*: We were there to confirm the transactions of the Managing Director.
> *Rufus Isaacs*: Can you tell me anything you did to protect the shareholders?
> *Mr Worters*: I never interfered with the Managing Director.

These extracts have been given, out of chronological order, to demonstrate the position of power which Whitaker Wright held in the office in Lothbury which housed his consortium of companies. Their Boards were interlocking, they shared secretaries, the same staff of clerks served them all. They were an orchestra under the baton of one conductor.

As may be imagined, the personal gain to Wright was enormous. Nowhere is it truer than in the City of London that money makes money. It was not only the manipulation of his personal stake and his founder's shares. He was not averse to more direct methods. It is recorded that on one occasion he discovered that certain speculators (market 'bears') were selling ahead a number of shares which they did not own. This was a not uncommon procedure. The 'bears' had calculated that the price of these particular shares would go down, so that when the time came they could acquire them cheaply, and fulfil their bargains. What they had not reckoned on was the fact that, in this case, Wright's group of companies owned or controlled all the shares in question. He proceeded to force their price up. Settling day cost the bears £120,000, which went directly into Wright's pocket.

At this period, as Betjeman noted, 'money was able to buy a position equal to that of good birth'. It had not always been so, but it was beginning to be true in the reign of Edward VII. Even then it depended a little on how the money was spent. Wright bought the obligatory 'gorgeously furnished' London residence in Park Lane and a yacht which was appropriately named *Sybarita*; but the greater part of his wealth went into land. Which brings us to Lea Park, later known as Witley Park, for, if Wright's name is remembered at all nearly ninety years after his death, it is not on account of his financial wizardry, or the legal proceedings which it gave rise to, or even the dramatic conclusion of those proceedings. It is what he did at Witley, in the county of Surrey, that constitutes his abiding memorial.

The country west of Guildford and south of the River Wey is sandy soil, much of it covered with heath, and woods of larch and fir. The Brook stream meanders north from Brook village, up a shallow valley which shows on the map as a series of joined lakes and waterways, dividing and rejoining until they reach the Wey at Royal Common and Royal Hostel; for all this land belonged at one time to the Crown.

Witley Park received its first mention in history when it was sold in 1599 to Sir George More, who built on it the handsome Elizabethan manor which formed the centrepiece of the much larger building which later engulfed it. The estate passed from country gentleman to country gentleman, gradually extending its bounds, and taking in surrounding farms, until, by the close of the nineteenth century, it was a single unit of about 2,500 acres, surrounded by a wall fourteen miles long and eight feet high.

This estate, with its farms, cottages and lodges, including two old iron mines and forges (a nostalgic reminder of his youth) all safely tucked away within its boundary wall, may well have appealed to Wright as the counterpart of the business enterprises which he had gathered together and housed in his fine office in Lothbury. He imposed his personality as firmly on the one as on the other.

Great improvements were planned for the residence. One army of workmen was engaged to turn the old structure of mellow brick and timber into a building which could, without exaggeration, be described as a palace. Two new wings were added. At the end of the west wing there was a huge plant house; at the end of the east wing an observatory with a dome and a revolving roof through which its owner might observe the march of the planets and the phases of the moon.

There were thirty-two bedrooms and eleven bathrooms. The main dining-room measured 50 feet by 10 feet. A smaller dining-room, for family use, was three-quarters panelled in oak, carved by craftsmen brought from Italy. The ballroom, cedar-panelled, with an oak and walnut floor, had at one end a fitted stage, with dressing-rooms for the professional casts that performed there.

One of the most spectacular apartments was the bridal suite. It was formed of two rooms, each 74 feet long, in the shape of a capital L. The furniture was Chinese and Japanese, and at the junction of the two arms stood a Chinese drum-gong, more than six foot tall. The dressing-table, 32 square feet of it, was covered with a tapestry embroidered with the words, 'Love Maketh a Feast With Most or Least'.

Most, in this case, without a doubt. But if the house was no more than the habitation of a very rich man with a love of extravagance, it was the grounds which became fabulous, and by which Wright's memory became enshrined in local lore.

The English, as is well known, like a 'character' and have a weakness for eccentricity. Here there was something to feed on. Four or five hundred workmen were kept busy in the grounds day by day. Among them stumped the massive financier, armed with a great oak stick, pointing to new improvements and fresh designs. The workmen enjoyed this. Every time they saw the stick waving they said, 'There goes another hundred pounds.' Sometimes Wright would remove his coat and take a pick or shovel, fancying himself back, perhaps, on the Snake River.

'Put your back into it,' he would say. 'When I dug, I worked a lot harder than you're doing now.' The navvy he was addressing was not at loss for an answer: 'Maybe you did,' he said, 'but you were digging for diamonds.'

So the stories circulated; and the extraordinary work went on. For it was, in every way, extraordinary. Lea Park, as has been mentioned, stood in a well-watered valley. It was not difficult, therefore, to construct a series of artificial lakes. There were to be three main ones. The first was a square one at the top of the hill, from which the water ran down, over a cascade, to the bathing lake. From here the water was carried into the Brook stream and down again to the main lake. A turbine house at the far end of the main lake carried water up again to replenish the top lake.

The centre of this chain of waterways was the point at which it entered the main lake, and here Wright planned to place something which would catch the eye and encapsulate the whole project. In a trip which he made to Italy, to enrol artists to decorate the house, he had seen a vast, and beautiful, marble dolphin. He determined that it must form the entrance to the lake. The difficulties in the way of getting it there were considerable. When this gigantic artefact arrived at Southampton Docks the railway authorities announced that they had no rolling stock which could transport it. Undismayed, Wright had a special 'float' constructed, and sent down one of his own traction-engines to haul it. The precise route which it took is not known, but it must have been along fairly minor roads, since on more than one occasion the roadway had to be widened to permit the passage of this monstrous transport. On one occasion there was a more severe hitch. It would not go under a bridge. Difficult to raise the bridge, but the road below it could be dug out. So the dolphin arrived. It can still be seen, brooding over the main lake.

The twenty-five acres of this big stretch of water formed the central point of Wright's outdoor wonderland. His guests could go on it in electric launches, or, if they felt more energetic, in rowing boats and penetrate the creeper-covered openings which led to grottoes under the trees. Leaving the boat you stepped on to a path carved out of the rock which led into a labyrinth of galleries and hidden chambers.

But these were minor extravagances. The one which really caught contemporary fancy, and has been elevated into a myth, was the room under the lake. To build this the lake was drained and a construction of steel and glass was run out across its floor. The waters then returned and covered it. The effect was described, with some truth, as a fairy palace. 'Outside the clear crystal glass', says a contemporary writer, 'is a curtain of water – a beautiful green at the bottom fading away to the faintest green at the top where little white wavelets ripple. Goldfish come and press their faces against the glass, peering at you with strangely magnified eyes. On summer nights one looks through the green water at the stars and the moon, bright and large, magnified quite ten times by the curved glass and the water.'

Was it only social climbing that drove Wright to pour out his money in this way? Surely it was a personal compulsion as well. Unquestionably it gratified his sense of power. When a guest pointed out that the lake could not be seen from the house because a hill shut out the view, the hill was ordered to be removed. An army of navvies sliced it away.

In some cases the results of this demoniac energy produced a result which was almost ludicrous. There was the stable block, with its loose boxes and stalls for forty-six horses, the ceilings moulded in relief with scenes of the chase. 'A blatant sumptuousness', says Rufus Isaacs' biographer, 'which must have embarrassed the horses.' Increasing age and girth made Wright an occasional and unenthusiastic rider, but it was all very useful for his guests, the business associates and rivals, the aristocracy; on at least one occasion their heir to the throne, with his coterie of German financiers and high-born hangers-on.

Did Wright himself enjoy it? The only comment he is recorded as having made about it was that he liked listening to the rooks in the evening. An agreeable change, no doubt, from the grunting and bellowing of the bears and the bulls in the jungle of the City of London. Did he sometimes sit alone, in his sub-marine parlour, smoking a cigar and reading his fortune in the ten-times-magnified stars?

As the century drew to a close it certainly appeared that this fortune was solidly founded. In a book prophetically entitled 'Wealth and Wildcats' the author, Raymond Radclyffe, wrote. 'The very title, "The London and Globe" is an ambitious one and conveys the idea that as its founder and leading spirit Mr Whitaker Wright has said, its operations are world wide.

The value of its interests in Western Australia alone may be fairly estimated to be worth, at the present time, between four and five million pounds. Mr Whitaker Wright, than whom no man in the City of London has a higher reputation for financial ability and business integrity, is something more than a mere financier and is no juggler with millions.' This was written in 1898. The New Globe was demonstrably prosperous. In its accounts for the year ended 30 September 1899, and the report which went out to its shareholders on 16 October, for the meeting held eight days later, two figures caught the eye. The profits for the year were £483,000 and the cash balance at the Bank was £534,455. In his speech to the shareholders (written by Whitaker Wright) the Chairman, Lord Dufferin, said that this cash balance was the best evidence of the prosperity of the Company. There was, as could be seen, a balance available for dividend of more than half a million pounds, and it would have been possible to declare a dividend of 25% or even more. However, the financial policy of the company had dictated a more conservative dividend – as in the previous year – of 10%. The shareholders were well satisfied.

The corresponding figures in the following year were as good, and in one respect even better. It is true that the cash at the Bank was smaller: in this case only £113,671. But the profit was almost as good at £463,672 and the shares held by Globe in other companies had reached the imposing total of £2,332,632. Nor, said Wright, in answer to a question, was this in any way an exaggerated figure. In arriving at it a million pounds had been written off during the year for possible depreciation. It was the lowest possible valuation. The dividend would be maintained as before.

There was only one shareholder who was not satisfied, and this was a typical English eccentric, the Rev. Randle Fielden, who had been for 44 years the Rector of Muggington, and was a noted controversialist. In village matters he could be relied on to oppose enclosures of land and the shutting of footpaths, and to fight for rent adjustments when crops failed. He had not sufficient expertise to question the figures in Wright's balance sheets, but he had heard stories of the mansion in Surrey and its underwater conservatory, elevated by local myth into a full-sized underwater ballroom. He felt that a man who held dances under water was not to be trusted. Having purchased a few shares in the Globe, he made a point of attending the second meeting, in December 1900, and stood up to denounce what he believed to be a misuse of invested funds.

No one paid much attention to the views of a country clergyman, and the bulk of the shareholders left the meeting of 17 December thinking only of their good fortune to be investors in such a sound concern, and looking forward, no doubt, to a very happy Christmas.

Ten days later the New Globe announced that it was unable to meet its obligations. In short, that it was insolvent.

If a bomb had exploded in Lothbury it would hardly have caused a greater, or a more painful sensation. True, one or two weather prophets had forecast hard times for the Globe, particularly when it had sunk a substantial amount of capital in the new Baker Street and Waterloo Railway. Trains under London? Clearly a nonsensical idea! But no one had expected anything like this.

There were two immediate groups of sufferers. First, the members of the public who had invested in the Globe and now found their shares worth little more than the paper they were written on. Secondly, and less justifiably, certain firms of stockbrokers. As was to transpire later, the real cause of the Globe's collapse was its attempt to shore up the value of what had been one of its finest projects, Lake View Consols. The discovery of a rich lode, and the enthusiastic reports of mining engineers, had pushed up its £1 shares to £28. Then something (it was not quite clear what) had happened. Had the lode failed? Were the engineers mistaken? Had they been dishonest? The matter was to be thrashed out later in a civil action which lasted for nine days without any conclusive answer being arrived at. But whatever the reason, Wright had felt that it was necessary to maintain the value of the shares and this could only be done by buying them in as they became available. It was in the middle of this operation that the Globe suddenly put up its shutters. Brokers who had been acting on Wright's instructions found themselves holding large blocks of shares without the money to pay for them. Of the £1,603,436 admitted liabilities of the Globe, £1,600,000 was due to London stockbrokers; £365,000 to one firm alone. Now they could whistle for their money. December 30th was settling day. A chief feature of *The Times* on the following day was the announcement of thirteen broking firms being in default.

To understand what followed one has to appreciate the difference between different forms of wrong-doing. If a man robs a bank, gets away with a few hundred pounds, and is unfortunate enough to be caught with the proceeds in his possession, it will be a few weeks, or at the most a month or two, before he finds himself answering for his actions in court. When a man defrauds his fellows of several million pounds the wheels of justice turn, if they turn at all, a great deal more slowly. One reason for this is that such frauds are, by their nature, immensely complex. Mention has been made of a dozen companies which Wright controlled and there were as many again in which he had an interest. Money passed between them with the speed of a three-card trick. As Rufus Isaacs was to comment later, 'as Chairman of one company, you could write yourself a cheque for a million pounds as Chairman of another.' Wright objected to this. He said 'It was not the Chairman who was transferring the money. It was the Company.' But in a Whitaker Wright company this was a distinction without a difference.

The second reason was the fact that matters fell to be dealt with under the Civil and not the Criminal code; and civil law is more careful, less draconian and above all slower than the criminal law.

To start with it hardly seemed that Wright, personally, was in any trouble. On 14 January he held a meeting of Globe shareholders whom he addressed with his usual skill and aplomb. If they were prepared to trust him, all would yet be well. The company had assets which had been greatly undervalued and for which offers were being made. American purchasers had shown interest. And so on. The shareholders were convinced to the extent of voting for a voluntary liquidation.

There are two routes by which a company which is in difficulties may slide down to final dissolution. Of these a voluntary liquidation is much the more agreeable. It is an 'in-house' operation conducted by the company itself, and sidesteps a number of awkward questions which might be asked by outsiders. The alternative route is a compulsory liquidation. This is conducted by the Court. The affairs of the company are examined by the official liquidator and the directors are subject to public examination.

For the moment the Globe had succeeded in avoiding this distasteful alternative and when, in June, the liquidators presented their report they even went as far as to suggest that, if a little more money could be raised, the Company might still be put back on its feet.

But, meanwhile, public opinion had been hardening. The City of

London is a whispering gallery, and some of the most virulent whispering was being done by the defrauded stockbrokers and their friends. 'We do not believe', said *The Times*, 'that the real interest of creditors, shareholders or the public will be served by allowing Whitaker Wright to raise five shillings, or any other sum per share, and continue to carry on this moribund and mischievous concern.' 'Old shareholder' wrote congratulating *The Times* on having consistently advocated a compulsory liquidation. Other papers followed suit. The sands were shifting.

Then some of Wright's other companies came under the hammer. At the end of June an order was made for the compulsory liquidation of British America. Later in the year the Standard and the two Leroys went the same way. But still the main fortress seemed unassailable. *The Times* returned to the attack. In a leading article on 18 October it said, 'it would seem that the penalties of the law, however terrible they may appear on paper, can be no real deterrent to the rogue. The chances are, particularly if his frauds have been bold, large and complicated, that he will never be prosecuted.'

It is not possible to say whether this weighty pronouncement tipped the balance; but four days later the disillusioned shareholders of Globe at last voted for compulsory liquidation. In December the expected orders were made for the public examination of Wright and certain directors and functionaries. Those who had been following the matter closely noted that the order did not involve the Marquess of Dufferin and Ava.

These examinations, and the long drawn-out liquidation proceedings, proved curiously disappointing. They may be said to have covered a lot of ground without ploughing deeply into any of it. One of the difficulties was that the new Companies Act which furnished the official Liquidator with a more formidable set of teeth, did not come into operation until 1901, and could not be used to attack the two really vulnerable positions, the balance sheets of 1899 and 1900. Under the company code it was a criminal offence to issue a fraudulent prospectus, but this did not at that time extend to a fraudulent balance sheet. The other difficulty was that the liquidator, Mr Barnes, was not really up to Wright's weight. He could make suggestions, and Wright could deny them, or evade them. *Mr Barnes*: 'Do you agree that the assets of Globe were increased artificially between October 1st and December 5th 1900 by not less than £1,300,000?' Wright did not agree. He said that he objected strongly to the use of the word 'artificially'. He stuck to two main points. First that it was his duty to present the best possible picture of the financial state of the Globe, and if this involved the transfer of assets from one company in the group to another, that was a matter for him. Secondly that it was no fault of his that the Globe finally got into difficulties. This was due to the malpractice and treachery at the Lake View Mines. He added that proceedings against the responsible parties had already been instituted.

On one aspect of the matter Mr Barnes did score some points.

> *Mr Barnes*: 'Will you swear that you have not paid between £8,000 and £9,000 to certain newspapers to puff every company you have promoted?'

When Wright indignantly denied that he had ever paid any sum to any newspaper, Mr Barnes explained that he was not referring to payments in cash. The arrangement had been that a block of shares in one of Wright's companies would be sold to the journalist cheap and bought back at a higher price.

When Wright denied this, too, Mr Barnes produced his trump card. The stockbroker opposition had got busy and turning over their records had unearthed two actual contract notes: Loddon Valley shares, sold on 26 November for £84,562; the same shares repurchased on 27 November for £93,537. One of the names mentioned on the notes was a Mr Benjamin. He was a broker, and coincidentally, said Mr Barnes, the brother-in-law of the owner of *The Financial News*. This produced a good deal of laughter, but Wright was not unduly disturbed. It was the universal custom of the financial press, he explained, to ignore all issues in which they were not personally involved. Unless a journalist held a few shares in a company, he would be unlikely to take much interest in its prospects and progress.

But Mr Barnes had the last laugh. He observed that in the case of the Loddon Valley shares this interest could not have been a very profound one. It had only lasted for one day.

After Wright had left the stand, with dents in his armour certainly, but no fatal wound, a number of other directors were questioned. Mr Barnes prefaced this part of the examination by saying that he had decided that no useful purpose would be served by bringing Lord Dufferin over from Ireland. The Marquess was seriously ill. Nor was this merely an excuse. The position into which Wright had forced him had so upset the Marquess that he had suffered from a brain storm and had been confined by his doctors to bed. Nevertheless he had offered to appear. He was prepared to face the music however unpleasant. His offer was refused. He died the following year.

The disingenuous answers of General Gough-Calthorpe and others have already been noticed and these, too, caused amusement, but it seemed to the ranks of senior counsel who were in attendance that little real progress was being made. The leaders of the Bar were there with watching briefs: Gore-Brown, Otto Danckwerts and Rufus Isaacs. All of them, Rufus, in particular, were awkwardly placed. In preliminary proceedings in a criminal matter counsel normally reserve the asking of really awkward questions until the actual trial. They know that if they ask them too soon the defence will have a chance to work out plausible answers.

Rufus knew, too, that if there were to be a criminal trial it was fairly certain that he would be entrusted with the leading brief for the Crown. He was at the zenith of his career at the Bar, and clearly the best-equipped to deal with a man like Wright. 'Very quiet,' says his son. 'Very courteous, rarely raising his voice, he never resorted to browbeating, though he could be severe enough if the need arose. Nor did he ever lose his temper or give the appearance of being ruffled by a witness, however insolent or obdurate.'

But the real question was, *would there be any further proceedings?* Unless a prima-facie case of fraud could be demonstrated, it was possible that there would not be. Accordingly Rufus confined most of his questions to one point which he knew could be attacked, the profits shown in the Globe Balance Sheet of 1900. Some of the explanations offered by Wright were so naïve as to be incredible. Asked about a liability of £150,000 which did not appear anywhere in the balance sheet, he said 'Mr Malcolm, the accountant, overlooked the contract notes for £100,000. He had put them together with contract notes for £50,000 in a drawer and he forgot about them.'

> *Isaacs*: 'The result of this, and the other points I have just put to you, was to swell the Globe profits by several hundred thousand pounds.'
> *Wright*: 'I cannot be responsible for other people's mistakes.'

Under Company Law it seemed possible that he could not be. The remaining chance was that the Attorney-General might be persuaded to instruct the Director of Public Prosecutions to institute proceedings. He was pressed to do so. Towards the close of the year he announced his decision. He could not, or would not, act.

It was a difficult position for him, too. The post of Attorney-General is an anomalous one. He is partly the head of the Bar and a servant of the Law; partly a politician and a servant of the Government. Some holders of the office have leaned markedly more to one function than the other. Very few have managed to maintain the delicate balance which the duality of their position demands. The present incumbent, Robert Bannatyne Finlay, was unquestionably a politician first and a lawyer second. In 1895 he had become Solicitor-General, attaining the senior position in 1900. He was a stalwart Conservative and supported the Balfour government, and this at a time when conservatism was under growing threat from the Left.

The reason for his blank refusal to permit a prosecution is not easy to pinpoint. Staunch Church of England men faced with any departure from orthodoxy, used to say that it 'would give a handle to the Nonconformists.' It is possible that Finlay simply felt that to allow a prominent member of the Establishment to be dragged before the Criminal Courts would give a handle to the Radicals.

When the Attorney-General's refusal was known its political implications did not escape comment. In February a well-known Liberal Member, George Lambert, moved an amendment in the debate on the Address expressing regret that no prosecution had been instituted against the directors of the Globe.

In the circumstances this amounted to a vote of no confidence in the Government. The lawyers, as is usual in such circumstances, blamed the weakness of the existing law, but this really satisfied no one. Mr Lambert's motion was defeated, but by no more than a handful of votes.

The politicians having been defeated on points, the brokers once more stepped into the ring, led by a Mr John Flower. They had been quietly collecting affidavits from defrauded firms, and funds from their supporters, and in March Flower made an application in the Chancery Division for leave to institute a criminal prosecution against Wright.

On this occasion the prosecution was not to be under the companies legislation, which had proved such a broken reed, but under the Larceny Act of 1861. Under Section 84 of this Act it was an offence 'to make a statement in writing, known to be false by the person making it, in a material particular, with intent to deceive or defraud'.

Certainly the Globe balance sheets of 1899 and 1900 appeared to come within this definition. But there was a difficulty. A prosecution under this section could only be brought with the consent of a High Court Judge. It was such consent that Flower was now seeking.

This was the historic appeal to the judiciary over the head of the Crown and it must have taken people's minds back to the battles which had been won in the seventeenth century. On this occasion its chances of success were not thought to be great, and it would probably have failed, but for one fortuitous circumstance. The case came into the list of Mr Justice Buckley. He was a notable man in many ways. It is likely that he knew more about company law than anyone on the Bench or at the Bar. His massive work, *Buckley on the Companies Acts*, is still the bible of lawyers. More important even than this, he had a remarkably independent mind.

The hearing started in chambers, but on Buckley's insistence was moved into open court. 'It is a primary consideration of English justice', he said, 'that an accused person should have an opportunity of the case against him being heard in open Court.'

The main opposition came from the creditors, mainly on the understandable grounds that they did not want the remaining funds of the company wasted on criminal proceedings.

Mr Astbury, KC, on their behalf, said that the application to use the company's money in such a way was 'unprecedented', and added that 'there was no case in which the Court had sanctioned a prosecution when the Attorney-General had refused his fiat.'

At the close of the arguments Buckley reserved judgment. It was an important matter and he needed time to consider it.

No one was watching these proceedings more anxiously than Wright. He had removed to Paris but was keeping in touch with his home by telegram daily.

On 10 March Buckley announced his decision. He started by switching the blame away from the Acts of Parliament and on to the people using them. 'The apathy of the public in setting the Law in motion has – I will not say encouraged – but has at least failed to repress grievous frauds which have been committed and have too often gone unpunished.'

He had little sympathy for the creditors. The Act gave the Court complete discretion. It could order a prosecution even if a majority of the shareholders and creditors were against it: *provided there was a prima-facie case*. This was the nub of the matter. The Committee of Inspection (a body appointed to assist the liquidator) had voted by seven to one in favour of a prosecution. The eighth, a Mr Brigstocke, Buckley pointed out, rather unkindly, was Wright's broker. The only matter which had weighed with him personally, he said, was that the Attorney-General, for reasons known only to himself, had declined to instruct the public prosecutor. 'However, I decided that I ought not to allow my judgement to be influenced by the fact that even the highest authority at the Bar and the First Law Officer of the Crown has thought proper to decline to put the Public Prosecutor in motion. I must accept the responsibility of determining the question for myself.'

This slap in the face did Robert Finlay no harm. When the Conservatives went out he returned to private practice and when they came in again was rewarded for his loyalty with the Lord Chancellorship and a Peerage. But to Wright, Buckley's words sounded the knell of doom. 'Everything looks bad' said the telegram. 'Case for prosecution settled.'

Wright then made a fatal mistake. He decided to bolt. He booked cabins for himself and his niece in the name of Mr and Mrs Andreoni on the SS *La Lorraine* bound for New York. But a warrant preceded him. He was arrested on landing, and lodged in Ludlow Street gaol.

Whilst he was there pending service of proceedings for his extradition, the American press took up the case with enthusiasm. They were not subject to the same restraints as their confrères in England, where Arnold White, a well-known journalist, had already been fined £100 and served a term in Brixton prison for daring to attack the actions of the Attorney-General. The *New York Times* not only slated the British Government roundly for taking the stand they had, but insisted that there were sinister reasons for the Attorney-General's obstinacy: 'It was an open secret that many great and even royal names were indirectly involved in the proceedings. Friends of Wright had said that if driven into a corner he would tell who had profited by his transactions.'

Wright briefed Samuel Untermeyer, of the leading New York firm of

Guggenheim Untermeyer and Marshall, to fight the extradition proceedings and managed to delay them for several months. Finally, when their outcome seemed certain, he announced that he would return voluntarily to face his accusers. The British authorities, who had their backs up, refused to compromise. In early September Wright returned to England in the custody of the City Police. As soon as he landed he contacted his old friend, Sir George Lewis, who obtained bail for him in the then unprecedented sum of £28,000 and hastened to brief Rufus Isaacs.

He was too late. Rufus had already been instructed to lead Horace Avory for the Crown. The defence was therefore entrusted to Lawson Walton (a very competent lawyer, later Attorney-General) and Richard Muir, who was afterwards to make his mark as Senior Counsel to the Treasury in numerous Old Bailey trials.

Muir, who is a primary source of the facts of Wright's early career, held long conferences with his client; and never wavered from the opinion, expressed in his memoir, that he was not guilty of any criminal intent. 'His head', he says, 'had been turned by the unending adulation he received in the highest circles of the land', and adds 'that there could be no doubt at all that there were other people who should have been arrested with him.' He was confident that Wright would be acquitted.

One of Muir's early decisions, whilst the preliminary proceedings were dragging on at the Guildhall, was that the trial itself should not take place at the Old Bailey. He already knew Old Bailey juries too well. They would be confused by the figures, would not listen to the arguments, and would bring in a verdict of guilty on the grounds that a lot of people had lost a lot of money and Wright had run away. Accordingly he applied to have the trial heard in the Civil Law Courts in the Strand before a Chancery Judge and special jury, that is, a jury of more responsible men with certain property qualifications. The application was granted, and the case was set down in the list of Mr Justice Bigham, an experienced commercial judge. It was a decision which was to have unexpected consequences.

Rufus Isaacs must have given long and anxious thought to the tactics of the prosecution. All the points against Wright had to be fairly presented to the jury. They were set out in a document known as the indictment, but this was lengthy and so full of the phraseology and repetition dear to the hearts of legal draughtsmen that when it was suggested that each member of the jury should be supplied with a copy, the judge was to say, 'you might just as well give them all a copy of *Archbold's Criminal Pleading* or the *Encyclopaedia Britannica.*'

It was the recurrent problem in all fraud cases. How to combine comprehensiveness with clarity. Rufus decided to compromise. He would cover the whole ground as clearly as possible in his opening speech, and he would call the minimum of witnesses to support the facts and figures which he had put forward. By that time he reckoned that the jury would understand the outline of the case but might still be hazy as to the details. This obscurity he intended to disperse in his cross-examination of Wright. This was his plan and he adhered to it strictly.

The opening of his speech set the tone. After referring to the proceedings in front of Mr Justice Buckley he said: 'If the facts which I propose to put before you are true, it would be scandalous if they did *not* constitute a criminal offence.'

He was on his feet for five hours. Sir George Lewis, a shrewd judge, said that it was one of the most masterly speeches he had ever heard. Rufus had an immense territory to map out. He had to introduce the jury to twelve different companies, their constitution and inter-relationship and their star-studded boards of directors. Then he had to deal with the figures. He started with the Globe balance sheet of 1899.

First to come under the spotlight was that famous 'Cash at Bank' figure of £534,455. There was no doubt about the figure itself. This *was* the amount that had stood in the bank to the credit of the Globe on 30 September 1899. But how had it got there? On the previous day the cash balance had been a mere £89,000. Where had the balance of £445,455 come from? Item by item Rufus explained. For instance, a sale of Lake View shares by Globe to Standard had produced £158,424. There were two points on this. The shares had been sold at £23. Their market price at that time was £8. Also, finding themselves 3,000 shares short in this curious transaction, Globe had had to borrow them from Wright. No one was worried about this. The transaction was reversed as soon as the meeting was safely over.

Even more curious was the International Nickel transaction. This time the judge took a hand. He said, 'It appears that on 30 September Globe sold 80,000 of these shares to Standard at 18/- thus raising £72,000. Two months later Standard bought back the shares, at par, for £80,000. Am I not right in thinking that the real effect of this remarkable transaction was that Globe borrowed £72,000 from Standard for two months, and paid £8,000 as a bonus for the loan?'

Rufus agreed with this analysis; but it was not his real point. Certainly it could be demonstrated that the cash-at-bank had been built up in the course of a single day by loans disguised as sales and other devices. What mattered was what Wright had said about it. He had said 'that the cash balance was the best evidence of the prosperity of the Company, and that it could have been used to declare a dividend of 25% or even more'. The implications of that were quite clear. Since a dividend could only be paid out of profits, he was saying that the cash balance represented a year of profitable trading. Not, as was the fact, a day of juggling with the figures.

Rufus then turned to the balance sheet of 1900. It had been postponed, unlawfully, from 30 September to 5 December. Had it been made up to its proper date, instead of a profit of £463,672 it would have shown a loss of £1,600,000. A particularly bare-faced example of how this apparent miracle was achieved was the switch of all the losses on Lake View Consols into the accommodating books of Standard. A simplistic method of turning a loss into a profit. There was worse to come. It will be remembered that the really striking figure in the 1900 accounts was the figure of £2,332,632 representing shares held in other companies, and that at the meeting a shareholder had asked whether this was a reliable figure. He had been assured that it was a minimum valuation. More than a million pounds, said Wright, had been written off for depreciation.

Rufus proceeded to demonstrate that this was the reverse of the truth. The shares had not been written down, they had been grossly written up. One example of this: they included 410,235 shares in Standard at 20/3d. Their market value was 9/9d.

By the time Rufus sat down the atmosphere in the court had changed. Before, shrewd observers had wondered whether the charges could be brought home. The question now was whether, when he gave evidence, Wright could make his way out of the net that was being woven.

One other matter was clear. The judge was hostile.

The first witness on day two was a Mr Edward Flowers, corn merchant of Portsmouth, a shareholder in Globe. Yes, he had seen the 1900 balance sheet and yes, he had attended the meeting on 17

December. He had been much struck by Wright's comment that the shareholders could look forward to an Easter egg. (Laughter.)

The Judge: 'If you wanted an Easter egg you should have stuck to Consols.' (Loud laughter.)

This was a comparatively mild intervention. At a later stage Walton was driven to protest at the Judge continually eliciting merriment from the gallery by comments which were both flippant and unfriendly to Wright. It was tending, he said, to prejudice the jury.

Mr Justice Bigham was not inclined to be apologetic. He said, 'It is better that my impression of the arguments of the defence should be made plain to them, so that they might be able to meet their difficulties.'

Thus, when Wright entered the witness stand, it was clear that he had two opponents. Counsel and Judge. It was a daunting prospect. Rufus' schoolboy son, who was paying his first visit to a law court, said: 'I have never forgotten the picture of Whitaker Wright as the relentless cross-examination went on and he found himself forced into admissions or evasions which he must have known to be having an effect on Judge and Jury. He took on, more strongly every minute, the appearance of an angry and bewildered bull. As question after question went home like darts driven deep into his shoulder, he seemed to back away from the front of the box, as if to put himself out of range of his too nimble enemy.'

It is sometimes said that the first question in a cross-examination is the vital one, setting the tone for what follows. Rufus was very simple. He asked, 'Why did you run away? And under an assumed name?' Wright denied that he had run away. He had been intending to visit America anyway. It was a mere coincidence that he had done so on learning of Buckley's decision. As for taking the name Andreoni, it had been easier to get a berth on a foreign ship by giving a foreign name.

When a witness gives a totally implausible answer Counsel are sometimes inclined to rub it in. This was not the Rufus Isaacs style. A moment of silence, perhaps a glance at the jury, then on to the important points.

When, towards the end of the second day of the cross-examination, they got on to the 1900 balance sheet Wright had his back to the wall. It was that £2,332,632 worth of shares which finally finished him.

> *Isaacs*: You said in your speech that over a million sterling had been written off for depreciation. That was untrue?
> *Wright*: I do not admit it. You must take the report as a whole.
> *Isaacs*: You said, 'Over a million sterling'.
> *Wright*: I should have said, 'for loss and depreciation'.
> *Isaacs*: Have you any doubt that this statement is absolutely untrue.
> *Wright*: It was an extempore utterance.
> *Isaacs*: That is, as it stands, the statement was untrue.

Wright made no answer to this. No answer was possible.
And a little later,

> *Isaacs*: You said you had marked the Lake View Shares as low as possible.
> *Wright*: Yes.
> *Isaacs*: Had you, in that list of assets, marked them down a penny? (No answer.)
> *Isaacs*: You said you had marked the Lake View Shares as low as possible.
> *Wright*: Yes.

When Lawson Walton made his final speech – having called no evidence except the accused, he was entitled to the last word – he started by accusing the Prosecution of vindictiveness. This cut no ice with the Judge. At the start of his summing up he said, 'The prosecution was carried on temperately and properly. If Mr Isaacs' view was the right view, it was scarcely possible to use language too strong in describing it.'

Whilst Wright was listening to the summing up, people who were watching him maintained afterwards, they noticed a change in his demeanour. Whilst he was giving evidence, he had been fighting. Now he seemed curiously resigned. Sir George Lewis noticed that he was drawing the Roman figure VII on a piece of paper in front of him.

The jury were out for little more than an hour before returning a verdict of guilty. Mr Justice Bigham said, 'I have no option but to visit you with the severest punishment which the Act permits. You will go to penal servitude for seven years.' Wright bowed and said, 'All I can say is that I am as innocent as any person in this Court of any intention to deceive or defraud the shareholders.'

It was at this point that the decision to hold the hearing in the Royal Courts and not at the Old Bailey became a matter of crucial importance. At the Old Bailey, or at any other criminal court, the police would have taken immediate charge of the prisoner, and, if they had not done so before he came into court, would certainly have searched him. In the Royal Courts things were not done like that. Wright was led back by the Assistant Superintendent of the Courts and a tipstaff to the private room which had been made available to him during the trial. This was the room in which he had had lunch every day, and some of the things, including a bottle of whisky, were still on the table.

A short conference took place. Sir George Lewis's son was there, also Mr Eyre, one of Wright's oldest friends and a bail surety. Wright left the room to go the lavatory, and when he returned helped himself to a glass of whisky. Eyre asked whether they should telephone his wife. He said, 'No. There's plenty of time for that.' He took his watch and chain out of his pocket and gave it to Eyre, saying, 'I shan't have any use for this where I'm going.' Then he seemed to stagger, and slipped down on to the floor. A few minutes later he was dead. The tabloid containing cyanide of potassium which he had washed down with the whisky had acted quickly.

After the formalities of inquest and autopsy the body was taken down to Witley. The funeral was attended not only by his family and city friends but also by a large number of villagers.

'The village of Witley', said the *Morning Post*, 'where the kindness and generosity of the dead man are held in high appreciation, closed its shutters out of respect and sympathy. Villagers, who came from far and near, carried in their hands bunches of violets from the neighbouring lanes and copses in which an abnormal season has brought them prematurely into bloom. After the coffin of light polished oak had been lowered into the grave these simple blossoms were laid reverently on the mound which marks the earthly resting place.'

The villagers cared very little about what the Squire had got up to in the City. They only knew that he had been friendly and generous. If his behaviour had been eccentric it had done them no harm. Which was more than could be said for his successor, Lord Pirrie, who bought in many of the farm leases on the estate and allowed the farmland to run wild so that it would form a pleasance for his herds of deer.

There were repercussions. Not least, on the formalities at the Royal Courts when it was found that Wright had on him not only a second tabloid of potassium cyanide but a fully-loaded Smith and Wesson revolver.

Mr Justice Bigham came in for some deserved criticism for the way in which he had conducted the trial. Said *The Times*: 'from the opening of the prosecution he made no secret of his opinion of the prisoner's guilt. There was a levity of demeanour and speech which exposed him to the most humiliating rebuke from Mr Lawson Walton for the merriment he elicited from the gallery.' The *Morning Post* reported that the Judge had received a number of letters threatening him with personal violence and as a result had been accorded police protection.

At the end of that dramatic week *The Saturday Review* summed up:

> So Whitaker Wright used his knowledge and his brains to the very last moment. Courage and ingenuity, even in crime, command a kind of respect. We cannot echo the cruel glee expressed so freely over this man's end. The world is not altogether free from responsibility for the commercial frauds which have been so frequent of late. A man is largely what his world makes him. The insensate luxury of society and reckless speculation, stimulated almost to madness by the example of American and South American millionaires, are the causes which produce Whitaker Wrights. There are many men flourishing today in Mayfair like the green bay tree who are only luckier gamblers than the poor wretch over whose grave we will chatter for another twenty-four hours.

American comment was shorter, and more to the point.

The fact that a conviction could be obtained under these circumstances illustrates the difference between the administration of the criminal law in other civilised countries and our own. In England and Germany those who direct the affairs of corporations are held to a higher standard of responsibility. If the rules of law that were applied to Wright were to be enforced here, some men prominent in this community would feel very uncomfortable.

Maybe he should have stayed in America.

HORATIO BOTTOMLEY

The Swindler as Lawyer

HORATIO WILLIAM BOTTOMLEY lived an exceptionally full life. He was born on 23 March 1860, of working-class parents in the London suburb of Bethnal Green. His father was a tailor's foreman, who died when Horatio was three, and the institution which accepted this apparently unremarkable child was Sir Josiah Mason's Orphanage. Here he was instructed in the elements of English and arithmetic. From that unpromising beginning, by intelligence, by guts and by a remarkable facility for lying and persuading people that he was speaking the truth, he carved out for himself a life with every semblance in it of success.

And, indeed, until the sad epilogue came to be written, it was successful.

He made a great deal of money. He converted a Sussex cottage into the likeness of a manor house. He owned race horses which won Classic races. He owned newspapers and magazines, the best known of which, *John Bull*, was to become synonymous, in the public mind, with its founder. He promoted eighty companies with a total capitalisation of twenty-eight million pounds.

He was elected twice to Parliament; on the first occasion, in 1906, on the tide which was sweeping the Liberals into power; on the second, in 1918, as an Independent, and very much against the tide. After a shaky start he made a good House of Commons man. He was accepted, as an acquaintance if not a friend, by many of the eminent people of his epoch. None of this might have entitled him to more than the sort of posthumous notice which attends any man who advances himself by his own efforts. But he had one unique faculty.

There was one field in which his accomplishments have never been equalled.

The best known story about Bottomley – of which he was very proud, and which he often recounted himself – was that after his first great law suit the presiding judge, the famous Mr Justice Hawkins, had congratulated him in unstinted terms, had advised him to take up the law as a profession, and promised to donate him his own wig.

This was his chosen field. The field of litigant in person. A mere recital of the facts is staggering.

He appeared, between 1891 and 1922, in more than forty major trials and numerous minor ones. There were prosecutions for fraud, in which he secured his own acquittal. In a number of cases he and his publications were sued for libel, rarely with success. In others he sued for libel and obtained substantial damages. In fair fight (or perhaps one should say in moderately fair fight – his tactics will be examined more closely later) he took on and triumphed over advocates of the quality of Sir Charles Russell, Horace Avory, Sir John Rigby and Richard Muir.

Such a remarkable body of achievements has naturally not escaped the attention of biographers. Well-documented books have been written, notably by Julian Symons in 1955 and by Alan Hyman in 1972. One of Bottomley's admirers, Henry Houston, has given us the favourable side of the picture. His enemies have produced an (anonymous) exposure of the darker side, under the title '*The Gentle Art of Exploiting Gullibility*'. Bottomley wrote two accounts of his own life, and many articles about himself in the newspapers and magazines. The *Dictionary of National Biography* has awarded him three full columns.

Clearly, a mere summary, in the space allotted to it here, would be pointless. It is proposed instead to concentrate on the heart of his success: his skill and technique in legal warfare.

Many qualified solicitors practise for the whole of their careers without entering a court of law. If litigation comes their way it is left to a managing clerk – often an unqualified managing clerk – who sets the case up for counsel to conduct it. It is these subordinates, schooled by experience not by study and book lore, who comprehend the practical side of presenting a case to judge or jury. If a woolly defence is presented to their claim they will divine when it is essential to press for further and better particulars – and when it is wise to leave well alone. They have studied the strengths and weaknesses of different sorts of witnesses.

Above all they understand the secret of timing. An innocent sub-subparagraph may lie buried in a statement of claim delivered a year before; waiting, like a time bomb, to be exploded when the right moment arrives. A last minute subpoena, hauling an unexpected witness into court, may have a more devastating effect than a dozen witnesses summoned in a routine way.

It was at a very early point in his career, at the age of fourteen, that Bottomley was introduced to the ground rules of this fascinating game.

One of his first jobs was as office boy to a city solicitor. It was, says Mr Hyman, 'a very small firm consisting of the solicitor, who tippled, the managing clerk who was as crooked as a corkscrew – and Horatio Bottomley.' Few clients, maybe fortunately for themselves, entered its doors. The main profits of the firm came from the crafty managing clerk. For many years he levied, upon unsuspecting city firms, a totally imaginary 'County Rate'. It was a simple fraud, needing only a one-room office and a quantity of impressively headed stationery. Noting its success the young Bottomley may have echoed the words of the Tichborne Claimant who, that same year, had been committed to gaol for perjury: 'Surely men with plenty money and no brains were made for men with plenty brains and no money.' Before this ingenious managing clerk was finally brought to book Bottomley, on whom most of the routine work necessarily devolved, had mastered the nuts and bolts of litigation: the serving of process and the swearing of affidavits, the mustering of witnesses and the briefing of counsel.

After the managing clerk had been marched off by the police, Bottomley removed to a respectable law firm in Essex Street and continued his studies. These took an unexpected turn when he left to join the firm of Walpole's, official shorthand writers to the Law Courts. It is clear that his years with them exercised a decisive influence on him. Day after day this impressionable young man listened to eminent Counsel, noting their phraseology, memorising their gestures. The end of the nineteenth century was the heyday of the jury trial, the day of Edward Clarke and Marshall Hall and Edward Carson. Concentrating on the jury rather than the judge they employed a style of emotional oratory which started to go out of fashion as the twentieth century brought in the drier, more factual approach of Rufus Isaacs, Norman Birkett and Patrick Hastings.

Bottomley learned something from all of them. One of his assets was an excellent memory, and he was capable of expounding, in the manner of Rufus Isaacs, a set of complex figures, without apparent reference to notes: an accomplishment which always impresses a jury. On the other hand, if he detected that the feelings of the jury were on his side he could finish with a peroration which would not have shamed Marshall Hall at his ripest.

He had other assets. His appearance invited confidence. A photograph of him as Sergeant Buzfuz in a performance of *The Pickwick Papers* illustrates this admirably. The solid figure, squarely planted on his feet, the broad shoulders from which the gown hangs, the strong hands grasping a law book. The resemblance to Hardinge Giffard, Lord Halsbury, was marked; but what Bottomley liked to emphasise was the facial similarity between himself and Charles Bradlaugh; even going further, on some occasions and suggesting that his true father was not the humble tailor's foreman but the great radical and secularist. The suggestion has neither been proved nor disproved, but it may have been a belief in it which first emboldened Horatio to get up on to his feet. His other unquestioned advantage was his voice.

A barrister who heard him in court during the Hess case in March 1902 wrote 'The voice is one of singular charm and power. Low, melodious, strong, it is an admirable instrument for an advocate. For five hours on end Mr Bottomley addressed the jury. For the most part, his tone was conversational – now and again the low voice would rise to indignant heights – ever and anon as the litigant appealed to the noblest instincts of the jury, or declaimed in accents of scathing reproach and scorn against the flimsiness and inadequacy of the case he had to meet his voice would be hushed almost to a whisper, which only the startled silence of the Court made audible.'

These were the personal attributes that Bottomley brought to the job. There were other, more dubious, ones which must be described if the full picture is to be painted.

The first was that, not being a barrister, Bottomley was not bound by any of the rules of professional conduct which constrain the Bar. This does not mean that his conduct and language were unseemly. Far from it; the usual description of those witnessing his performance was that he was 'more barrister-like than the barrister opposed to him'. His stance and delivery were impeccable. He never lost his temper except on purpose and as a tactical move. But he was in a position to flout two of the main rules which bound his professional opponents. These were, and still are, that nothing must be stated as fact in a speech unless it rests on evidence which the speaker has adduced. The second is that he must not put forward evidence which he knows to be false. Bottomley drove a coach-and-horses through both of these rules. His supporters gave evidence which he must have known to be false, and he repeated in his opening and closing speeches both this suspect evidence and further facts of which he had produced no evidence at all.

A further point was that since he was acting for himself in defending a criminal charge he was normally allowed to speak from the solicitors' bench and not from the dock. A small point, but one which was bound to affect the minds of the jury.

Mention has been made above of Bottomley's supporters. These were of two sorts. There were the members of his own organisation, and clerks and accountants who might not be giving evidence, but were prepared to assist in other ways. They worked in the offices from which Bottomley controlled his many Company interests. The ethical standards of the office were not of the highest. When an office boy was caught helping himself to the petty cash Bottomley refused to sack him, merely remarking, 'We've all got to start somewhere.'

Such men were able to help the boss in a number of useful ways. If it was essential to the plaintiff that a minute book should be produced, it was curious how often it had been dispatched to one of Bottomley's corresponding offices in Guernsey or Paris. Or perhaps a member of his staff might have taken it home to work on it and left it on the train. In either case, of course, strenuous efforts would be promised to recover the missing volume.

On one occasion the opposition had obtained a judge's order enabling them to examine the share certificates and counterfoils in the London office. These were known to be available and any attempt to remove them would have constituted a serious contempt of court. When the examiners arrived they found drawerfuls and cupboardfuls of documents. Working through the day they succeeded in putting them into order for examination. When they came back the next day, alas, the confusion was worse than before. The documents were scattered all over the place. Someone must have left the window open. Also, an important section of share counterfoils was missing. As Bottomley blandly observed, 'You were the last people handling them. I can only suppose you took them away with you.'

This did not make it easy for the opposition to mount their case in the systematic way that the court requires. There were darker devices.

Leonard Levie had worked for Bottomley's Joint Stock Trust for many years. After a time it occurred to him that he might be able to butter his bread on both sides. Either Bottomley would pay him for what he described as his 'special services' – meaning no doubt the part he had played in the devices described above, and other unscrupulous manoeuvres – or else the opposition might be prepared to reward him for the evidence he could give if called as their witness.

It was a dangerous game to play with Bottomley.

It came to a point in 1908 when Bottomley and three of his associates were charged with conspiracy to defraud the shareholders of the Joint Stock Trust and Finance Corporation. Levie, who had by now changed sides, gave evidence of the curious arrangements made for books and documents in the offices of that company. Bottomley started his cross-examination by asking him, 'Did you, during the whole period you were in my service, ever report to me any irregularity in the office?'

Levie found this carefully phrased question difficult to answer. Having been himself fully involved in the irregularities he would, after all, have been unlikely to have reported them. He had to say 'No'.

Bottomley then drew his sword.

'Did you ever have a little lapse?'

'I might have done. I once had a little too much to drink.'

'Were you suspended for being intoxicated and fighting in the office?'

'I was knocked about and, I did not understand the position. I think it was arranged somehow.'

Levie was then forced to admit that, after being dismissed, he had written a number of letters thanking Bottomley for sums of money which he had sent him. When these payments ceased his letters became threatening.

Bottomley was now able to cast Levie convincingly in the role of a disreputable blackmailer and his evidence was correspondingly depreciated. Fair tactics, one might suppose. But there is a footnote in Hyman which opens up another possibility: 'It is practically certain that Bottomley had arranged to get Levie intoxicated in the office because he wished to get rid of him; but he was an expert in covering up his tracks.'

He has certainly covered up his tracks this time, for Hyman can offer no actual authority for the suggestion, but it has a horrible plausibility. The staged fight in the office; the correspondence (copies carefully retained); first sending money, then withholding it.

One final point. It was noticeable that when Bottomley made a joke in Court, and he made several very good ones, the laughter was hearty and immediate, and that the end of one of his perorations was normally greeted with applause. The applause was immediately suppressed by the judge, but not before it had had some influence on the jury as a demonstration of popular feeling. None of this was spontaneous. The claque was most carefully organised by an ex-medical student called Tommy Cox, a life-long friend of Bottomley, ably seconded by the leather-lunged John Harrison, a demagogue known as 'the People's Perkins'. The claque performed with equal efficiency in courts of law, at political meetings and on first nights at plays which Bottomley was supporting. They were paid for their services. Three shillings, apparently, in the nineties, but the rate rising to ten shillings as the new century progressed.

Thus equipped, and thus supported, did Bottomley wage legal warfare. His first major battle occupied the spring months of 1893.

The Hansard Publishing and Printing Union had obtained its Stock Exchange Quotation in April 1889. Its board of directors was headed by Sir Henry Isaacs, Lord Mayor of London, and included a banker, Coleridge Kennard, a publisher, C. Kegan Paul, Sir Roper Lethbridge and Henry Isaacs' younger brother, Joseph. Horatio Bottomley was Managing Director. Its share capital of £500,000 had been quickly subscribed. The investing public had confidence in such an impressive board and were beginning to associate the name of Bottomley with financial success. Had he not secured for the company (as its name signified) an exclusive contract for the publication of all parliamentary debates?

The first step was to put together a consortium of printing and publishing businesses. No time was wasted. That same April Bottomley signed, with a Mr John Phillips, a contract to purchase five companies: McRae Curtice and Co., Clement Smith and Co., Wyman and Sons, Vanoni and Co., and Henry Vickers. The overall cost to Hansard was £340,000.

There was still capital to be laid out. In May a Mr Charles Dollman had written to the Board mentioning that there was an opportunity for them to purchase the Athenaeum Printing Works at Redhill and the Bridge Papermills at Cullompton for £105,000. The Board dispatched an accountant called Dalton Easum to investigate (the name is spelt in different ways in different accounts but this seems to be the popular version). Mr Easum reported that the properties were worth the price being asked. His report was in front of the Hansard directors, with Mr Dollman's letter, on 26 August and the offer was accepted with the proviso that £70,000 should be paid immediately in cash, the remaining £35,000 'to be settled in account'.

The next steps which the Company took were not so well advised. The nominal capital was increased to a million pounds, and in order to encourage the public to subscribe this further half million a dividend of 8% was declared on the existing capital, involving payment out of £40,000. It is true that the profit for the year was declared to have been £40,877, but when the company had to find hard cash this 'profit' seemed somewhat elusive. In fact, at the time, there was little more than £1,000 in its bank account. Coleridge Kennard, the banker, came to their rescue. He negotiated a loan of £50,000 from the Debenture Corporation. If the public responded and subscribed the new capital all would be well. Unfortunately rumours were already current that the Hansard Union was not soundly based. Very few of the additional shares were taken up; and soon the Debenture Corporation was clamouring for payment of the 20% interest it had exacted on its loan. The money could not be found. The Company defaulted, and in May 1891 a compulsory liquidation order was made.

The next, and inevitable, step was the public examination of the directors; in particular of the Managing Director. These proceedings were conducted by the Official Receiver, Mr C. J. Stewart. Bottomley made it clear, then and later, that he did not care for Mr Stewart: 'What a vicious examination! Fraud and fraud only was the essence of every question?' Equally Mr Stewart did not care for Bottomley's answers. They seemed to him to be evasive.

In such matters no steps are taken hastily; and it was nearly two years later that criminal proceedings followed. The selected victims were Sir Henry Isaacs, his brother Joseph, Mr Dollman and Bottomley. The charges were, fraud and conspiracy to defraud. This is a simplification of an indictment which contained twenty-five separate counts, but it is what the sum total amounted to. Fraud, against Bottomley in connection with the five original company purchases. Fraudulent conspiracy against all four of them in connection with the Redhill/Cullompton transaction. Certainly the Company had been unfortunate, but how could any idea of fraud have arisen; particularly, how could it be suggested in the case of the five Company purchases? 'The properties', as Mr Justice Hawkins was to comment later, 'were thriving and genuine businesses. The scheme seems to have been rational, to amalgamate them into one large company.'

The prosecution was in the hands of Sir Charles Russell, the Attorney-General, assisted by the Solicitor-General, Sir John Rigby, and two juniors, 'Charlie' Matthews and Mr Gill, both of whom attained subsequent fame. Charles Russell was a host in himself, the most formidable barrister practising at the Bar, before the scourge of whose Irish tongue witnesses wilted and barristers and solicitors ducked into cover. He was, in a sense, too great a man for this particular job. He had other more important assignments on hand and the highest legal office was pending. After his opening speech, examination of witnesses and the day-by-day conduct of the case tended to be handed over to his juniors.

However, his opening made certain facts very plain. He dealt first with the financial side of the two transactions. His figures were quoted down to the last shilling and penny, but have been rounded off here for clarity. The five companies had cost Mr Phillips £238,000. He had sold them to Hansard for £325,000. A profit of £87,000. And who was this profit made by? Not by Mr Phillips because he did not really exist; or was, at the most, a sort of legal fiction. He was a clerk in Bottomley's office, and anything he made went straight into Bottomley's pocket.

Russell then turned to the Redhill-Cullompton transaction. The Redhill property had been bought for £7,500. There were some allowable expenses involved. Call the figure £8,500. Cullompton was a little more complicated, since there was an intermediate purchaser, none other than Joseph Isaacs. He had snapped it up for £15,000 from its owner, Mr Hall, and since there were liabilities to be taken over amounting to £12,500, in fact the only cash which had to pass was the balance of £2,500, and a cheque for this amount was paid to Mr Hall when contracts were exchanged.

The profit in this case was not as great as in the previous instance, but was substantial. Joseph Isaacs had sold to Mr Dollman for £22,000. Mr Dollman had sold both properties to the company for £70,000 with £35,000 'to be settled in account': there were some allowable expenses here as well but, on a cash basis, Mr Dollman's profit was at least £40,000.

However, it seems that Mr Dollman was an equally fictitious purchaser. He was Bottomley's brother-in-law. Any money paid to him was immediately paid over to Bottomley, a sensible precaution since Dollman himself was an undischarged bankrupt.

'If you are standing', said the Attorney-General, 'in no confidential position to a company, you are entitled to demand a largely enhanced value when selling to that company. If, however, you are in a fiduciary position to the buying company, Company Law, honour, justice forbid you to take advantage of that position . . . If the defendants are proved to be parties to a scheme by which persons were put forward as ostensible vendors, they were guilty of an offence against the law as well as against common honesty.'

He concluded, 'These facts reek of fraud, and are incapable of an honest explanation.'

Bottomley, sitting impassively in his place, must have noticed that the Attorney-General's summation, though vehement, was vague; there were a lot of conditional clauses hanging about. '*If* you are in a fiduciary position.' '*If* the defendants are proved to be parties to a scheme'. He knew more about fraud than Russell, and it was clear to him that if the charges were to be brought home, two things at least would have to be established. First, that the companies and properties purchased were not worth the money paid for them. Secondly, that an attempt had been made by the 'conspirators' to bamboozle the other directors, all of them shrewd business men, on this vital point. *And he noticed that the prosecution did not, apparently, intend to call any of the other directors to give evidence.*

By this time the outline of the way in which he would conduct the defence was becoming clear to Bottomley. To him a Court of Law was a chessboard. The pieces on it were judges, barristers and witnesses. The judge he encountered here was that notable figure Mr Justice Hawkins, known to the man in the street as ''anging 'orkins'. Known to the bar as a very difficult man.

Travers Humphreys, who was only twenty-five at this time, but has an important part to play later in this account, described him as 'an elderly but vigorous man, very sure of himself, very certain of the law', who had a beautiful voice with a slight purr in it 'resembling the sound made by a pleased cat'. One of his peculiarities was that he delighted in inconveniencing and upsetting the barristers who appeared before him. But he did not upset Bottomley, who managed to establish a curious rapport with him. One possible explanation is that it amused Hawkins to let Bottomley, the amateur, show up his professional rivals. Whatever the reason, their exchanges were amiable. The purr was a friendly one.

Bottomley (cross-examining): Would it surprise you to hear—?
Hawkins: No, no. I can't have that. His surprise doesn't matter one way or the other.
Bottomley: I thought I was following a time-honoured legal formula.
(Laughter, in which the judge joined)

When the prosecution produced Bottomley's diary, the judge asked for it to be handed up and read out '"The Reverend J. Macneil preached". Has this anything to do with the case? And on 25 May there is an entry "Paddington 11.45".'

'That is to prove that you can get to Exeter by the Great Western,' suggested Sir Edward Clarke, who was representing Sir Joseph.

One of the exchanges may have been due to Bottomley's quick wits. The Court was listening, with barely concealed boredom, to a rereading of all the questions and answers at the preliminary hearings. The point had been reached at which Sir Henry Isaacs was describing a visit paid by himself and Bottomley to the Cullompton Mill.

'They had been introduced to Mr Hall's family, and they had a very pleasant evening, as provincial evenings go – music and singing. Sir Henry Isaacs sang and Mr Hall prayed.'

Hawkins: Should that not be 'played?'
Bottomley: No. Prayed is correct.

It was not only the claque who laughed at this. By that time Mr Hall's anxiety to dispose of the Cullompton Mill had become clear to everyone.

And Hawkins was getting tired of the whole affair. In particular he saw no point in reading out pages of previous questions and answers.

'As a matter of curiosity, how many questions are there?'
Bottomley: My lord, there are 11,460.

The jury were not only getting bored, they were getting confused, and understandably so.

After Russell had concluded his opening speech a number of witnesses were called, presumably to establish and clarify what the leader had said. The effect they produced was exactly the opposite. Instead of repeating Russell's figures, they produced ideas of their own.

Frederick Barrow, a solicitor, had evidently noted the payment by Joseph Isaacs of £2,500 to Mr Hall on exchange of contracts. Being wedded to the idea that a purchaser normally paid a 10% deposit he seems to have assumed that the purchase price of the mill was £25,000.

The air became thick with figures.

Ernest Day, a clerk, said that Joseph Isaacs had bought the mill for 'the liabilities of the firm and £26,171'. The liabilities were £12,588. Mr Annan, the receiver appointed by the Debenture Corporation, put it another way. He said that Joseph Isaacs' profit was £8,590, which meant that he must have bought it for £17,581. When pressed as to how he arrived at this figure he said that Collumpton, including stock, had been sold for £26,000. When this was queried he corrected it to £23,000.

By this time the jury must have been in much the same state as the jury in *Alice in Wonderland*, who 'wrote down all three dates on their slates, added them up and reduced the answers to shillings and pence'. But relief was at hand.

On Friday 17 February one of the jurors, a Mr Hodge, failed to appear. Dr Pettifer rose in court to explain that Mr Hodge was incapacitated by a severe attack of influenza. The judge was sympathetic. 'No one', he said, 'would wish this gentleman to leave his house sooner than it is safe for him to do so. Attendance in court is a strain even on a strong man.' He ordered an adjournment until Mr Hodge had fully recovered. One feels that he was not sorry to have an unexpected holiday himself.

Mr Hodge's influenza must have been severe, since the Court did not reassemble until 14 April. In the interval something had happened which had a decisive effect on the trial. Sir Charles Russell, whose elevation to the High Court Bench was imminent, was invited by the government to present the British case in the Bering Sea Commission then about to open in America. He accepted, leaving the prosecution in the hands of his number two, Sir John Rigby, a man more used to the legal niceties of the Chancery Court than the hurly-burly of a criminal trial. Hawkins seems to have listened to his efforts with barely concealed impatience. 'Sooner or later,' he said, 'we *must* have our attention drawn to the precise criminal charge. We must draw a line between a criminal offence, a breach of trust, and a misfeasance. I don't say there has not been the sort of laxity one meets with in company cases. The law might well be amended. But in criminal cases we must be strict.'

Bottomley was allowed to intervene in a way which a hostile judge would have checked at once.

> *Rigby*: There is a further £18,200 in cash paid upon Mr Bottomley's own figures.
>
> *Bottomley*: Subject to the payment back of £10,000 upon the very same day.
>
> *Charles Matthews* (springing to the rescue): There was nothing of the kind.
>
> *Bottomley*: Mr Julian swore that he drew a cheque for £10,000.
>
> *Matthews*: Nothing of the kind.
>
> *Rigby*: When we know that Mr Bottomley had transactions of a very great magnitude with the company.
>
> *Bottomley*: What you know is not evidence.
>
> *Rigby*: I do not think you will improve your position by interrupting me in this way.

Bottomley thought differently. He continued to interrupt him at every opportunity.

The episode is worth bearing in mind, if only by way of contrast, when the closing case in this series comes to be considered. But Bottomley's principal target was not the opposing counsel. He made a point of selecting a villain for each piece, and this villain had been selected – or, one might say, had elected himself – during the preliminary proceedings: Mr C. J. Stewart, the Official Receiver. A tool in the hands of the Debenture Corporation, said Bottomley, who were using him to wreck a well-found and potentially prosperous company.

His cross-examination of Stewart was masterly.

When taken through the cash books, item by item, he was forced to admit that numerous payments had been made to the five companies who were the subject of the first alleged swindle. Since he agreed that he had not followed up these payments, they could now be safely labelled by Bottomley as 'expenses'. Then Stewart had criticised the 8% dividend declared by the Company as illegal, since it was not paid out of profits. Bottomley produced a number of cases in which Waterworks Companies had borrowed money to pay dividends. Their accounts were audited by the Board of Trade. Was Mr Stewart accusing the Board of Trade of dishonesty or incompetence? Neither, said Stewart hastily.

Bottomley then turned to more personal matters. A criminal information had been sworn against him. Why had it been kept secret? Surely he was entitled to know about it and not have it sprung on him during the hearing? The judge agreed with him. 'I think it is a very questionable thing to say that an information can be sworn against a man and then kept secret.' Gill, who was holding the prosecution fort at that point, objected, 'No, my lord, it was no secret.' But Hawkins was not having this sort of thing from junior counsel. He said: 'Mr Gill, please remember that the jury have to deal with the evidence which is before *them*. Not what was before the magistrate.'

The attack grew sharper. Mr Stewart was accused of personal bias against the defendants. He protested, 'I have no personal feeling against Sir Henry Isaacs or yourself. I have never expressed to anyone a desire to bring about a prosecution of either of you. Most certainly I never said that if I succeeded it would be a great feather in my cap.' He had fallen into a carefully prepared trap. 'Do you know a solicitor named Farman?'

Mr Stewart had to admit that he knew him.

'I am calling him as a witness. He will confirm that you made precisely that comment to him.'

Mr Farman was called, and did confirm it.

It must not be supposed, however, that Bottomley's tactics were simple harassment. When the time came for his final speech it could be seen that he had prepared his ground very carefully. First he dealt with the case against Joseph Isaacs. He had bought the Cullompton Mill for

£15,000 and had sold it for £22,000. He had taken his profit. There was no concealment. What motive thereafter had he to conspire with anyone about anything? There was no need for him to trouble the jury about Sir Henry Isaacs. Sir Edward Clarke, one of the shrewdest jury advocates of the day, had already extracted from Mr Stewart the admission, 'No single entry that I can point out shows that Sir Henry made anything.' The Isaacs brothers were honourably dismissed from the case.

In his own defence Bottomley hammered home three points. First, if there was a conspiracy to rob the Hansard shareholders by buying properties at an inflated price it must have been a conspiracy by the whole Board. Why had three directors been selected as guilty; and if this was the prosecution's idea, why had they not called the 'innocent' directors as witnesses? No. This had been left to the Defence to do. They had called Mr Kegan Paul. What had he said? 'We thoroughly and entirely agreed with every word said by Mr Bottomley, I had implicit confidence in his ability and integrity.' And, incidentally, how viciously Mr Gill had cross-examined him. 'He adopted a manner which reminded me of the hissing of a cobra.' Secondly, *was* the price an inflated one? What evidence had been called as to the real value of the properties? None at all. In fact, attempts had been made to exclude it. One such attempt had been thwarted by the judge. The Attorney-General had objected to the production of a report given to the Board by Mr Birt, the Hansard General Manager. Hawkins had insisted on seeing it. It said that Mr Birt, an experienced printer, had inspected the Cullompton works and had been impressed by their potential.

Finally, and most important, what exactly was it suggested that he and his so-called 'accomplice' Dollman had made out of these sales?

So far as the five companies were concerned he was prepared to agree, with certain reservations, the prosecution figure of £87,000 profit. But this was a paper profit. What had to be deducted were his expenses. The jury would remember how Mr Stewart had dealt with that point: he had queried them but he had not troubled to investigate them. He was throwing mud without even bothering to see if it was genuine mud.

As for the mills, the figures were even more revealing: £70,000 had been received in cash. Clearly nothing further was going to be paid. From this he had repaid Joseph Isaacs £22,000, which included his perfectly legitimate profit. The price of the Redhill property had been agreed at £8,500. There were other expenses which had raised the total laid out on the two properties to over £40,000. This meant that his actual profit was something under £30,000. And what had he done with it? Here Bottomley played the card which he had been hugging to his chest. He had at once repaid £26,000 to the Company by subscribing for £26,000 shares, thus demonstrating his confidence in the Company.

The prosecution had no chance, now, of investigating this remarkable statement, which was supported by Bottomley's confidential clerk, Julian, and the books of the Company. The shares were there, all right, registered in his name. If Bottomley had played this card sooner – at his public examination or during the preliminary proceedings – the prosecution might have demonstrated, as was almost certainly the case, that no money had passed. Now it was much too late.

Bottomley concluded: 'I refused to be a party to wrecking the Company, and have therefore been singled out for prosecution. I do not plead for sympathy. I ask you simply to do your duty. No criminal intention has passed my mind. I ask with confidence for your verdict.'

Vigorous applause from the *claque*.

The Solicitor-General then spoke at great length, reducing everyone to a state of apathetic inattention, but when, on the twenty-fifth day of this marathon, the judge summed up, it was clear that he was following Bottomley's line almost all the way. He had asked for accounts and they had not been produced. He had asked for independent evidence of the value of the mills and this had not been forthcoming. He discharged a final dart into Mr Stewart's hide, saying that he thought the Receiver had shown animus unbefitting a man in his position.

'In a complicated matter, one is apt to say, "Well, there is an air of mystery about the whole thing," but it is necessary to put down one's finger and say, *"There is the illegality".*'

The jury had to ask themselves whether this had been done.

In the face of such a clear hint it took the jury only twenty-five minutes to bring in a verdict of 'not guilty' on behalf of both the remaining defendants.

Sustained applause.

It was more than fifteen years later that Bottomley faced the second serious attack upon himself and his companies for fraud. This was an inquiry into the affairs of the Joint Stock Trust and Finance

Corporation. Again there was the examination by the Official Receiver (3,267 questions this time); but this time the preliminary hearing did not take place in Magistrate's Court, but in the Guildhall, in the City of London. It was responsible for the nervous breakdown of two Aldermen and ended, on its twenty-eighth day, in front of a third Alderman who found that there was no case to answer.

It was in so many ways a replay of the Hansard Mills case that to deal with it in like details would be repetitious. There was the same calculated confusion over figures; the same relentless cross-examination of witnesses; the selection, this time, of two 'villains', one of them being Leonard Levie, the ex-clerk referred to above, and the other a fellow clerk, Bowden, both of whom had been rash enough to offer evidence against their old employer. But now there was something more. By 1908, with a wealth of experience in the courts and in parliament behind him, Bottomley had gained in maturity and self-confidence.

His opponents on this occasion were of a different calibre. Avory and Muir. 'Avory for law, Muir for facts' was a saying in the Temple. They were a formidable team.

Richard Muir, later Chief Prosecuting Counsel at the Old Bailey, was, according to his admirers, a master at the marshalling of evidence. Norman Birkett, who disliked him, said he was 'a silly, pompous, self-opinionated, vain, hard, emotionless despicable ass'.

His leader was Horace Avory. Comments on Avory's character are reserved for later pages. At the moment all that is necessary is to say that he was an excellent lawyer, and normally reserved to the point of frigidity. It was one of Bottomley's most remarkable feats that he not only made him lose his temper more than once but bested him on actual points of law.

An opportunity arose when the Second Alderman, Sir Horatio Davies, took over from the first sufferer, Sir George Smallman. The question was whether the evidence of witnesses heard by Sir George could simply be read to the Court, or whether the witnesses should be recalled and heard all over again. When one considers that it was more the impression that witnesses like Levie and Bowden had made in the box, and not what they had said, which was important, one can see that this was a vital matter indeed to Bottomley.

It produced the following exchanges at the outset of the new regime:

Sir Horatio: I shall come to a decision on the evidence before me.

Bottomley: If the learned counsel says that he discounts the evidence already given and proposes to rely exclusively on the evidence he now calls before you I have no objections to make, except that one must assume that the earlier evidence was unnecessary, or redundant, or unsatisfactory.

Avory (annoyed): Of course one must not assume anything of the kind. Nobody but a lunatic would.

Bottomley: That is mere vulgar abuse.

Sir Horatio: I think, Mr Avory, you should withdraw that. (Applause from the gallery).

And again, when a Mr John Lever, an architect, was giving evidence Bottomley asked him, 'Did the Crown Solicitor tell you that he had been all over the country to try to rake up evidence against me?'

Avory: The witness must bear in mind that he cannot accept a statement that is embodied in a question.

Bottomley: I hear learned Counsel with the utmost amazement saying that you cannot put, in cross-examination, a fact that has not been proved. At a later stage (if ever we get there) and these facts are proved, I shall be met with the objection 'Why didn't you put it to the witness when he was in the box'.

Bottomley was right and the question was allowed. But that was not the end of the matter. For when Levie was being re-examined he stated that he had invested £2,000 for which he had received 'some scrip'. He thought the shares were worth £1 each.

Avory: But did you know that they had already been mortgaged?

Bottomley: I thought a witness was not allowed to assume a fact that had not been proved.

(Prolonged – and in this case deserved – laughter)

Knowing that City aldermen sometimes resented the patronising airs of judges and magistrates in the more orthodox courts, he closed on precisely the right note: 'I say in conclusion, Radical and Democratic as I call myself, I am one of those who honestly has always revered the traditions, the prestige and the power of this Corporation, and I do not hesitate today, hunted, hounded and harassed on all sides as I am, to come to you as not the least respected and one of the senior members of the Aldermen's Bench to give me sanctuary.'

Case dismissed. Prolonged cheering and the singing of 'For he's a jolly good fellow'.

When Bottomley was being sued for fraud he fought hard and unscrupulously. His liberty and his career were at stake. In the other types of case in which he was involved, cases involving charges of civil and criminal libel, slander, contempt of court and winding-up orders the atmosphere was lighter.

There were two notable libel cases. The first in 1902, in which Bottomley was the plaintiff; the second in 1911, in which he appeared as defendant.

Henry Hess, an Austrian by birth who had adopted South African nationality, had come to England in 1900 and had established a financial newspaper called *The Critic*. Each week one of its features was entitled 'The Black Book', the content of which can be guessed from its name. An article devoted to Bottomley appeared on the eve of the poll when he was making his first and unsuccessful attempt to obtain a seat in Parliament. There was no mincing of words.

> Since the day when this bare-faced swindler had the luck to escape conviction over the Hansard Company's frauds he has engineered one imposition after another upon the credulous public ... with the result that many of his victims are now in the workhouse, and he, without thinking of their ruin, is bribing with their money the unwashed of South Hackney to send him to Parliament. His place is at the Old Bailey, not at Westminser.

These were expressions which no modern journalist would have dared to use without the fullest evidence of justification. Bottomley was forced to sue. He may even have welcomed the opportunity. The case came before Mr Justice Grantham. Hess was represented by Mr McCall, KC.

Bottomley, as usual, appeared for himself.

Being plantiff it was for him to open proceedings, which he did in his blandest manner: 'So far as I am concerned unfortunately my name has been before the public somewhat prominently during the past few years, both in connection with financial concerns, and later as a parliamentary candidate. I am unfortunately well known in the law courts too, and if my name has not become eminent, at all events it has become notorious.' (Laughter.)

He then turned to the matter of the Hansard Union Trust. It had been unwise of Hess to open this matter since it was almost entirely creditable to Bottomley. When the Hansard Union Company had failed he had established a trust to alleviate the losses of the poorer shareholders. It is true that he had not managed to carry out all that he had promised, but he had paid into it a substantial sum of his own money and, as Sir Charles Turner, one of the Trustees, was to state in evidence, by June 1900 £9,042 had been distributed to the poorest and most distressed shareholders and £24,500 to others.

'Was this a fraud? Mr Hess would not leave one act of my life untouched by his poisoned pen. He tried to suggest that when I did a good act I did it out of duplicity and fraud.'

On the allegations of bribing the press to give him favourable notices he agreed that he had purchased *The Sun* (a short-lived evening paper, no connection with the present daily) and that a number of comments favourable to himself happened to have appeared in it.

At this point the judge was moved to intervene.

'Do you mean to tell us, Mr Bottomley, that you had not sufficient influence to ensure favourable notices?'

Bottomley's reply to this was an excellent example of his court sense. A weaker man would have said something about editorial independence, and would have been believed by no one. Not so Bottomley. 'Well, my Lord, I think I may say that I did acquire sufficient influence over the editor to make him put anything I liked in the paper.' (Loud laughter.)

After dealing with the specific allegations which he proposed to demonstrate as false, Bottomley said that he had made a bargain with the defence. He would submit to cross-examination if Hess agreed to do the same. From his point of view this was an excellent arrangement. He was a good witness. Hess was a very bad one.

Bottomley concluded his opening late on the second day. 'It has been said that Mr Hess proposes to return to South Africa. I ask you, members of the jury, by your verdict to award me such damages as will expedite his departure.'

He then offerred himself as a witness. McCall was not at his best. He started with questions about the Hansard prosecution. Justifiably Bottomley refused to answer him. 'I decline absolutely', he said, 'to reopen the Hansard prosecution.' The judge supported him. McCall then plodded, at great length, through a maze of other company transactions. Eventually the judge intervened: 'I suppose you have some reason for going into all these questions about the Companies but I do not know that the jury will be any wiser.'

The jury felt that this was understating the case.

One has to remember that this was a special jury – composed mostly of business men who had made some way in the world. They were both bored and vocal. One of them said, 'What we want is that some material case of fraud should be gone into.' Another juror supported him: 'The end is not likely to be attained by lengthy cross-examination. We would like some material matter of fraud dealt with.'

McCall did his best. He pointed out that he had not been allowed to inspect the private books of the company. A juror: 'Then how are we to form an opinion?' Taking this question as directed to him, the judge said 'I don't know.'

Nobody seemed to know.

Dismissed from the witness box, Bottomley called his principal witness, Sir Charles Turner, the ex-Chief Justice of Madras. He testified that Bottomley had paid £15,000 into the Trust and that it had been able to alleviate the distress of many of the shareholders. Bottomley always liked to finish his examinations on a high note. He said, 'Are *you* of the opinion that the Trust was a fraud from its inception?'

Sir Charles: 'If I had thought that, I should not have devoted a year to it.' This was received with applause so prolonged that Mr Justice Grantham threatened to clear the Court. When it had subsided, Hess took the stand. He had a rough passage in front of him, made no smoother by the fact that he had a poor delivery and an imperfect grasp of English.

He had to admit writing in *The Critic* that the Hansard Trust had not distributed any money.

Bottomley: And you know now that that is untrue?
Hess: Well, I had read it somewhere. It was in the *Times* report of the case.

Bottomley: Then let us read what *The Times* said.

McCall jibbed at this. He knew what *The Times* had said.

Bottomley (unperturbed): If we are not to hear this report perhaps I could mention another case. Did not counsel, in Sutherst v. Hess, say that Hess had had a very lucky escape from conviction? And, yet, within a few months, here he is, distributing more than a thousand copies of *The Critic* to private detectives to hand round in Hackney. Why should he do it?

Hess protested that he had no animus against Bottomley. Everything he did was to protect the public. To protect them from investing in Bottomley's companies.

Bottomley: Why? When you knew that two committees of inspection had given the companies a clean sheet?

A difficult question but there were worse to come.

Bottomley: What statements did I make about mines knowing them to be untrue?

Hess could not recall any actual statement.

Bottomley: You say that I used my shareholders' money to send me to parliament whilst they went to the workhouse. Names, please.

Hess did not actually know of any that were in the workhouse.

Bottomley: What about the allegations of bribery? Who did I bribe?

Hess did not know of any specific acts of bribery, but the *Sun* newspaper had been founded to ingratiate him with the public in Hackney.

By this time Bottomley knew that the jury were with him. His last question was much appreciated by Mr Asquith, himself a lawyer, who happened to be in court.

'Now, Mr Hess, do you still persist, after all you have learnt in the course of this trial, in these charges against me?'

'Yes. In all of them.'

'And you say you are worth £7,500.'

The suggestion was clear, but the jury was not prepared to go the whole way with it. After a short deliberation they awarded Bottomley £1,000 damages and costs.

In the 1911 libel case Bottomley appeared in his more usual role as one of the defendants, the others being *John Bull* and its publisher, Odhams Press. The plaintiff was a young man called Francis Joseph Ronald.

The pieces on the chess-board were different, but no less impressive. The judge was the notorious judicial humorist Mr Justice Darling. *John Bull* retained F. E. Smith, KC, and Odhams Mr Hemmerde, KC, with Harold Smith as his junior. Ronald was represented by that formidable Ulsterman, Edward Carson. But for all this galaxy of legal talent the man the spectators had come to hear was Horatio Bottomley, by this time as certain a draw as any actor on the West End stage.

The case sprang from the failure of the Law Trust and Guarantee Society. It was attributed to a series of ill-judged loans on the security of commercial premises, hotels and flats. *John Bull* had taken up the cudgels on behalf of the shareholders who had lost their money. In an article which appeared in July 1910 they attributed the loss largely to the incompetence of the Society's valuer, F. J. Ronald, son of the General Manager. 'Gross nepotism', said *John Bull*.

Carson opened his case on the expected lines. It was an unfair attack. The liquidation was not young Mr Ronald's fault. He was a qualified valuer, and had displayed great care and devotion in his work. But when Carson handed him over to the opposition for cross-examination it must have been with trepidation, fully justified by the outcome.

F. E. Smith and Bottomley were both in excellent form, and had been supplied with ample ammunition by their instructing solicitors.

'Why', asked F.E., 'had his father appointed him?'

Mr Ronald explained that his father had not appointed him. He had merely put forward his application, with others, to the Board. Now this was not a bad answer; but the witness made the fatal mistake of embellishing it. 'In fact, my father had said that he didn't like relations in the office,' 'Then, no doubt,' said F.E. smoothly, 'you can explain to the Court why your brother, your brother-in-law and two relations by marriage were all employed?' As F.E. was to comment in closing, 'We might apply to this case the epigram that the more the society contracted, the more the Ronald family expanded.'

By the time F.E. had finished with the witness it was clear that Carson was getting worried. He objected to the scope of the cross-examination. To what extent did the defendants intend to justify the alleged libel? Bottomley was happy to enlighten him: 'My attitude need not be in any way doubted, Sir. I charge the plaintiff with inefficiency, incompetence, and dishonesty.' His first question was 'Are you a member of the Surveyors' Institute?'

> *Ronald*: No. But I have been a member of the Auctioneers' Institute since 1905.
> *Bottomley* (innocently): Having, of course, passed their examination.
> *Ronald*: Actually, no.
> *Bottomley*: Is there any book or document in your office setting out the work you have done which had brought you in fees of between £10,000 and £12,000?
> *Ronald*: No.

The cross-examination contained two excellent examples of a Bottomley speciality, the prepared trap; a series of innocent-sounding questions which ended with a question to which no answer was possible.

As part of his duties Mr Ronald had been allowed to occupy one of the Company's flats rent free.

> *Bottomley*: Now this flat in St James Mansions which you occupy free of charge. Worth £350 a year is it not? Beautifully decorated, too.
> *Ronald*: Certainly, as an advertisement for the other flats.
> *Bottomley*: Are they all beautifully decorated?
> *Ronald*: We have decorated them as well as we can.
> *Bottomley*: Then perhaps you could explain how you came to be convicted and fined in 1908 for allowing a part of Albermarle Mansions to be let in a state unfit for human habitation?

The second example is quoted by J. O. Casswell, QC, in his book *A Lance for Liberty*.

Ronald had already been questioned at considerable length by F. E. Smith and Harold Smith. Bottomley, suave and unemotional, proceeded to demolish him as follows:
'Do you put yourself forward as an expert on the valuation of furniture?'
'Oh, no.'
'So when it became necessary to assess the value of the furniture of the Waldorf Hotel did you employ an expert?'
'Yes.' Mr Ronald named him. 'The best man in London.'
'Then why did you take it upon yourself to add £3,000 to his valuation?'
'I considered his valuation too low to that extent.'
'But you are not an expert.'
'No.'
'And he is.'
'Yes.'
'Suppose you had found a discrepancy of say £10,000 what would you have done?'
'In that case, undoubtedly, I should have sought the advice of some other eminent valuer.'
'Well then, now add up your figures again and see whether you have not made a mistake of exactly that amount.'
Mr Ronald had, in fact, made such a mistake; which Horatio kept in secret storage for his cross-examination.

For once his cross-examination justified the brutality of Bottomley's closing: 'The facts show that this sordid family group has battened and fattened on the carcass of that unfortunate company.'

But he had also learned the virtue of a show of moderation: 'All I have charged Mr Ronald with is dishonesty as a valuer. I want the charge put no higher than that. But when one considers the manner in which fees have been obtained one wonders whether the charge should not have been one of obtaining money by false pretences.'

The judge's summing up was largely in favour of the defendants, who had, he considered, exposed an undesirable state of affairs. He was unable to refrain from one piece of Darling-ism: 'It has been put against the plaintiff that he had passed no examination. Was it always necessary to pass examinations? Where did Napoleon's marshals learn their duties? What military academy did Murat and Massena attend? If these marshals had been asked to show their certificates from the Staff College they would have said, 'We will leave that to other generals who cannot show the number of victories we can claim.'

The jury ignored this flight of fancy and returned a verdict for Bottomley and *John Bull*.

Not all Bottomley's cases ended in triumph. People were beginning to understand how he worked; and to work out how to deal with him. His jokes and his repartee were as good as ever, but the result at the end of the day was not always satisfactory. The young John Simon was reading to the Court a letter in which Bottomley had postponed an appointment 'being very busy with the Budget.'

'I didn't know, Mr Bottomley,' said Simon, 'that the Government was consulting you on the Budget.'

This got the first laugh.

'I don't suppose you did, you lawyer-politicians know so little about what goes on in the house, you're so seldom there.'

This produced a second, and louder laugh. But Bottomley lost the case.

'He that runs against time' said Johnson 'has an antagonist not subject to casualties.' By 1920 Bottomley was running against time, and his casualties were mounting. In one way he had become a more difficult man to attack. By his activities during the war (all, as he pointed out, paid for out of his own pocket), by his recruiting speeches, by his lectures, by his visits to the front he had acquired political muscle. A public idol may have feet of clay but he is a dangerous man to attack.

On the other hand, people were learning. They were studying his tactics and working out ways of countering them. 'The only way to beat him', said the financier Osborne O'Hagan, 'is to hold yourself in. Smile when he insults you. Laugh more heartily than the rest when he scores a point against you.'

He had made personal enemies too. Carter and Bell, solicitors whom he had tried, and failed, to bribe. Most menacing of all, a man of Bottomley's own stamp, Reuben Bigland.

The difficulty which most of Bottomley's accomplices encountered when they were induced to give evidence against him was that, having been involved in his skulduggery, they hesitated to go too far from fear of incriminating themselves. Bigland felt no such hesitation. He was a fanatic. Many people went further and called him a monomaniac. His mania was the destruction of Bottomley. It meant nothing to him if he went down too. He was delighted to be arrested and wanted nothing better than to turn the trial into an anti-Bottomley show. He published a pamphlet, *The Downfall of Horatio Bottomley M.P. How he gulled poor subscribers to invest in his great Victory War Bond Club*. He put on a black mask and sold the pamphlet for a penny in the streets of London. Friends, similarly masked, sold it through the Midlands, with a special visit to the Trades Union Congress at Cardiff. Bottomley was forced to act.

The difficult decision was exactly what step to take. He could charge Bigland with criminal libel, but this was playing into his opponents' hands. Bigland had prepared a Plea of Justification in fifty-seven folios which he was longing to read out in court. Bottomley therefore decided to concentrate on a criminal charge of trying to obtain money by menaces.

This move back-fired. The criminal charge was dismissed by the magistrate at Bow Street and Bigland was committed on the libel charge at the Old Bailey. He was delighted. Pending the hearing he had been allowed out on bail. When he surrendered to his bail and presented himself at the Court a further difficulty arose. The case had aroused such public interest that the Court was crowded and the entrances strongly guarded. Bigland found considerable difficulty in getting into the building. Finally, he forced his way to the dock, and stood ready, with his Plea of Justification in one hand and a glass of water in the other.

The cup of victory was dashed from him. Marshall Hall, appearing for Bottomley, said that the prosecution had decided to offer no evidence. Bigland left the Court; surely one of very few men who had fought to get in and had been bitterly disappointed to be let out.

But if this was a victory for Bottomley it was a hollow one. His friends were dismayed, his enemies more rampant than ever. *The Times* printed the complete Plea of Justification, so the public were able to read it at leisure and form their own conclusions. It was a surprise to no one when Bottomley received a summons charging him with fraudulently converting money belonging to the War Stock Combination and the Victory Bond Club.

Bottomley's personal prestige in the immediate post-war years, bolstered by the popularity of *John Bull*, ensured that any attractive gamble which he proposed would be immediately taken up. The scheme in both cases was much the same. Subscribers to the 'Combination' purchased 15/6d. War Savings Certificates which would mature in five years and be redeemable at £1. The Trustees were authorised to raise £10,000 on the security of the certificates and distribute it in prizes to those who were lucky in the draws which would take place periodically. It was a safe two-way bet. Your capital was in government stock, slowly appreciating in value, and you had the chance of a large money prize. It was, in fact, almost a replica of the modern Premium Bond Scheme. But there was one significant difference. In this case the £80,000, which was quickly raised, went into Bottomley's own bank account.

The Victory Bond Club was even simpler. The contributor paid one pound and this gave him the opportunity of winning a £20,000 prize. A simple sweepstake. The money was invested in Victory Bonds, and the Bonds were under Bottomley's control. He explained, later, that he had tried to find reliable trustees, but failing in his efforts was forced to act as sole trustee himself. He also conducted the draw for prizes himself.

The task which faced the prosecution was to show what had become of the moneys so trustingly handed over; and to do so without allowing Bottomley to employ his normal tactics of confusion over figures and destructive cross-examination of witnesses. The pieces on the chess board were different once more, this time not to Bottomley's advantage.

The judge was Clavell Salter, and the prosecution was in the hands of Travers Humphreys and H. D. Roome. Humphreys was one of the group of Treasury Counsel, headed by Richard Muir, who conducted Crown prosecutions at the Old Bailey. By tradition these men did not take silk and he was therefore technically only a junior counsel; but if a junior, a very capable one. He also had some accountancy experience. Nor was this his first encounter with Bottomley. In 1914 he had prosecuted him at Bow Street on a charge of promoting an illegal lottery. The magistrate convicted him. The Court of Appeal disagreed, and Bottomley emerged, once more, triumphant. But Humphreys was learning. He had absorbed the advice of Osborne O'Hagan, and had made his plans accordingly. In his autobiography, written many years after the event, he puts down his success in this case to the deterioration of Bottomley. 'The clever scheming rascal, who had never confided in anyone over whom he had not such a hold that they dared not betray him, the liberal employer of other equally unscrupulous creatures like his dupe Bigland who eventually turned upon him, had become careless.'

This is unduly modest. Humphreys' success was due to minute attention to detail in preparing the case, and to keep his temper whilst it was proceeding.

He dealt first with the fate of the 'combination' funds. From the £80,000 subscribed, £10,000 had gone to a Mr Howard, a stockbroker to whom Bottomley had owed money since 1912, and £7,500 to the liquidator of the John Bull Investment Trust. Both payments, said Humphreys, 'in violation of the undertaking upon which the money had been subscribed'.

From the money of the Club – advertised as a 'New Road to Fortune' – £41,500 had been paid through Mr Cohen, Bottomley's solicitor, for the purchase of the *National News* and the *Sunday Evening Telegraph*. Further sums had been paid to tradesmen, including £1,050 to Mr Jelama the wine merchant, for champagne.

'For myself and a syndicate,' interjected Bottomley.

'Certainly.'

'I wouldn't wish it to be supposed that I drank it all myself.'

Humphreys allowed him this joke and moved smoothly on. It was noticeable that his witnesses were mostly junior men: bank clerks, cashiers, and shopkeepers. The advantage of this was that it gave Bottomley no scope for cross-examination. The cashier produced a cancelled cheque to self or a paying-out slip, and deposed that Mr Bottomley had drawn the sum shown on such-and-such a day. It was no use questioning him about why the money was wanted or whether payments had been made into other accounts. The cashier did not know and could not say.

Not all witnesses were of this type. It was necessary, for instance, to call Mr Cohen to speak of the newspaper purchases. Humphreys did so reluctantly, aware that he was one of Bottomley's friends. Sure enough, in cross-examination he said that Mr Bottomley had an interest in the bonds he deposited with him to raise the purchase price. This adumbrated the defence that Bottomley was going to put forward; almost the only defence possible, that the money he withdrew was reimbursement of sums which he had paid in to the Combination or the Club.

At one point Humphreys used one of Bottomley's own devices against him. He stated, as a fact, that £5,000 of the Club money had been transferred to a bank in Belgium to pay his racing expenses. This was too much! Bottomley shouted 'Rubbish'. This time he had himself fallen into a carefully prepared trap. At that date anyone wishing to transfer money abroad had to sign a Bank of England form, asking permission and stating what the money was required for. Humphreys produced the form, completed in Bottomley's own writing. 'Purpose of transfer: upkeep of Belgian racing establishment.'

The most damaging of Humphreys' witnesses was his last one. Owen Wyatt Williams, a clear-headed chartered accountant, had been appointed by the Receiver to examine the books of the Club. He was able to show that, far from the Club's being in Bottomley's debt, on balance of payments in and out Bottomley owed the Club £56,842. He apologised for the length of his evidence. It would have been shorter, he said, if the Club had kept books.

Bottomley got no joy out of his cross-examination.

'What books do you suggest I should have kept?'

'A cash-book, a ledger and a register of certificates.'

'Assuming a club of one million members would *you* have done the necessary work for £5,000?'

'Yes, and done very well out of it.'

'If 50,000 people were clamouring for their money back, that would require a large staff?'

'Yes. But it ought to be done.'

'If the scheme was honestly conducted, would there be any disadvantage in not having a large staff?'

To which Mr Williams said coldly, 'I always think it is an advantage to keep books.'

So the prosecution case ended, after three and a half days, and Bottomley rose, once more, to his own defence.

'Few ordeals are more trying than for a man to sit practically silent while all kinds of charges are being hurled at his head. It matters not how spiteful or irrelevant their remarks may be, or whether the evidence supports them or not.'

He went on to detail the very large sums he had paid into the Club – £200,000 in 1920 alone. He would call the manager of the Paris office to support him. Finally, almost in tears: 'I tell you, there are times in the silent hours of the night, when I think of all I have endeavoured to do to wipe out my sordid past and to justify the confidence of the fighting man, my troubles have almost overwhelmed me.'

When he presented himself for cross-examination the sharpest attack came from an unexpected quarter. Had he been paid, Humphreys asked him, for his efforts during the war? Had he, in fact, made considerable sums from his patriotic lectures?

Bottomley denied this, but found it hard to explain a letter to Farrow's Bank asking for a loan of £3,000, repayable at the rate of £200 a week, charged on his lecture receipts, which, at that time, were averaging between £300 and £400 a week. This might not seem directly relevant to the charges being preferred, but Humphreys knew his jury. The author of *The Gentle Art of Exploiting Gullibility* prefaced each chapter with a revealing quotation; none more apt than the quotation from Pope:

> Once, we confess, beneath the patriot's cloak
> From the cracked bag the dropping guinea spoke
> And jingling down the backstairs told the crew
> Old Cato is as great a rogue as you.

The cloak had been stripped off, and Bottomley was revealed as a swindler trying to bluff his way out of trouble.

Humphreys, in his closing, was almost brutally brief. Did the jury believe the evidence of witnesses and documents, or did they believe uncorroborated statements? The judge repeated this straightforward summation of the position. 'If these great sums of money came from the sources referred to by the Defendant, where are the documents, where are the receipts?'

The jury took less than half an hour to arrive at their answer to these questions. They found Bottomley guilty. The judge, after making the expected comments about 'a long series of heartless frauds', sentenced him to seven years' penal servitude.

Bottomley's last campaign was over. He had met his Waterloo. His spirit was not entirely crushed. During his sojourn in Wormwood

Scrubs he had from time to time to attend the Bankruptcy Court, where he appeared in civilian garb. A friend remarked on the creases of his coat. 'Never mind,' said Bottomley. 'When I get back I change for dinner.'

IVAR KREUGER

Internationalist

'His thirst for experiment was frequently due to his desire for testing how far the things that he had set in motion would develop. And he was never afraid to bear the consequences. If something dangerous was undertaken, Ivar had to have a part in it. But he did not care for slaving. Even in those days he appeared fully determined to arrange all the small unimportant things into a system. He did not waste time over side issues. His principle was the law of the least resistance and the realisation of the maximum results with the minimum of effort.'

The speaker was a school friend of Kreuger. He is quoted by George Soloveytchik, whose book appeared within six months of Kreuger's death. Of all the dozens of books written about him subsequently, in Sweden, in Germany, in America and in England, this one is, in many ways, the most revealing. The author knew Kreuger personally, and was much moved by the tragedy which had overtaken him.

It is a pity that the commentator is not awarded his name, for his comments must rank among the most percipient ever made by one schoolboy about another. It summarised, in a hundred words, a character that it took the noted Swedish psychoanalyst Dr Poul Bjerre a complete book to describe.

There are anecdotes galore about Ivar's schooldays. He was comparatively young when he died, and he was extremely famous. Everyone who had a story to tell was urged to tell it.

So we hear about the Kreuger system for co-operative cheating, under which each boy in his class concentrated on the particular subject in which he was most proficient and allowed the other boys in the favoured clique to copy his results in return for theirs.

An even less creditable exploit was when he succeeded in breaking into the study of the preceptor who was setting the end of term exams and copying the questions in the papers. These were sold to his friends at twenty-five kroner for each paper. Subsequently, by the same means, he seems to have got advance information about the results, and sold this too.

Then there was the Kreuger method of passing exams. Riding to school on his bicycle, conscious that he was inadequately prepared for the test in question, he happened to spot the Mayor with some of his Council in informal conference on the pavement. The next moment he had skidded to a halt in front of them, falling off at the Mayor's feet. The Mayor was all sympathy. He suggested that Ivar should go home and have his scrapes and scratches – not, in fact, at all serious – attended to. Speaking in a dazed and shaken voice, Ivar said, 'No. It is an important exam. I must do my best to be there.' The Mayor was much impressed by this display of fortitude. He walked with Ivar to the classroom and explained what had happened. He suggested that the master should go easy on the boy and allow him to pass. Which, naturally, was done, since the Mayor was the schoolmaster's employer.

Who was this boy with cool eyes, a sharp nose set in a pale face, and a mop of brown hair much darker than the blond of the traditional Swede; a boy who was capable of organising a co-operative of cheats, making split-second decisions and acting a part? He came from an entirely orthodox and respectable background. His birthplace was Kalmar, a prosperous seaside town, part of which lies on the mainland and the other part, across the Kalmar Sound, on the Island of Oland. It is some two hundred and fifty miles SSW of Stockholm, facing the East and the menace of Russia, against whom the castle of Kalmarnahaus had been built. It was close under this fortress that Ivar was born, on 2 March 1880.

His ancestors came from Germany; their name had originally been Kroger and they were bakers. The first of them to achieve a position of local prominence was Ivar's grandfather, Peter Edvard Kreuger, who followed his own father as a partner in the shipping firm of Kreuger and Jennings and followed him also in the distinction of being Russian consul, a post often held, in those days, by prominent local business men.

Peter, already wealthy, entrenched his position still further when he married Amelia Von Sydar, the daughter of the richest man in the neighbourhood. He liked to be referred to as 'Consul Kreuger', in the same way that his famous grandson, in years to come, liked to be called 'Engineer Kreuger'. The addition of a sobriquet seemed, somehow, to add a touch of reliability.

The consul's oldest son was Ernst August. He took no part in the shipping business, but starting at the bottom of the ladder rose to be manager, and ultimately owner, of a match factory in the adjacent town of Fredricksdahl. Since much of Ivar's story centres around the household matchbox, a short digression is necessary here.

History does not record the precise moment at which the flint and tinder of an earlier age became the match. But it is clear that, as first conceived, it was a fairly dangerous device. The original substance on the match-head was yellow phosphorus which, when scraped vigorously against a roughened surface, would perform in the fashion of a small firework. Readers of *Struwwelpeter* will remember that when Harriet was forbidden by her mother to light one she said 'Oh what a pity! For when they burn it is so pretty. They crackle so, and spit and flame.'

Gustav Pasch is generally regarded as the father of the safety match since he made two important improvements. He substituted for yellow the more inert red phosphorus, and transferred it from the tip of the match to the striking surface of the box. Another Swede, Alexander Lagerman, invented a simple machine for making matches; and the Jonkoping match boom got under way. As will be seen (when the subject falls into place with the main story) it was a boom which carried the seeds of its own destruction: too many factories competing with each other for too few markets. None of this was apparent at the date of Ivar's birth.

From his mother's point of view he was an ideal baby. 'Quiet, obedient and gentle,' says Soloveytchik, 'he gave his elders and betters no trouble of any kind.' His mother reported that he took his three meals regularly every day, and one at midnight, and never cried if he was fed late, or, for that matter, about anything else at all. He took care of himself. 'He was just an angel.' It seems as though the fairy godmother who hovered over his cradle presented him with many desirable gifts: placidity, self-control and ingenuity. But was there in the background, perhaps, one disgruntled fairy who had not been invited to the christening? Did she murmur in the infant's ear, 'I will give you a further gift. The gift of total amorality. You shall never be motivated or hindered in any of your actions by considerations of right and wrong'?

This began to be borne out, in a small way, by his behaviour at school, though it seems that his extracurricular activities did not make him unpopular with his fellows. 'It wasn't that he cheated,' said one of them, 'it was just that he was more successful at it.'

In 1896, at the age of sixteen, Kreuger left school and joined the Tekniska Hogskolen, the Technical High School at Stockholm. He enrolled for Mechanical Engineering, possibly following the example of the most colourful of his family, his maternal grandfather, who had emigrated to Pretoria and had risen to become Surveyor General to the Dutch government.

With the onset of puberty there was a development in Kreuger's character. At school his nickname was said to have been 'the sneak', though this may be a mistranslation of the Swedish word which could better be rendered as 'the clever cheat'. At college he was known as 'the solitary' or 'the silent one'. He had not abandoned his disposition for taking short cuts. When the task was to produce a model – in one case of a steam engine, in another of a drawbridge – he borrowed the models of a number of his more expert fellow students, copied a single part from each, and reproduced it in his own. This was prudent. If he had copied the whole of the best model either the owner might have objected or the plagiarism might have been spotted by the superintendent. By dividing his fraud into a large number of component pieces he baffled detection. This was a method he was to adopt later in his career, when investigators who suspected his bona fides found themselves lost in a labyrinth of interlocking companies and organisations.

It is at college that we can see planted the seeds of the character which ultimately emerged. 'Reticent,' says one biographer, 'distant, unpersonal, secluded in himself'. The face a little paler, a little more inscrutable. Was he, at this comparatively early stage, practising for the part he was going to play on the world's stage? In exactly this way, did

Philby, at an early stage, plan *his* public persona? Kreuger would have made a secret agent of the highest class.

His only physical activity was walking. Like Charles Dickens he was a compulsive night walker. But as he pursued his solitary course through the dark streets of Stockholm it was plots of a very different type that he was composing.

Also, he achieved one physical distinction. He became an expert pistol shot; a facility which he retained until the end of his life.

In August 1900 he crossed the Atlantic, in search of fortune. His early experiences, and his reaction to them, revealed his character clearly. He had landed in a foreign country, thousands of miles from home. He had £30 in his pocket, and had soon spent that. Yet from the dispassionate, amused tone of his letters home he might have been enjoying a subsidised holiday at the seaside. And he kept his wits about him. Some of the first money he earned, in Chicago, came to him when he found that the previous tenant of the lodgings, an architect, had left behind the almost completed plans of a small house. When the client turned up Kreuger explained that the architect had been called away unexpectedly, but added that being himself an architect he could take over the job. He was draughtsman enough to complete the plans. Result, a satisfied client and fifty badly needed dollars in Kreuger's pocket.

Of the jobs, and travels in search of jobs, which followed, two episodes are worth mentioning as demonstrations of his character. Of the first we have to rely on his own account. He was, he says, taking a trip on an excursion boat from New Orleans when a small girl fell into the sea. He was a good swimmer, jumped in after her and supported her until a boat could be launched to pick them up. For this he was awarded a medal, of which he was very proud and which, later in his career, he kept on his desk. He never actually showed it to people, but if they happened to notice it he was prepared, with becoming modesty, to tell them the story; which may have been true, but people who examined the medal closely pointed out that although it had an inscription ('Only a hero would risk his life for others') it did not carry his name. And the date on it, 6 November 1900, did not seem to correspond with the times he was in New Orleans, before or after his visit to Vera Cruz.

About the second episode there was no doubt, and it demonstrates the same sort of enterprise and disregard for danger that led Whitaker Wright to the Snake River. Volunteers were wanted to build bridges at

Vera Cruz in Mexico, in those days a notoriously unhealthy part of the globe. He went, with ten other engineers. There was a rhyme about the East Coast of Africa: 'The Gulf of Benin, the Gulf of Benin. One came out where three went in.' The proportions in this case were even starker. Ten of the eleven perished from yellow fever or from the attentions of the local Indians. Kreuger alone returned, and he came out with the after effects of fever which weakened his heart and affected his eyesight; and were to exempt him from national service.

After a brief spell back in Sweden to recuperate, it was New York once more. Here, possibly as a result of his experiences in Vera Cruz, he seems to have had no difficulty in finding work, first for Purdy and Henderson, then for the Fuller Construction Company. He also found a friend, one of the closest he ever made, a young Norwegian called Anders Jordahl. When an attractive proposal was made to him by Waring and Gillow, to go to Johannesburg and take part in the designing of the engineering work for the Carlton Hotel, he refused the offer, but put in such a warm recommendation for Jordahl that his friend got the job. A little later Jordahl reciprocated by securing a job for Kreuger to oversee the installation of the steelwork which Jordahl had designed.

The next step was an unexpected one. With their joint capital the two young men opened a restaurant, working there themselves in the evenings. It was a success, too. But oddly enough a success that was never to be mentioned to any of their family or friends in Sweden. They must have considered serving food and washing dishes to be below the dignity of up-and-coming engineers. However, the money was useful to Kreuger, as also were his gains from trafficking in gold. Together they were sufficient to fund a leisurely journey back, which took him first to India and after that to Paris and London. But all the time America was calling. America was the new centre of the financial world. It was the place for a young man of ambition.

But in what direction, precisely, was that ambition to lead? He wrote to his family, 'I am bursting with ideas. I am only wondering which to carry out first.' Chance played a part.

At that time he was manager of the Consolidated Engineering Company and one of his jobs was to oversee a number of new buildings at Syracuse University. The material which was being used was reinforced concrete, which is concrete formed round an inner core of iron rods. The iron, to stand up to this usage, has to be of a special type. Technical matters of this sort always interested Kreuger. He made enquiries, and found that the holder of the patent for this iron was one Julius Kahn, who happened to be in Syracuse. Kreuger arranged to meet him. Both men liked each other, and Kahn suggested that Kreuger might represent him in Europe where, at that time, reinforced concrete structures were practically unknown. Kreuger jumped at the idea. For one thing he was longing to introduce American technology and American hustle to his sleepy, backward homeland. There was only one snag.

When, on his way back to Sweden, he stopped off in London to make his number good with the English end of the Kahn firm he found that someone was threatening to get ahead of him. A twenty-five-year-old engineer, Paul Toll from Stockholm (be it noted that Kreuger himself was only twenty-eight at the time) had already offered to represent the Kahn firm in Sweden. Instead of insisting, as many men would have done, on the prior rights he had obtained in America, Kreuger at once proposed a joint venture.

So the world-famous firm of Kreuger and Toll was born.

It was formed on generous terms, since Toll put up no money and Kreuger supplied all the capital (which he borrowed from his father). The division of labour was that Toll, the practical man, acted as overseer or clerk of the works at the building site, while Kreuger, from their two-roomed office, handled the logistics – the paperwork, the supplies of raw material, the dealings with the local authorities over matters of safety and health and (more important than any of these) the scrupulous costing of each project. The Swedish building fraternity observed the efforts of these two young men with the mixture of uneasiness and cynicism always accorded to the arrival of energetic newcomers in an exciting field. They were soon to change their minds. The new boys' opportunity came when Kreuger secured the contract to put up the Myrstedt & Stern building at the corner of Kungsgaten and Norrlandsgaten, in the centre of Stockholm.

One of Kreuger's biographers suggested that Swedish building firms often employed the tactics of delayed construction. When a building was half completed they would inform the unhappy owner that some unforeseen development (escalation of the cost of materials or workmen's wages) necessitated an increase in the price they had quoted. This placed the owner in a difficult position. He had either to pay up, or spend even more money trying to get another firm to finish the job.

Possibly with this in mind, the Myrstedt and Stern lawyers inserted a clause in their contract under which Kreuger and Toll were obliged to make a penalty payment of twelve hundred dollars a day if the work was not completed in four months. This was reckoned to be a fairly short time for a building of this size, and they did not, therefore, raise any objection when Kreuger, in turn, inserted a clause which called for a similar daily payment for each day that the building was completed ahead of schedule.

This was the opportunity for a demonstration of modern American methods. It was midwinter, and night-work was thought to be out of the question. Kreuger disagreed. He had the building draped in canvas covers, fires were lit to supply warmth and light, double shifts were worked and double wages were paid.

Stockholm was not enthusiastic about this exhibition of American hustle. People living or working in the neighbourhood complained of the unceasing grind of the concrete mixers. (Luckily for them that this was before the days of pneumatic drills and power-riveting.) Somehow their complaints were overcome or sidestepped. 'It will only be for eight weeks,' Kreuger promised. And, incredibly, this was achieved. The building was completed nearly sixty days ahead of schedule.

This result meant not only some seventy thousand dollars in the coffers of the firm, but an excellent advertisement for the potentialities of reinforced concrete.

The years 1908–1913 form a separate chapter in the Kreuger story. It was a chapter of continual success. Kreuger and Toll grew in size and in financial muscle. In 1911 it was incorporated with a nominal and issued capital of one million kroner (the exchange rate at that time was approximately four kroner to the dollar). A year later the capital was increased to two million kroner. Many office buildings were erected in and around Stockholm; and there were more grandiose undertakings, such as the Stockholm Civic Hall, and the stadium for the Olympic Games. 'A structure with a fine massive gateway like that of a castle' says a contemporary account, quoted by Allen Churchill. 'The whole combining beauty with utility.' And George Soloveytchik tells the story, which he must surely have had from Kreuger himself, of the amusement park in the Stockholm Exhibition.

On this occasion, Kreuger being in America, the initiative had been taken by Paul Toll. He was offered the chance of erecting what is described as 'a sliding track' and seems, in fact, to have been a giant helter-skelter. The expense was substantial but the attraction was that the firm's name was to be displayed, in large letters, on the front of the track. Additionally they were to receive ten ore (a tenth of a kroner) for each person using it. Kreuger's first reaction on his return from America was alarm at the expenditure. This was 1908, in the early days when every kroner had to be watched. Toll said, 'Well, let's go and see how many people do use it.' So out the two partners went, on that lovely evening in July. The slide certainly seemed to be popular. Telling the story afterwards Toll said, after thirty respectable Swedish citizens had come down the slope to be 'fielded' by the catcher at the foot, 'See, Ivar, we've made three kroner. That's enough for a cup of tea for you and a beer and a sandwich for me.' To which Ivar said, 'Let's remain a few more minutes and we shall have enough for a bottle of wine.'

It may have been that evening which planted in Kreuger's mind the idea that his young partner was, as well as a builder, a sound business man. This was an idea which was to bear fruit in 1913.

Meanwhile the success story continued. It was not confined to Sweden. Branches were set up abroad. The first, and the more remunerative, was in Germany. Here, true to his principle of helping his friends, he installed Anders Jordahl. Further branches were set up in the other Scandinavian countries, and, cautiously, in Russia where the red regime had come into power. If Kreuger hesitated he had good reason to do so. The immediate results were satisfactory, from a financial point of view; but in the long run the Russian connection was to prove unhappy.

In 1913 Kreuger came to one of his sudden decisions. He would abandon building, and concentrate on the traditional family business of making matches. Many explanations have been offered for this, some of them romantic, some clearly mythical. The simplest seems the most probable. Success once attained was unattractive to Kreuger. What he relished was the struggle to succeed: the overcoming of difficulties, the defeat of enemies, the luring of rivals away from the opposition and into his own camp.

As a first step he separated Kreuger and Toll into two divisions. A new company, Kreuger and Toll Building, was entrusted entirely to

Paul Toll. From this point it became successively more remote from the main company which gradually, and in a way that was unnoticed by financial observers, became that most powerful and most dangerous of all modern institutions, a one-man finance company. For a comparison one need look no further than the New Globe Company of Whitaker Wright.

For the moment, however, it was matches, not finance, that occupied Kreuger's attention.

The position of the Swedish match industry in 1913 has been mentioned. Too many producers, fighting with each other, for a market which was not large enough for all of them. There had been a measure of rationalisation. One of the leading firms, Jonkoping, had merged with their rivals, Vulcan, and the joint enterprise, capitalised at 17 million kroner, was the largest in the field. Kreuger's plan, from the very first, was to take it under his own wing. It was an ambitious conception. Initially he had only the two family companies, the one which belonged to his father, and a second one built by his brother Torsten. Both were operating at a loss.

The situation was tailor-made for Kreuger's almost hypnotic powers as a negotiator. In a little over a year he succeeded in bringing together the ten smaller factories outside the Jonkoping-Vulcan combine and forming them into 'United Swedish Match Factories' or, as they soon came to be called, 'The Kalmar Trust', a company with an issued capital of four million kroner.

This seems an extraordinary accomplishment for a man who, a few years before, had been worrying about single kroner. He needed outside money and this had to come from the banks. In the end three Swedish banks agreed to support him. The main one was Scandanaviska, the Swedish Credit Bank. They stipulated, when making their loans, that the combine should be under Kreuger's personal control. They were able to recognise the coming man. No one supported him more wholeheartedly than the Scandanaviska manager, Oskar Rydbeck, who was to take a prominent part in all of Kreuger's future enterprises.

Circumstances sometimes played into Kreuger's hands, sometimes against him. The outbreak of the First World War in 1914 operated in both directions. On the one hand there were the armies, good customers for the Swedish match-box. On the other hand, blockade and war-time restrictions made it difficult to obtain the necessary raw materials. Kreuger had dealt with this problem with foresight.

The materials mainly needed were wood, potash and phosphorus. So far as wood was concerned he already had options on ample supplies from the forests of Scandinavia and he now set up a wood-conversion factory to manufacture the billets which would be fed into his matchmaking machinery, all of the most up-to-date type. This cost money. In its first year the Kalmar Trust lost seven thousand dollars.

The next step was to construct phosphorus-producing factories of his own and, in 1917, as a protective and an aggressive measure, he bought outright the large phosphorus firm of Hamilton and Hansell. By this time he could afford such an outlay. The Kalmar Trust had turned a loss into an annual profit of two million kroner.

His rivals had been neither so prudent nor so successful. By December 1917 the Jonkoping-Vulcan supplies of phosphorus were running out. It was they who came to Kreuger with proposals for amalgamation.

In his book *Il Principe*, Machiavelli warned princes against making alliances with states stronger than their own. It was into this trap that Jonkoping had fallen. Not only were they short of supplies, but they were losing their markets. The war had cut them off from the Far East and the Japanese were invading the profitable Indian field. This was an invasion which, tradition maintains, had been started by a Japanese hat trick. When a party of Japanese business men had visited the Jonkoping factory one of them had allowed his hat to fall off into a vat of secret chemicals. The hat was returned, with many apologies; and the secret of the chemicals was a secret no longer. Kreuger, one feels, would have been equally apologetic. But he would not have returned the hat.

The Kalmar Trust was having less trouble with its markets. They were mostly in northern Europe, and Kreuger had laid down the lines before war broke out. He was therefore in a strong position when the joint organisation, Swedish Match, was incorporated with a capital of 45 million kroner. In theory Jonkoping and Kalmar had equal shareholdings, the balance being held by the small firms who had been bought out. Kreuger soon had the majority of these in his pocket. As soon as he had acquired an overall majority shareholding Jonkoping realised the unpalatable truth. They were a minor cog in a Kreuger machine.

1920 was a difficult year for everyone. It was, as Hatry was to discover, the first of the post-war slumps. Not as bad as 1929/30, but disturbing to a business community that had come to expect, now that the war was over, steady progress in an upward direction. Sales fell off, the markets in different countries fluctuated.

From now on, in each of the headquarters that Kreuger built, a special room, usually on a top floor, at the back, was set aside. It was known as the Silence Room. No one but Kreuger was allowed into it. Here he sat, alone, and worked out answers to his problems. What was the answer to this one?

The first solution was one which might have occurred to any enterprising man of business. Many states, in the difficult post-war years, had tried to protect their home industries by erecting tariff walls against imported products. The answer was to organise production *inside* the country concerned. Kreuger descended on Europe like a tiger – if one can imagine a tiger in a well-cut suit, wearing a Homburg hat, carrying a slim brief case. (He never had much use for paper. Figures were always in his head.)

Before the tiger arrived, the jackals had scented out the prey. These were a special brand of helper, politely referred to by Kreuger as 'observers'. Sometimes they were empowered to make actual offers for businesses, but always at a derisory figure; so that when Kreuger arrived with the real offer his victim's first reaction would be relief.

Later there were to be suggestions that Kreuger employed more questionable methods, bribery and blackmail. There was never any clear proof of this, and to start with, at all events, his methods were straightforward enough. Belgium can be taken as an example. Here the 'observer' was young Gunnar Cederschiold. He nosed out two factories which had been badly damaged in the latter stages of the war, but which, he estimated, could be repaired. Using local banks Kreuger snapped them up. In the next few years he bought four more. The six were then merged. That left one major competitor. For a time there was a system of 'co-operative trading'. Then the tiger's mouth opened, the competitor was swallowed, and Kreuger's control of the Belgian match business was complete.

It was Kalmar and Jonkoping all over again.

Sometimes Kreuger even got ahead of the governments. Learning that it was probable that India would shortly be introducing a tariff of import duties he rapidly constructed his own factories in Bombay, Calcutta, Karachi and Madras, and had them in full working order by the time the new duties were imposed.

Not all of the money for these projects came from bank loans. Some of it Kreuger made by his own efforts. There were two transactions at this time which demonstrated his grasp of world finances. He knew that the war had left the United States 'cash rich'. He guessed that they would want to place some of their surplus money into real estate in Europe. Accordingly he bought up house properties in France and Germany – in Germany, owing to the fall of the mark they could be obtained very cheaply – and sold them at a profit to Americans. His second coup was even simpler. He concluded that the dollar was undervalued against the kroner. At the end of the war the exchange rate was 2.80 kroner to the dollar. Following the Napoleonic dictum that war should pay for war he first borrowed a large sum of kroner from the banks. These he at once changed into dollars, and used the dollars as security for the loans. By the end of 1919 the dollar had risen to a value of 4.83 against the kroner. Which enabled Kreuger to repay the bank loans and put some five million dollars into his own pocket.

All the operations so far described could be classed as orthodox money-making. It was the second idea which Kreuger worked out in the calm of his Silence Room that put him into a class by himself as a financier.

His conception of the state monopoly was simple but majestic. It demonstrated that Kreuger's ideas had now left the narrow bounds of Sweden and had become international.

At the end of the war most of the states of Europe and the smaller emerging states in other parts of the world, were short of money, and lacked the financial muscle to raise it. To such a country came the benevolent Swede from Stockholm. He would lend them money, at a reasonable rate of interest, and on easy terms for repayment. In return he asked for a monopoly to manufacture and market matches in their territory. If there was an existing state monopoly he would take it over. If not, one would be created.

Nor was the State to be excluded from future benefits. The monopoly would be run by a company in which the State would have a half share of the profits; after repayment of the interest on the loan, of course. It was an idea with undeniable attractions.

The first two monopolies were organised in Poland and Peru. Poland was prototype. Kreuger was feeling his way. It was, at first, only a monopoly of production. There was to be considerable doubt about the subsequent marketing monopoly. Kreuger certainly said that it existed, and preliminary conversations had been held with Dr Glowacki from the Polish Ministry of Finance. When doubts arose later Kreuger was prepared to let the doubters glance at an impressive document with Glowacki's signature at the foot of it. That was for the future. At the moment no one saw any reason to question the arrangements.

Nor was there any doubt about the other monopolies. As soon as the first ones had been arranged the idea gained force and credibility. Greece, Yugoslavia, Hungary, and the new states of Latvia, Lithuania and Estonia had all suffered financially in the war, and were embarking on the expensive road of rehabilitation. Romania, Danzig and Turkey followed their example, echoed on the other side of the Atlantic by Ecuador and Guatemala. When, as will be recorded in due course, the list was completed by the massive addition of France and Germany, it was calculated that the equivalent of more than a hundred million pounds sterling had been laid out in these loans.

The benefits they conferred were unquestionable. To take a few examples: five million dollars in Greece went to the repatriation of refugees scattered by the war; in Poland, six million dollars for flood relief; in Yugoslavia twenty-two million dollars to assist economic development in this newly created state; in Hungary a massive injection of thirty-six million dollars for land reform; in little Latvia six million dollars for farm relief.

However, as was not uncommon in Kreuger transactions, there was a reverse side to the coin. When the German journalist Richard Katz learned that Germany was negotiating for a monopoly loan, he published a warning from Peru. It is quoted *in extenso* in Allen Churchill's book *The Incredible Ivar Kreuger*. It starts: 'Before a steamer arrives in Peru the captain puts up a notice saying 'Passengers are warned that an agreement has been made between the Peruvian Government and the Swedish Match Trust to regulate the production, distribution and sale of matches in the Republic of Peru. In accordance with this agreement, the import of all foreign matches is prohibited. Offenders are liable to a fine of fifty Peruvian pounds. The fine is imposed for the import of even one foreign match . . . Anyone who discovers a match can claim half the fine [worth twenty pounds sterling]'. Katz concluded that this was not only making life difficult for tourists, but was having an unhappy effect on the national character. 'Peruvians do not beg much and they hardly ever steal. But the agreement with Mr Kreuger is gradually training them to be sneaks.'

This warning did not stop the German loan, which was to be the last and the largest of the lot. But where was all this money to come from? The answer was predictable. The war had impoverished a great many countries. It had made one country rich. This imbalance should be redressed. The money would come from America.

To follow this part of the story, it is necessary to go back a few years. In 1919 Kreuger paid an exploratory visit to New York. He had last seen it twelve years before. Then he had been Engineer Kreuger, a young man on the make. Now he was beginning to be recognised as the Swedish Match King. The success of the Kalmar Trust in the past six years had enlarged him in every particular.

His headquarters was no longer two rooms in a Stockholm back street. It was a four-storey building in the centre of the business zone. George Soloveytchik knew it personally and had described it in loving detail. Kreuger's own room was panelled in rosewood and mahogany. His desk was in the window, opposite a Gobelin tapestry. One of the interesting objects on the desk was a dummy telephone. By pressing a bell hidden under his desk Kreuger could make this telephone ring. This gave him a double advantage. It would either be an excuse to get rid of a visitor who was outstaying his welcome, or it might be made to play its part in an imaginary conversation designed to impress.

The other rooms in the building were on a similar scale. Notably the Board Room which was, says Soloveytchik, the *pièce de résistance*. Somewhat detached from the director's rooms, in the curved upper part of the house; its construction had raised a number of problems. One wall had to be windowless. It was divided into vertical panels in proportions corresponding to those of the windows, these panels being united by a large colour composition harmonising with the panelling. The work was called 'Dawn'. 'Through the rainbow, Prometheus on a winged horse comes rushing down to earth bringing fire to man, and bidding the darkness flee.'

Visitors from America who had seen this magnificence were impressed. On their return they carried accounts of it home. When

Kreuger arrived in New York he was already a personality. On his visit in 1919 he was content to plant the seed for future operations. With the faithful Anders Jordahl he set up American Kreuger and Toll. This was a company with (on paper) a six million dollar capital entirely represented by shares of that value in Swedish Match. It involved itself in a number of purchases of stock in sound American companies.

One of its most important acquisitions was a substantial block of shares in the Diamond Match Company. It should be noted that the money for this purchase came out of Kreuger's own pocket, being part of the proceeds of his dollar/kroner gamble. This was the sort of transaction which caused no comment at the time, but was destined to drive to distraction the accountants who had, ultimately, to disentangle the financial position.

By the time that he made his second visit, in 1922, Kreuger was ready for his real business: the raising of large sums of money from American investors and the transfer of those sums to certain carefully prepared 'pockets' in Europe. It was boom time. American money was searching for outlets. Two factors drew it in Kreuger's direction.

The first was that Americans, like most capitalists, great and small, resented paying taxes on their gains. It was made clear to them that if these gains were transferred to, or retained in, Kreuger's European companies they would not be subject to any tax at all. The second reason was more one of psychology. Swedish businessmen had a well-deserved reputation for probity. John Kenneth Galbraith, the author of the standard work on the American financial crisis of 1929, said in his introduction to Robert Shaplen's book, 'It is the nature of the boom that the men who have confidence and do not ask questions look with uneasiness on the suspicious men who do. And we may lay it down as an absolute rule that, given an excess of confidence, there will be confident men to take advantage of it.'

At this point readers may very well ask, 'Why is Kreuger featuring in a book about swindlers? All he is doing is to induce Americans, who have money to spare, to invest some of it in a company, to be known as the International Match Corporation (or IMCO) so that such money can be reinvested in the form of loans to governments, mainly in Europe, who will use the money for a number of beneficial purposes. What's wrong with that?'

Here we reach the heart of the Kreuger mystery. It is as much a mystery of character as of actions. Many children have cheated at school, but have grown up to be tolerably honest citizens. This may have been a normal progression as they grew older; or maybe it was prudence. They have observed that the penalties for cheating in adult life are more severe than they are at school. Could it be said, then, that Kreuger never grew up? Or would this be an over-simplification?

The psychologist, Dr Bjerre, propounded the idea that it was Kreuger's very success in obtaining money from the Americans that tipped the balance. This may be so in a historical sense, since it is certainly true that it was at the time of the two American visits that Kreuger started, in his European dealings, to depart from the high road of hard, unscrupulous, but lawful dealing, and to descend into the byways of criminality. But does this explanation untie the interior knot in his character? Was the whole explanation not afforded more simply by the school friend quoted at the outset? Kreuger was a gambler. If the gamble was a dangerous one, so much the more interesting. He was also a pragmatist. Obstacles were there to be surmounted or avoided. Corners were for cutting. If the resulting track led outside the bounds of legality, that was a consideration to be weighed up, certainly. But the real criterion of any move was, would it work.

There we must leave the psychological problem. It can never be definitively solved.

The steps which Kreuger took, at this time, were to establish a number of 'pockets' in Europe, into which the money derived from America could be transferred. In the end he had constructed a maze of enormous complexity, involving some four hundred subsidiary and sub-subsidiary companies; a maze in which teams of investigating accountants were to find themselves lost and baffled. Two examples from 1923 and one from 1925 may make the idea a little plainer.

In 1923 one of Kreuger's employees, Bror Bredberg, was sent to Zurich to incorporate a private limited company with the impressive name of Finanz Gesellschaft fur die Industrie. Its nominal capital was stated to be three and a half million dollars, in Swiss francs. Under Swiss law 20% of the nominal capital had to be paid up in cash. Bredberg produced two certified cheques for the requisite amount. As soon as Finanz Gesellschaft was in existence Bredberg proceeded to the nearby Principality of Liechtenstein. This was a very convenient birthplace for companies. Its laws were permissive, its taxes non-existent. Here, in what Shaplen describes as 'this happy fiduciary cove', Bredberg founded the Union Industrie A.G. It had a nominal capital of a million and a half dollars, but this offered no difficulty. The sum was transferred, on paper, from Finanz Gesellschaft. The only cash that had to be found was the forty-dollar formation fee.

These, and the other companies that followed, had certain attributes in common. Their assets were either non-existent or grotesquely inflated. They were formed in areas which did not insist on any government control or inspection. Their managing directors were, in every sense of the word, Kreuger's creatures who could be relied upon to ask no questions, to do as they were told, and to sign the accounts at the end of the year.

How does one create non-existent assets? Consider *Union Industrie*. Bredberg was told to insert in its balance sheet seven million francs' worth of real estate in Berlin. Next year he was told that this property had been sold to a certain E. G. Lehmann for twenty-one million francs, partly in cash, partly in the form of an eighteen-million-franc 'note'. But where exactly was the property? No one knew. Who was Lehmann? No one had ever met him. These facts did not worry Bror Bredberg, and were unknown to the rest of the world.

The third of these 'shadow' companies was the most remarkable. It was founded in Amsterdam, another 'happy fiduciary cove', late in 1925. It was christened, in the sumptuous Kreuger manner, 'N.V. Financeaelle Maatschapp Garanta' and in charge of it was placed one Karl Lange. Karl was an admirable figurehead. He was an imposing, portly man and had (clinching sign of honesty) a long white beard. Unfortunately his story, when unravelled, did not quite live up to his appearance. He had been employed in one of the banks of which Kreuger was a director and had been dismissed from it for organising an illegal loan for himself. However, in the same spirit in which Bottomley said to the dishonest office boy, 'We've all got to start somewhere', Kreuger was prepared to forget and forgive. He had a use for Lange and his beard.

The principal and possibly the only asset of Garanta was a contract which Kreuger affirmed that he had entered into with the government of Poland. It will be remembered that there was already a genuine contract with Poland under which Kreuger had obtained a state monopoly for the manufacture of matches. This new contract was to be one covering marketing and distribution. Doubts as to whether it ever existed have been mentioned. But even if such doubts were well-founded this did not prevent Kreuger from assigning the benefit of the agreement to Garanta. Clearly it was a very profitable asset, since it enabled Garanta to declare handsome yearly dividends, supplied by Kreuger. The company, it is true, was not housed in the same style as Swedish Match. It had a bank address in Amsterdam, but its registered office was Lange's flat, where the company books and records were kept in an untidy pile in one corner of the living room. They were not of great importance to Lange who supposed that Kreuger himself must maintain detailed records of receipts and outgoings upon which the annual accounts were, no doubt, based. Lange's duty was to sign them. They were impressive documents, showing that IMCO had granted Garanta two loans, one for seventeen million dollars, and one for eight million dollars, at the handsome rate of 24% interest.

On one occasion only, scared perhaps by the magnitude of the sums in which he was (theoretically) dealing, Lange had raised two points with Kreuger. First, what had actually happened to the twenty-five million dollars? The answer was simple. It had been paid to Poland for this valuable monopoly. Lange accepted this but, not being entirely stupid, he said, 'If Garanta has paid away all its money, where is the annual interest coming from?' Simple again. 'I pay it,' said Kreuger. Lange raised no further questions. He knew which side his bread was buttered.

It has been necessary to go, in some detail, into the Garanta case since it demonstrates how the Kreuger system worked once he had crossed the line between fair dealing and crooked dealing. From the viewpoint of the American contributors to IMCO, they were purchasing shares in a well-found company which enjoyed the profits of numerous equally prosperous subsidiary companies in Sweden and elsewhere, and was so prudently managed by the reliable Ivar Kreuger that it never failed to pay them a handsome tax-free dividend. From Kreuger's point of view the situation was equally satisfactory. He was controller of all the subsidiary enterprises, and there was thus no difficulty in diverting the American money into his own account, or the account of Kreuger and Toll.

The moneys received were very considerable. When a final accounting took place it was estimated that of $148,500,000 received in

Whitaker Wright (*centre*) and his solicitor, Mr Lewis, in court. From an artist's sketch.

Horatio Bottomley

Sentenced to seven years' penal servitude: Horatio Bottomley leaving the dock.

Left:
Ivar Kreuger

Below:
Lange (*left*), Huldt and Holm, directors of the Kreuger company, in court with (*right*) Wendler, the accountant.

Right:
Leopold Harris.

Below:
Capsoni, whose evidence caused a sensation in the trial of Harris.

Left:
Clarence Hatry

Below:
Crowds of stockbrokers outside the Stock Exchange after business hours because of the Hatry case.

The Hatry case hits the headlines.

John Stonehouse

American cash 144,000,000 disappeared into the Swiss-Liechtenstein pocket. The balance was utilised to pay the handsome dividends to the shareholders, who, had they realised it, were paying themselves out of their own money.

One of many unsolved problems is what Kreuger did with all this money. He had, of course, a certain style of life to keep up. There were his apartments in Park Avenue, New York, and the Avenue Victor Emmanuel III in Paris; his suite permanently reserved for him at the Carlton, London, and his three summer residences in Sweden. They were part of the public persona of the millionaire. Everyone knew about them. Very few people knew of his more private hideaways such as the flat in the Eriksberggaten, to which came secretive men, by night. For Kreuger was now leading part of his life in the shadows.

Bredberg may have been stupid and easily intimidated and Lange under Kreuger's thumb on account of his past indiscretion, but there were other men, lower in the scale of operations, shrewd and not easily intimidated. Although the matter was not susceptible of proof, there seems to be no doubt that Kreuger was now paying heavy and regular blackmail.

Additionally, of course, part of the American money did go to the purchase of state monopolies, the two largest of which were now being negotiated.

In 1927 the French Government was in difficulties, temporary as it turned out, but none the less distressing. Poincaré was aiming to stabilise the franc, and to do this he needed a large loan, which could only, he thought, come from America. The obstacle was the banker J. P. Morgan, to whose bank France already owed seventy million dollars. Morgan and his fellow American bankers said 'No more, until that is repaid'. It was a critical moment, but as happens in the best fairy stories, a good fairy stepped out on the stage. Kreuger offered Poincaré a loan of fifteen million pounds (equivalent, at that date, to seventy-five million dollars) at the low rate of 5% interest. In return he wanted the monopoly right to import certain match-making machinery and his new and improved safety match. This was a compromise proposal after his first offer had fallen foul of the opposition and the Chamber of Deputies. It was accepted.

One of Poincaré's first steps was to pay off the whole of the Morgan loan. Since this had carried an 8% ticket, he was thus able to save the country many millions of dollars in interest payment. The only person who did not think this a happy result was J. P. Morgan. It was the beginning of a personal enmity as fatal, in the end, to Kreuger as was the hostility of Montague Norman to Hatry.

The immediate results were beneficial. As a timely infusion of blood will restore the health of the whole body, so did the French economy turn the corner and more than recover its balance. The first instalment of Kreuger's loan was repaid with interest – and gratitude. His services were rewarded by the Grand Cross of the Legion of Honour.

All commentators who have followed the career of Kreuger, noting its ups and downs, and its overall steady climb from small beginnings to international power and affluence, have marked this as the point when the graph climbed to its peak. He was more, now, than a successful financier. He was a superman. He was the saviour of Europe.

Paramount in Europe, Kreuger turned his brooding eyes on the East. He had been born and brought up in the shadow of the fortress of Kalmarnahaus and like Napoleon before him and Hitler after him he was conscious that his conquest of Europe could not be complete until Russia had been brought to heel. He had had trouble with the Russians before. Direct trouble in Estonia and Latvia where, although he had a monopoly of match production, every time he tried to widen it and branch out into other related fields Russian opposition had either blocked him or forced the price up.

In Germany the trouble was indirect. Here Kreuger had reached a position where he controlled two-thirds of the match-making factories. This was satisfactory, as far as it went. But the sales of his own products were being seriously curtailed by an influx of Russian matches, not as good as his own but being sold at a price which undercut his; a consideration in a country which was still so impoverished that single matches were split into two.

The answer to this was simple. What Kreuger needed, to round out his German production monopoly, was a German marketing monopoly. The Russian matches could then be kept out. The situation was complicated by the existence of the American loans. The first of these, the Dawes loan, had been accepted and, by the end of 1929, largely exhausted. There was now a proposal for a new loan, the Young Loan. The conditions on which this was to be granted were under discussion, and it seemed that it might not come to fruition. There were difficulties in both countries. The American bankers, influenced by J. P. Morgan, were averse to pouring more money into what seemed to be a bottomless pit. The Germans were quarrelling among themselves over what they should do with the money when, and if, they got it.

The Times reported: 'The Reichstag is talking about the possibilities of using the Young Loan to effect tax reduction. Most of the members said "no". It should be used in social directions. However there were reports of a possible deal with Kreuger –.'

Once more the eyes of the world were on him. It was a situation he relished. Oskar Rydbeck, writing some years later, recalled the course of the negotiations, between Kreuger, Herr Luther, the German Finance Minister, and Dr Schact, the Director of the Reichsbank. To start with, the highest price mentioned for the sort of monopoly Kreuger wanted was 400 million marks, but this had to be fitted in with the reparation payments under the Young Loan when, and if, this was finalised.

It was at this point that a curious and almost inexplicable duality in Kreuger's nature was exhibited. It was a moment when his finances, stretched by the French loan, had almost reached breaking point. He should have been driving the hardest possible bargain with Germany. Instead he elected to behave like a modern Maecenas, a fount of inexhaustible bounty.

First, he insisted that his loan was bound in with the American 'Young' loan. Germany needed the American money. The loan must go through. If this was agreed, he said, he would increase his own loan to 500 million marks *and would concede that repayments of the American loan should have priority over repayments of his loan.* Small wonder that this was accepted by Germany with acclaim. It was Kreuger's friends who were worried.

'But', said Rydbeck, 'where will you get the money from?' 'From America, of course,' said Kreuger. 'I've already arranged it.'

But had he?

Oskar Rydbeck, speaking after the event, said, 'At first the international transactions of Kreuger and his trust were financed almost solely abroad.' Meaning, by this, largely from America. 'At any rate, the Scandanaviska Credit Bank was not called upon to help. But when, towards the end of the year 1930 the situation on the International Lending Market changed decidedly for the worse, the Trust found itself in need, in increasing measure as time went on, of financial support from Sweden in order to meet the obligations it had incurred in respect of the grant of loans to foreign states.'

In speaking of these large sums – fifteen million pounds to France, five hundred million marks to Germany – it must not be supposed that all the money had to be found at once. It was to be paid in agreed instalments. There was an element of budgeting in this. The annual repayments of interest due to Kreuger from the smaller states would roughly balance the payments out to France and Germany. Unfortunately this was 1930 and the depression was becoming world-wide. A number of states were either defaulting on their interest payments or asking for time to pay. What this added up to was a simple, deadly fact. For once in his career, Kreuger was short of cash.

It was particularly deadly in his case, because the whole of his financial empire was founded on trust. If he defaulted in a single payment doubts would begin to creep in. People would start to look through the impressive front that he had created. They might begin to suspect what Kreuger alone knew. That behind the façade there was very little substance.

The first steps that Kreuger took to remedy his cash deficiency, if injudicious, were not actually criminal. In the days of his prosperity he had acquired the L. M. Ericsson Telephone Company. Now he was able to drain off all the liquid resources of this formerly prosperous company and use them to bolster up his own position. More dubious devices followed. He moved large sums in marks from one German bank to another. At each move he obtained a receipt, on the strength of which he could borrow again and again. This version of the 'long firm' operation is rightly described by Allen Churchill as 'a trick of the shadiest sort of confidence man'.

An even more flagrant coup was his dealing with the Boliden mine, and it demonstrates the lengths to which Kreuger was driven. Boliden was a copper mine in northern Sweden that he had acquired some years before. There was gold there in small quantities, too, though insufficient to make the recovery of it a commercial prospect. This did not deter Kreuger. He started a whispering campaign about a gold strike which was so successful that he was able to approach the central government bank, Riksbank, and obtain from them a loan of forty million kroner, to develop the mine. The bank required security for the loan. Kreuger offered them the existing Boliden stock, and this was accepted. What the Riksbank did not know, and found out too late, was that the Boliden Stock had already been fully pledged to the Scandanaviska Bank, when the mine was originally acquired with its money.

Then came the final manoeuvre. The moves made by Kreuger in his dealings in German marks and the Boliden transaction were swindles. When they were discovered the banks concerned could have sued Kreuger and sought to recover the sums they had been induced to lend him. Now came a clear breach of the criminal code. Kreuger turned to forgery.

That he was able to do so demonstrates the difference between him and Clarence Hatry. Hatry was to be accused of forging Corporation Stock Certificates; although, in fact, this was something he did not do, and could not have done. Kreuger, with his enormous prestige, and his shadowy army of accomplices, was better placed.

The facts were established later beyond dispute.

In March 1931 he sent for the assistant director of a Stockholm printing company, asking him to bring with him samples of the paper used for printing bonds. He was deeply impressed when Kreuger showed him a personal letter from Mussolini. At the head of the letter were two devices, the royal Italian coat of arms and the fascist emblem of a shield. He told the printer that he wanted a plate embodying both the arms and the shield. The director saw no difficulty about this. He had done similar jobs for Kreuger before. He was warned that the whole affair was top secret. Any disclosure might jeopardise a deal which he had set up with the Italian government.

The next step was to imprint the heading, together with wording which was supplied to him by Kreuger, on forty-two sheets of bond paper. These now resembled, closely enough, forty-two Italian Treasury bills, each worth £500,000. All that was missing from them was the signatures of Mosconi and Finance Minister Boselli. This omission was remedied by Kreuger. Oddly enough this last item was handled carelessly. Boselli was spelled in three different ways on different bills. Either Kreuger had reached a stage where he could no longer bother about details of this sort; or, more probably, he never intended to use the bills as anything but stage props. He talked a lot about them, at suitable moments, but seems only to have produced them once, to Anton Wendler, the auditor of Kreuger and Toll.

Wendler accepted them without demur and an item 'Foreign Bonds. £7,000,000' duly appeared in the company's audited accounts.

It has to be borne in mind, however, that at this point we are privileged to look through the curtain. To the world at large, Kreuger was still a successful, impeccable financier of international standing. When, in the early spring of 1932, he crossed to New York in his search for ready money his optimism and smiling face spread a little cheer in that city, still shaken by the after-effects of the 1929 stock market crash.

He had a new proposal to put forward. One of the soundest of his purchases had been the well-known telephone company, L. M. Ericsson. He now approached a company of similar standing in America International Telephone and Telegraph (IT&T). He proposed an exchange of shares. He would hand over a number of Ericsson shares, receiving IT&T shares in exchange. Since, on current quotations, the Ericsson shares were worth more than the IT&T shares, the balance in his favour, a matter of eleven million dollars, would be settled in cash.

This cash was desperately needed to enable the current instalment of the German loan to be paid — so desperately that Kreuger agreed to something which he must have known was ill-advised.

It was a condition of the deal that American accountants should be allowed to examine the books of Ericsson, an examination which could only reveal that the bulk of their assets had disappeared into Kreuger's pocket. They were at least seven million dollars short of cash they should have held.

Conference after conference failed to produce the agreement Kreuger wanted. Sosthenes Behn, the IT&T president, had only one answer to Kreuger's arguments and protestations. 'Show me the seven million dollars.' And behind Behn, and supporting him at every turn, was the vengeful figure of J. P. Morgan. By 20 February Kreuger knew that he had lost. There was only one way out, and he decided to take it.

When George Soloveytchik wrote the first draft of his book, in the autumn of that same year, the facts of what happened on 20 February 1932 were not known. When they came to light he was forced to add an appendix, which he must have written with grief. Kreuger spent that night in his office. Everything indicated that he had determined to end his life. Farewell letters were written — so many of them that the staff found a large box of stamps they had left out for him empty. Some of the letters enclosed bank notes. He was particularly anxious that his family should not suffer. It is surprising that after that night of activity and torment he was still alive.

He was, but it had printed its effect on him.

Soloveytchik reports: 'When, the very next day on Sunday morning the manager of his New York office calls on him, Kreuger is quite broken. He is so nervous that at times he appears absolutely demented. He seems to be unconscious of himself and his surroundings, to be suffering from hallucinations. He has repeated heart attacks, and can hardly breathe. The telephone rings in his imagination, and time and time again he pulls up the receiver and shouts "Hullo" into it. Yet there is nobody at the other end. Suddenly he calls, "come in", but there is nobody knocking at the door. He gives instruction after instruction, merely to cancel them again a few minutes later or to repeat them, having forgotten what he had just said . . .'

Two events rallied Kreuger. The first was the request from the prestigious *Saturday Evening Post* for an interview. The second, even more gratifying to his shattered ego, was a personal interview with President Hoover at the White House. The interview was private, but afterwards Kreuger summed up for the press the message he had given to the President. No reason for America to worry about Europe. Europe could look after its own problems.

On 4 March he boarded the *Île de France* to return to France. There were to be discrepant accounts of how he passed his time on the voyage, but the more reliable and less sensational stories are of a normal ship-board routine, with Kreuger taking part in the various festivities. The Norwegian skating champion Sonja Henie, who was returning from her triumph at the Winter Olympic games, reported that she found him 'a friendly fellow'.

When the ship docked at Le Havre on 11 March Kreuger caught the boat train for Paris and went straight to his apartment in the Avenue Victor Emmanuel. There was no rest for him there. Through that long afternoon three of his accountants and one of his directors questioned him. There were matters that had to be cleared up. Kreuger fenced with his questioners. Sometimes answering their queries, sometimes evading them. But eventually, and inevitably, they reached those Italian bonds.

Like all bearer bonds they had interest coupons attached to them. Some of them, which were overdue for payment, had come to light in

Kreuger's office in Stockholm. Had they been cashed in? asked Sigmund Henning, the Chief Accountant. Yes, said Kreuger. Then to which account had the money been credited? And why had the coupons not been stamped as 'paid'? The unbelievable truth was emerging. He could read it in the eyes of his friends. They knew him for a swindler and a forger.

Meanwhile his friend and staunch supporter Oskar Rydbeck had arrived in Paris and was staying, with another old friend, Krister Littorin, at the Hotel Meurice. Kreuger called on them there, but refused their invitation to stay for dinner. He said that he had an important matter to attend to, and prepared to make an early night of it. What that matter was became known later. Kreuger went from the hotel to a gunsmith whose shop was not far from his flat and there purchased a nine millimetre automatic pistol and two boxes of cartridges. Then he went up to his bedroom.

How he spent the night is not known. There is a record of one telephone call before midnight to a business associate in America and it is clear that he wrote some letters. In the early hours of the following morning he organised the final act of his life with all the care and precision that he had devoted to his business affairs. He had lain down on his bed fully dressed. Now he opened his waistcoat, took the gun in his right hand, and pressed it against his body, pointing it in a left-hand downwards direction. He had always prided himself on his shooting. The bullet went directly into his heart.

Next morning, when Kreuger failed to appear at the important meeting which had been arranged for him at the Hôtel du Rhin, Littorin was deputed to go across to the Avenue Victor Emmanuel and find the missing financier. He found him, and found also three letters Kreuger had written, including one to himself, which dispelled any doubt about what had happened. It stated, 'Dear Krister, I have made such a mess of things that I believe this to be the most satisfactory solution for everybody concerned –'

When giants die, myths start.

There was some delay in notifying the correct authorities, a delay compounded by the fact that on that same day was taking place the funeral of the great French statesman Aristide Briand. This was sufficient to start the rumours. Was something being hidden? Had Kreuger not committed suicide at all? Had he been murdered? Or was he still alive? When his coffin was carried to its resting place in the Gustav Vasa Chapel in Stockholm was it simply an empty box?

There was no truth in these theories, and no harm in them. They may have afforded some relief to those of his family and friends who could not believe that Ivar Kreuger was dead.

The reactions of the press were, at first, muted. *The Times*, on 14 March, said, 'If we are to see Mr Kreuger's work in its true perspective we must try to forget what happened in 1931 when the depression, which began in 1929, took an entirely unexpected turn. During those years the USA and France had taken the place of England as the most important creditor nation, but neither Paris nor New York was playing London's part as an international lending centre. Loans were certainly being made, but they were either given indiscriminately, which was dangerous, and we are suffering today from the effects – or with a distinct political bias, which tended to create financial air-pockets, resulting in instability. It was here that Kreuger saw his chance. Central and Southern Europe were getting into difficulty, owing to inadequate credits, while money was piling up in the United States inflating Stock Exchange values . . .'

This was before the committees of investigation and the auditors had got down to the labour of disentangling the mess that Kreuger had left behind him. Then the tone was very different: 'Little more than three months after his death the whole imposing structure is shown to be nothing more than a sham and a fraud . . .'

Other papers were less restrained than *The Times*. But the man who had most reason to vilify Kreuger proved to be one of the most reasonable. Oskar Rydbeck suffered a stroke as a result of the revelation which followed Kreuger's suicide. He was indicted for failure to carry out his proper duties as a director of Kreuger and Toll, was sent to prison for ten months to appease the feelings of the thousands of his fellow-countrymen who had lost money in Kreuger enterprises, and emerged a financially broken man.

His comment about Kreuger was, 'He thought he was superhuman, and so superior to any other intelligence that he could scorn ordinary mortality. Time and time again he seemed to lose the spiritual faculty of recognising the connections between things. He despised concrete facts . . . and was convinced that he could master everything himself.'

It had all been said, forty years before, by a schoolboy.

CLARENCE CHARLES HATRY

The Swindler as Victim

THE trial of Clarence Hatry and three of his business associates opened at the Old Bailey on Tuesday, 21 January 1930, before Mr Justice Avory and a jury of ten men and two women. There were thirty-nine separate charges of forgery and fraud and the hearing was expected to last for at least two weeks, possibly three. Owing to a surprise decision by the defence, it was over in four days. On the morning of the fifth day, which was a Saturday, Avory pronounced sentences.

This timing was of considerable assistance to the Sunday newspapers. The Hatry Case was accorded a leading article in most of them. Since all the accused had, ultimately, agreed to plead guilty, an appeal, if there were to be one, could only be for some reduction of the savage sentences which Avory had imposed on them. This left the editors free to say what they liked. Yet, as one reads the articles, one cannot help noticing a curious difference, not so much in their contents as in their tone.

Organs of the popular press, such as the *News of the World* and the *Sunday Express* confined themselves to more or less factual accounts of Hatry's career, trial and sentence. The *Sunday Express* even started to serialise Hatry's own story. ('I have been vanquished within sight of the end of the most important task an Englishman has ever undertaken. The motives that impelled me on this course were influenced by a genuine desire to be of service to the country.')

It was the posh newspapers that let fly. They spoke with the voice of the suburban and upper middle classes: people to whom the concept of property is all important. And Hatry's real offence was that he had threatened the sanctity of property. He had, or so it appeared, forged stock certificates and used them to defraud members of the investing public. How right and just that he should have received a heavy sentence! 'A strong judge has restored, with cleansing severity, the full significance of the maxim, "He who steals what isn't hissen/When he's cotched, he goes to prison." False sentimentality about his sentence is contemptible. Humble rascals get seven years for smaller offences. In this case a man who gets fourteen years leaves some of his victims to ruin and misery for life.'

Thus the editor of the Sunday *Observer*.

James Louis Garvin, always magisterial, was normally rather more accurate in dealing with facts. He would not have had to follow the proceedings very carefully to discover that the victims in this case were four of the leading banks and five well-known finance houses, none of whom appeared to suffer either ruin or misery.

He had opened his editorial in schoolmasterly fashion: 'This clever little man began in his father's modest business. Plush silk for top hats. Not a bad preparation for the external effects in which he undeniably excelled to the very last.'

A joke. Hatry wore top hats. His father used to make top hats.

Some of the factual misstatements in this particular article will be noted later. What is significant, at the moment, is the venom behind it.

Who was the man thus pilloried? He was born on 16 December 1888. His father, Julius, was a Frenchman, a native of Seurre on the river Saône. His mother, Henriette Katzenstein, was half English and half Hungarian. The mixture of these nationalities may account for some of the contradictory elements in his character. Michael Pearson, in his book *The Millionaire Mentality*, says: 'He has great wisdom, but is quite extraordinarily foolish at times. He is generous to an extreme, but he can also be tough. He is a shrewd judge of men and yet hopelessly naïve in the selection of some of his colleagues.' This was a retrospective judgement on Hatry near the close of his life. At the moment we are considering a schoolboy, educated at St Paul's, 'a contemplative child, ingrown, inventive and self-sufficient'.

It was noted by more than one person that he was at odds with his mother and that this had the effect of driving him in on himself. (Is it too far-fetched to see a comparison with another old boy of St Paul's who had similar difficulties with his mother, a greater and more successful eccentric, who led the Eighth Army to victory at El Alamein?)

In 1905, at the age of seventeen, he was sent abroad for a few months to improve his French and German, and returned to lend a hand in the family business. Within a year his father was dead, the business had failed, with liabilities of £8,000, and Hatry himself had been struck down by rheumatic fever, the first of a series of physical afflictions which were to bedevil him at critical moments throughout his life.

What happened next is curiously significant. It is almost as though fate had planned a little prologue to the main drama of Hatry's career. When he hobbled into the Court of the Official Receiver it was clear that he was under no personal obligation to pay the debts of his father's company. He had taken no part in the business for nearly two years and was only technically involved on account of one or two guarantees of questionable validity. In the event, as he records, 'I was discharged without having to make any payment at all.'

But that was not the end of the matter. He had resolved that the creditors of the company should not suffer. He would make sufficient money not only to pay them, but to support himself and his wife in appropriate style. For he was by now a married man and had started a family.

He had met his wife, Violet Ferguson, then a girl of seventeen, when he was convalescing in Brighton. She had some sort of business job, which she probably did not need since her father, Charles Ferguson, was a man of independent means. As was to be proved later, she had a more realistic idea of the value of money than her husband. But how was Hatry, without capital, without any special training and without any valuable connections, to make the money he so urgently required?

The fact that he did make it is on record. 'By the time he was twenty-three,' says the *Dictionary of National Biography* 'Hatry was earning £20,000 a year.'

Pause for a moment to consider this remarkable statement.

Hatry would have reached the age of twenty-three in the year 1912. Using even the modest multiplicator of twenty, this means that, in terms of today's money, Hatry was earning £400,000 a year – and that within two years of his appearance before the Official Receiver. How did he do it?

Although all of Hatry's later dealings were to be unravelled and scrutinised in the bright light of criminal proceedings, this incredible start to his career has received little attention. All that survives of it is a handful of stories, recollected *ex post facto*, which may, quite understandably, have become embellished in the telling.

There is the Deighton Patmore story, which Michael Pearson records. It seems that Patmore was engaged in arranging loans for young men and women who had expectations. The problem was that the companies putting up the money insisted on two acceptable guarantors. Often only one could be found. Hatry's solution has a 'Monty' ring to it. 'Identify the problem. Work out the solution. Apply it!' He pointed out that Patmore's clients were numerous. Why not put them up to the lending company in pairs? They would produce one guarantor each. Twice one was two. The company's condition was satisfied. QED.

It seems incredible that this simplistic idea should have worked, but apparently it did. The money started to roll in.

Hatry himself has recorded another of his schemes. In the last years before the outbreak of the First World War there was a steady flow of Austrians who, nervous of the way matters were developing in their own country, wished to emigrate to America. Many of them had made London a staging-post. They would have money, raised by the sale of house or business in Austria, and it would be from Southampton or Liverpool that they would set sail for the Land of Promise.

But suppose, when they got there, the Americans refused them entry? This could be disastrous. Hatry's answer was the Austrian Immigrants Insurance Association which, for a substantial premium, would cover the expenses of return and re-establishment in England or elsewhere.

Hatry must have chosen his clients wisely. By the time that the outbreak of war put an end to the emigrant flow he had recorded a profit of £35,000.

What these initial manoeuvres put into Hatry's hands was the capital he needed to launch out into the main stream of company dealing. From his office in Austin Friars he now embarked on the work he really enjoyed and for which he had a flair which was not far short of genius. He was a master of the buying and selling of companies. He seemed to have the ability to look beyond the shares themselves, to penetrate the smoke screen put up by the published balance sheet, and form an accurate estimate of the potentiality of a business. He was the forerunner of the modern assets-stripper and dawn-raider.

Stories began to circulate about this financial wizard. It was reported that he had purchased Leyland Motors for £350,000 and sold it within twenty-four hours for twice that figure. He purchased and amalgamated a number of ship repair firms; a venture which could hardly go wrong at a stage in the war when more merchant ships were being sunk than could be built. But his main field was insurance.

He bought an interest in the City Equitable through his friendship with the managing director, Gerald Lee Beavan, an unscrupulous operator, himself heading for trouble. Then, in 1915, he was able to purchase the Planet Insurance Company. He did not intend to keep it. His objective, as always, was to reconstitute it, improve its image and sell it. He added a number of prominent figures to the Board. Figureheads more than figures. It was understood that they were not intended to play any part in the actual running of the company. They had no authority to sign cheques and rarely attended board meetings. What was being purchased, in return for a generous annual director's fee, was their names.

The board of the Planet was enriched by the addition of Lord Ribblesdale and Lord March, later Duke of Richmond.

One of the most famous soldiers at the close of the First World War was the New Zealand VC, Bernard Freyberg. Hatry asked him to lunch at the Savoy and offered him a seat on one of his boards. Recalling the incident in later life Freyberg said, 'I was on the point of accepting when I remembered my father telling me – "Never trust a man who talks money at meals." And I said "no". I had just transferred to the regular British Army and if I had said "yes" it would have been the end of my military career.' A number of eminent people must, later, have wished they had been as sensible as the New Zealander.

In addition to buying and selling existing companies Hatry occasionally formed and floated them himself, usually with the idea of fitting them into one of his large combines. At the first company meeting following one such flotation he was called on to address the body of the shareholders. This was a job he disliked. He was not, as was Bottomley, an orator and a demagogue. He preferred his contacts with the general public to be at second hand. On this occasion it is recorded that he 'fainted on his feet and gracefully slid under the table'.

His health had not been good. Throughout the war years one operation followed another. This lack of physical robustness was to constitute a fatal flaw at two important points in his life.

In those days the alternation of boom and slump was a phenomenon less understood than it is now. The Victorian and Edwardian eras had been a time of steady prosperity. To be sure, the war had been a violent interruption, but it was assumed that its victorious conclusion would herald a further steady and permanent rise in the national economy. There were a few shrewd people who took a longer and a deeper view. John Bruce, managing director of one of the great Merseyside cotton firms, explained. 'In our business we had to buy the cotton crop before it was sown. I used all our resources to buy for 1918, 1919 and, with some hesitation, for 1920. Then I cut down all our commitments.' He had realised the truth. That it would be a buyers' market for a year or more as the servicemen were demobilised and spent their savings and gratuities on new clothes for their wives and themselves and on furnishing their homes with curtains, sheets and table-clothes. 'I gave it two years,' he said. He was almost exactly right.

Hatry said, 'During the boom I had made a lot of money. I had speculated in oil shares, Shell and Mexican Eagle and I had bought at least fifty businesses and sold almost all of them at a profit.' They included Clarke Chapman and Company, Burton Son and Sanders, the London Public Omnibus Company, British Glass Industries and Swan and Edgar. Some of these were single purchases. Some were the basis of that Hatry speciality, the combine.

The takeover of Swan and Edgar was a one-off operation. Its assets and goodwill were acquired from Harrods, in association with the Charterhouse Investment Group, and a new company was formed with a capitalisation of £1,250,000 and an impressive Board. After that came the Jute Trust. This was Hatry at his best. Michael Pearson tells the story.

> The family jute firms of Dundee had been at loggerheads for years and were driving themselves down by cut-price competition. A Scottish firm of accountants, who saw that the industry would decline if something was not done to stop it, asked Hatry to negotiate. Hatry took a train to Dundee and interviewed all the families concerned. He did something that no one else had ever been able to do. Meeting each

family in turn he persuaded the dour Scots to work together in a giant combine under the title Jute Industries Limited. He says today that the secret of his success was the determination that none of them should be allowed to sleep on the proposals he made. He knew that, if they were allowed to go home and think about it, there would be no hope of a deal. The fact that these tough Scots could be persuaded to take immediate decisions of such importance is hardly credible. But Hatry managed it.

It is important to realise that already, by the end of 1920, when he was just thirty-two years old, Hatry, though hardly a figure of national importance, had achieved a position of real authority in the City of London. He had a string of sound successes behind him. He was a director of the prestigious London Assurance and he was, in terms of modern money, a multi-millionaire. To his contemporaries he seemed a curious and contradictory person. In appearance shy, timorous and self-effacing. 'An odd, almost Chaplin-like figure, dapper with a small black moustache, straight hair combed tight to his head and a limp inherited from rheumatic fever.' Or, according to another observer, 'A neat if unostentatious dresser. To save his tailor trouble he had whole wardrobes of similar suits all cut from the same bale of cloth.'

The trappings of millionairedom were there all right, but as one reads about them one gets the impression that Hatry indulged in extravagance simply because he understood that it was the correct thing for a millionaire to adopt such trappings. He neither valued nor despised them. He was almost, in the Huxleyan sense of the word, non-attached.

His first big London house, in Upper Brook Street near Grosvenor Square, was bought off the peg, complete with furnishings and fittings from Louis Duveen, brother of the art collector, Sir Joseph Duveen. From time to time he possessed other houses in the country, at Wargrave, Fairmile Court at Cobham, a cottage at Alfriston in Sussex and another at Birchington–on–sea. During the war these were mostly locked up, as he had found it more convenient to live a hotel life in London where he maintained a suite of rooms, first at the Savoy and afterwards at Claridges.

Inevitably he bought a yacht. It had been built for an American millionaire, had a crew of forty and cost £15,000 a year to keep afloat. When one of his race horses, Furious (naturally he owned race horses;

that was another thing that millionaires did) won the Lincolnshire Handicap at long odds, he was so uninterested in the financial implications of the matter that he not only refrained from backing his own horse, but donated the prize money to charity.

The truth seems to be that his only real interest in money was in the mechanics of making it. Once it had been made it ceased to be important. It was a decoration. On one occasion, when he gave a birthday party for his wife, the guests admired the many streamers floating from the ceiling. Closer inspection showed that they were made of £1 notes: his birthday present to her.

By 1920 the Hatry graph had reached its first peak. The successful Jute combine had been followed by an equally ambitious glass combine. It was a well-conceived idea. Its drawback was that, owing to technical difficulties over an American automotive glass-blowing machine in which the combine had acquired patent rights, it was slower in arriving at a successful conclusion. By this time 1920 was turning into 1921 and now black clouds were piling up on the horizon.

Hatry was not unaware of this.

By the end of 1920 all of his business projects were owned and controlled by his own private company, the Commercial Bank of London, which had been incorporated in that year and operated from an office near Austin Friars. It was to this office that Hatry departed every morning, rising at 6.30, leaving the house at eight o'clock and often not returning until eleven at night. Sometimes he would have eaten practically nothing between breakfast and a late supper. It was not a sensible regime for a man in a precarious state of health. The gastric troubles which always plagued him became worse. There was another abdominal operation. The doctor ordered him abroad for a prolonged convalescence.

Before going into hospital he had left instructions to his fellow directors. They were to make no further purchases, were to sell whatever was easily realisable and remain liquid. This was common sense. If a storm was coming it was prudent to take in sail.

Unfortunately his instructions were ignored. The directors could not resist the chance of further speculation, but they were speculating on a falling market and lacked the master's touch. The Commercial Bank found itself in difficulties. Hatry was on the point of departure. The tickets for his South American cruise were already bought. He cancelled the trip and returned to his desk. 'It was', he said, 'a great mistake.'

With the wisdom of hindsight one can, indeed, see what a mistake it was.

Hatry had, by that time, acquired a very substantial personal fortune. He could easily have stepped aside. As the liquidator of the Commercial Bank admitted, he was 'neither morally nor legally obliged to shoulder its debts'. Yet he did so. He realised the whole of his assets, gilt-edged securities and deposits in England and America. He sold his London house, his yacht and his race horses. He even turned to his wife, who produced, from a small safe in her bedroom, bank deposit receipts amounting to £120,000. 'Saved from the housekeeping,' she explained.

The reason for Hatry's action is fundamental to an understanding of his character. As has been said, the trappings of wealth sat very lightly on him. There were things he valued above money and one of them was his financial credibility – 'Hatry always pays'. Hatry did not let down the smaller men who entrusted their money to him and his companies. Maybe the ancient Greeks would have classified this as a form of 'hubris' or spiritual pride. Certainly, like all hubris, it bore within itself the seeds of destruction.

On this occasion Hatry was successful. The money he realised paid off the current creditors and enabled the company to escape the disaster of a compulsory liquidation and go through the more leisurely and hopeful process of voluntary liquidation. As with all companies dealing extensively in shares and share options, many of its liabilities were future and contingent. These amounted to approximately £1,500,000. Hatry accepted liability for all of them. He hoped to recoup himself by a gradual disposal of the Bank's remaining assets. But the state of the market was against him. Shares taken into the books at full par value had dropped to a few shillings. There was further embarrassment when one of the firms of brokers with whom he dealt, Ellis & Co., failed as a result of the defalcations of Hatry's old acquaintance Gerald Lee Beavan.

But Hatry was persevering and determined. The scheme which he finally devised was based on the construction of a new vehicle, the Austin Friars Trust, destined to feature largely in the second phase of his career which was now opening. For the moment it was designed as a lifeboat.

The scheme which he worked out was as follows. The whole of the ordinary capital, 50,000 £1 shares, was allotted without payment to Hatry. A cash working capital of £100,000 was supplied by Kleinworts, the well-known merchant bankers, who took up the debenture issue at 6%. (In parenthesis, it was a tribute to Hatry's financial standing in the City at that time that they should have agreed to do so.) The remaining shares were called income shares and were entitled to three-quarters of all the profits made by the company. These were offered, pro rata, to the creditors of the Commercial Bank in satisfaction of their debts. Of creditors with debts of £1,500,000, more than 90%, representing £1,400,000, accepted. Its first two years of trading were modestly successful. In the first year it made a small loss; in the second year a profit of a million pounds.

So, whilst the Commercial Bank plodded on, coming closer and closer to the final step of liquidation, relinquishing one by one the companies it still owned, many of which were purchased by Hatry out of his private fortune, alongside it a new commercial empire was rising. The Austin Friars Trust was the sun and centre of it. The four planets were the Oak Investment Corporation, the Dundee Trust, Retail Trade Securities Limited and the company which was to play a main part in the new enterprise, Corporation and General Limited.

Garvin was to describe them as 'the most dangerous things in the world of finance; jerry-built sky-scrapers, connected by a labyrinth of underground passages.'

This is imaginative, but quite misleading. There were no underground passages. The connection between the companies was simple and overt. They were all owned by and controlled by Hatry. The routine company work was carried out by a fifth company, Secretarial Services Limited, which acted as secretary and registrar of all of them.

Compared with the constructions of a real company wizard like Terence Hooley ('the modern Midas'), who was said to have operated through twenty-six companies, this was a comparatively simple organisation. The companies had separate existences because they had separate functions and separate boards. There were, as before, a number of figure-head directors. There were also working directors, four of whom now step on to the stage.

His operations in Scotland had brought Hatry into contact with Edmund Daniels, then in his late twenties. In the course of the next few years he became Hatry's right-hand man, starting as assistant to the General Manager and working his way up until, by 1929, he was Managing Director of both Corporation and General and the Dundee Trust. He brought in with him John Gialdini, a forceful and trilingual Italian who had started his working life in the Anglo-Egyptian Bank, had moved to England in 1912 and had met Daniels when both were working in the same London bank. Gialdini became a director of the Dundee Trust and secretary of the Oak Investment Corporation.

By the end of the Twenties it was this trilogy of Hatry, Daniels and Gialdini who ran the joint businesses at Pinners Hall. Equally it was clear that all important decisions until the climax came in June 1929 were taken by Hatry and by Hatry alone.

The formation of Secretarial Services Limited brought in a fourth man, John Graham Dixon. It was an unfortunate chance for him that he acted personally as secretary of Corporation and General and thus became involved in the final unhappy manoeuvres of that company. Much less directly involved was the fifth man, Albert Tabor. Roland Oliver, KC, who represented him in the court proceedings, explained his position in the hierarchy with unkind accuracy. 'If he was wanted, someone sounded a buzzer.'

As the slump levelled off and business got under way again, this was the team which controlled the operations of the Austin Friars Trust. It was a busy and a hopeful period. The General Strike had collapsed, the City had recovered its nerve and everyone was looking forward to a decade of prosperity. Across the Atlantic the United States was also enjoying its return to normalcy and a booming stock market. It did not occur to anybody that this Wall Street boom might be artificially inflated and as fragile as a balloon which has been blown up too tight. That was a realisation that was to come with dramatic suddenness on one October day in 1929.

Meanwhile the sun was shining on both economies. Hatry's operations in this period included the purchase of the Wood-Milne Rubber Tyre Company and its sale to British Goodrich Rubber; the flotation of the Inveresk Paper Company; and the setting up of the First Dundee Trust.

The next of Hatry's new combines was the Drapery Trust which brought together such well-known stores as Bobby's, Marshall's, Swan and Edgar, the Scottish Drapery Corporation and others. This was an unqualified success and is probably the one referred to by the *Observer* when it made the grudging comment that 'there were some failures in this new phase of Hatry's career, but one success was conspicuous and admired'.

In the light of what was to come, the mechanics of the Hatry combine merit study. Birkett was to refer to it later as a 'self-financing operation'. It was based on the proposition that, in share dealings, the value of the whole is greater than the sum of its component parts.

To look at a simple example.

If it was thought desirable to amalgamate companies X, Y and Z, the first step would be to make an offer for all the shares in company X. It would only be necessary to pay for them in instalments: a down payment, followed by further payments at stated intervals. The shares so acquired could *at once* be lodged as security for a substantial bank loan which would form the preliminary payment for company Y. The shares in the second company could then be used to raise further money for the acquisition of company Z. As soon as this was done the shares in the three companies would be transferred to a master company, the X Y Z corporation. If the combine had been put together intelligently the shares in the master company would be of such value that, once they had been floated on the market, the cash received would more than discharge the bank loans and would leave a handsome profit in the hands of the organiser.

This was an operation with undoubted attractions for a man who understood the market. It required strong nerves and accurate timing. Its dangers were also apparent. If some last-minute difficulty arose and the final package could not be assembled and marketed – even if there were only an unforeseen delay in reaching this final stage – then the promoter would find himself stretched to make payments for his earlier acquisitions. If he had a sufficient reserve of capital to tide him over this awkward hiatus, well and good. If not, he was skating on very thin ice indeed.

However, nothing succeeds like success and the Drapery Trust had been an unquestioned success. It was followed by the merger of a number of privately owned bus companies and their sale to the General Omnibus Company (not, incidentally, a development much favoured by the man in the street, who preferred to have a number of small bus companies competing for his custom rather than one large one ignoring him). Then came the penultimate and the largest to date of Hatry's amalgamations.

Before 1927, when Hatry took a hand in the game, there had been a number of abortive attempts to bring together the twenty or more firms, mostly small family firms, which specialised in light metal casting. Most of them were under-capitalised and all of them were suffering from the competitive nature of their business. This was a re-run of the Jute situation and one exactly suited to Hatry's talents. By personal appeal he brought all these firms together under the £3,000,000 umbrella of Allied Ironfounders. This was an acclaimed triumph, a company which successfully weathered the slump of the early thirties and was so evidently prosperous by 1938 that its debenture-holders had converted their securities into ordinary shares, the ultimate token of public confidence in an organisation.

So, by 1928, the graph of Hatry's progress had reached its second peak. He was again a leading figure in the City and again a very rich man. He did not revert to all of his former extravagances. There was no yacht and no string of race horses. But money was poured into his new London house in Stanhope Gate off Park Lane. 'A palace in miniature,' his wife recalled, 'with a spacious lofty hall and leaded windows.' One room on the ground floor was converted into the replica of an Elizabethan inn ('Ye Olde Stanhope Arms'). On other floors were installed a swimming bath, which Hatry occasionally used for a dip before breakfast, and a fully equipped gymnasium. His friends used to pull his leg about this, since he had never been known to use it. Physically he was an inactive and indolent man. It was his brain which he over-used, more than his body.

On 16 December 1928 Hatry held a party in his new house to celebrate his fortieth birthday. He had never, so he assured his guests, felt more healthy or more hopeful. There were fresh worlds to conquer, fresh ventures to be undertaken. Two, in particular. The venture into the field of Corporation Loans, which had already begun. And a venture, (a logical development of his light metal combine) into the field of the heavy metal industries.

Lord Beaverbrook once stated that the commonest cause of failure in a business man was undertaking too many things at once. The Emperor Maximilian put it more graphically. 'If you try to drive two mules they will tear you apart.'

The history of the next twelve months can be seen as the interaction of these two new projects.

Before Hatry took a hand in the matter, the business in floating Corporation Loans had been a monopoly of three large firms of brokers: Mullens & Co., then and until very recently the Government brokers; Nivison & Co., under the direction of that shrewd Scotsman Robert Nivison, later the first Baron Glendyne; and Messrs J. and A. Scrimgeour. It was a trouble-free and profitable line of business. Since it was inconceivable that a public authority would default on its repayment covenant, all that was necessary was to calculate the rate of interest realistically and the stock would command a ready market. The brokers or their banker friends would underwrite the issue – that is to say they would undertake to purchase any stock which the public did not take up – and would be paid a commission for this service. This commission might seem small, but 1% on a stock of a million pounds was undeniably attractive when the risk was small also.

Hatry forced his way into this market by making friends with Arthur Collins, a respected financier, formerly the City Treasurer of Birmingham and now acting as financial adviser to the Corporation Loan brokers. Hatry persuaded him that it was not satisfactory, either for the reputation of the City or for the Corporations themselves, that this business should be the monopoly of a small group. The market should be set free. Once it was free, of course, he proposed to enter it himself and did so with the assistance of a shrewd advertising campaign.

He offered Corporations two inducements. He cut the traditional commission and he offered not merely to underwrite the loan, but that one of his companies would subscribe the whole issue, thus saving the Corporation the hassle of dealing with it in the market themselves.

Corporation and General had been incorporated in December 1926 for this purpose. It proved so successful that, by the end of 1928, Hatry had dealt with forty such loans and had cornered 90% of the market. He had also made a number of powerful enemies. It was not only the brokers he had ousted, it was the financial establishment. Mullens, in dealing for the Government, had close connections with the Bank of England, then under its famous Governor, Montague Norman.

At a critical moment this fact was to prove crucial.

In a statement which he made in February 1931, Hatry explained the procedure which he always followed in dealing with these loans. The important point to bear in mind is that once the deal with the Corporation had been finalised and the first down payment had been made, *the whole of the stock in question belonged to Hatry's company* and could be dealt with by that company on the market, even though the definitive stock certificates would not be issued by the Corporation until the 'due date' arrived and the final payment had been made. Hatry wrote: 'Corporation and General Securities Limited made it a practice, when sponsoring a Corporation Loan, to issue its own scrip certificates (i.e. receipts and contracts) in various denominations of £50 upwards. These temporary scrip certificates would, in due course, be forwarded by the holders to the officials of the Corporation concerned, to be exchanged for the actual security, namely the definitive stock certificate of the Corporation. It will thus be seen that these temporary certificates, in addition to being receipts for money received by Corporation and General, were nothing more nor less than undertakings by that company to procure delivery of the real security. And, but for the high reputation and credit enjoyed by the Hatry companies, it would not have been possible to obtain advances against them.'

Nor, it might be added, to deal in them. Until final registration these temporary certificates ranked as bearer securities and could be freely bought and sold, passing from hand to hand without the formality of a written transfer document or, more important, the necessity of paying stamp duty. This freedom continued until 'due date' when the scrip certificates had to be sent to the Corporation for registration. During the interim they were a very useful and very popular, form of security.

Three of these Corporation Loans were in course of negotiation in the first half of 1929: with Swindon for £500,000, with Gloucester for £500,000 and with Wakefield for £750,000. All were dated stocks with 1949/59 redemption dates and rates of interest between $4\frac{1}{2}\%$ and $4\frac{3}{4}\%$.

Such a programme might have been thought more than adequate for a one man financier and his small band of helpers. In the event it was overshadowed by Hatry's second venture: the Steel Industries of Great Britain Ltd.

Using, once more, Hatry's own words from the 1931 statement:

At the beginning of 1929, having completed the amalgamation of a number of the principal businesses engaged in the manufacture of light castings through the medium of a holding company called Allied

Ironfounders it was suggested to me that I might, with advantage to the industry and to my group, undertake an amalgamation of the leading 'heavy' steel manufacturers on somewhat similar lines. After an exhaustive examination I decided to proceed with this second amalgamation and, as a first step offered to purchase for cash the whole of the issued debenture and share capital of United Steel Companies Ltd. [Itself an amalgamation of a number of well-known companies]. This company was to serve as a nucleus for the combine. The joint stock banks, as well as the industry as a whole, acclaimed this initial step as sound and constructive and other leading steel manufacturers readily entered into negotiations for inclusion in the contemplated merger. I put my offer to purchase United Steel through the Austin Friars Trust. As a commercial proposition United Steel was a sound undertaking. But it had been vastly over-capitalised in the post-war boom and possessed a very complicated financial structure. The company was financially embarrassed and its shares were practically unsaleable. There were some 40,000 debenture-holders and shareholders in the company and the offer by Austin Friars Trust, in due course accepted by substantially all such holders, was to purchase their holdings (originally issued for £14,000,000) for £5,000,000. Thus it will be seen that the total sum to be written off debenture and share capital was £9,000,000. In addition Austin Friars Trust was to provide the company with £3,000,000 for the purpose of paying off bank indebtedness. Thus our total offer amounted to £8,000,000.

Translated into terms of modern currency, whilst absorbing the floating of three Corporation Loans totalling thirty-five million pounds, Hatry was proposing to raise a further hundred and sixty million.

Had times been normal there seems little doubt that he would have done it. Unfortunately they were not normal. In the early months of the year the first ripples of uneasiness were beginning to spread from across the Atlantic. Then, in May, there was a General Election and a Labour Government was returned to power.

This combination of events had two effects on the City. The first was a general fall in the price of all shares, including those in the Hatry group. The second was that the banks and finance houses lost their nerve.

Hatry had made what seemed to him to be firm arrangements to cover the inevitable gap which occurred in all his combines, between the last individual purchases and the sale of the joint enterprise. One bank had offered him the four million pounds he needed. Now it had second thoughts. There was no firm contractual undertaking to make the loan. The bank regretted that in the changed circumstances, it could offer only one million.

The situation was difficult, but not yet desperate. Hatry had security that he could offer and his name was good. There were surely finance houses who would accommodate him – at a suitable rate of interest. He decided to go, first, to the fountain head. He approached the Governor of the Bank of England.

For what happened then, Michael Pearson quotes as his authority Lord Grantly, who was working for one of the finance houses behind the steel deal. Not only did Norman refuse to help. He did his best to persuade the finance houses backing the Austin Friars Trust to withdraw, and was partially successful in doing so. 'Norman could have saved the steel project. The moral here is uninspiring, but that does not detract from its truth. You should avoid making big and powerful enemies if you can. You never know when you are going to expose your flank.'

The real difficulty was that Hatry was short of cash. The slump in the Stock Exchange had hit a number of the small companies in his group. To take one example, the shares in Photomaton Limited, a company that marketed an automatic photographing machine (the forerunner of Instamatic) were beginning to drop. It was one of Hatry's favourite companies. He loved mechanical inventions and he had encouraged people to invest money in it. He was determined that they should not suffer. The remedy was to support the market by buying in any shares which were on offer. This policy was successful, but was a serious drain on his liquid resources.

For the first three weeks in June of that unusually hot summer, Hatry, Daniels and Gialdini conferred for long hours, on every day of the week including Sundays, in an endeavour to rectify the situation. And in spite of the nervousness of the City and the hostility of Montague Norman, they had succeeded in raising most of the £8,000,000. By the end of the third week the situation could be reduced to one of simple and frightening clarity.

The remaining £4,000,000 which they needed had, originally, been more than covered, on paper, by a number of smaller loans on parcels of the securities. The total so raised was, in fact, £4,200,000, but this was only a paper figure since £1,500,000 of it had been diverted from its primary purpose and expended in supporting Hatry's other companies. The final payment of £2,200,000 to the share and debenture holders of United Steel was due on 1 July, but only £1,300,000 was available. Once this final payment had been made the formation of Steel Industries of Great Britain Ltd. was complete. Offers had already been received from a powerful Anglo-American group to purchase shares of the combine at a figure which would have covered all the expenses of its formation and left a profit of £1,600,000.

Between ludicrous failure and triumphant success stood a figure of £900,000.

One thinks of an angler who has hooked a record fish and drawn it near to the bank. The gut on which it is held may snap at any moment. All that is needed is a landing net. In this case the landing net was the temporary availability of £900,000.

Where was it to come from?

All of Hatry's securities were fully pledged. They included the stocks which Corporation and General had subscribed in the Corporation Loans. These were mortgaged to the hilt. In fact, such had been the confidence in these stocks that they had raised very nearly their face value. Of the Swindon £500,000 for instance, £275,000 had been deposited with brokers, Cohen Laming and Hoare, for £250,000 and the remaining £225,000 with Lloyds Bank for £200,000. The Gloucester and Wakefield stocks had been similarly used. Gloucester had raised £450,000 from the Westminster Bank, Wakefield £675,000 from Barclays Bank.

The ease with which these substantial sums had been obtained may have been at the back of all their minds when the five of them met on the evening of Sunday, 23 June, at Hatry's house in Stanhope Gate. For on this occasion, Dixon and Tabor were there too, no doubt to their subsequent bitter regret.

There cannot be many stories of complex financial dealings spread over many years in which it is possible to say – 'At this time and place and at no other the wrong decision was made and the wrong turning taken.' Up to this point, although Hatry's schemes may have deserved criticism as rash or unconventional, there was no element of criminality in any of them. From that point onward, and for the next two months, it was fraud upon fraud and lies upon lies.

First, the *Observer*: 'On a Sunday evening, June 23rd 1929, the desperate clique of gamblers met at the palazzo in Mayfair with its sham classical swimming bath above and its sham Tudor cocktail bar below. What was to be done? On this pretty Sabbath they decided on the wholesale forgery of municipal stock.'

It needs only an instant's reflection to see that this was *not* what they did. Even had they wished to do it, it would have been impossible. The stock certificates of Swindon, Gloucester and Wakefield were impressive examples of the security printer's art, on special paper, embossed with the Corporation Seal and witnessed by the Chairman and Treasurer. Hatry and his colleagues had as much hope of forging these, as of forging five pound notes.

What they decided to do was simpler; fatally simpler. On the following day Dixon informed Mr Page, the Chief Issue Clerk of the Austin Friars Trust, that five hundred new Swindon Temporary Stock Certificates were wanted. They were to be in units of £500. The existing temporary stock certificates, he explained, which were all in £1,000 units, had proved too big for easy dealing on the Stock Exchange. Mr Page, who knew that temporary stock certificates had already been issued and pledged covering the whole of the Swindon Stock, may have expressed some surprise, but Dixon assured him that they would, of course, get back an appropriate number of the pledged certificates before using the new ones. The new temporary stock certificates were ready by the following day. The Austin Friars printers kept a supply of them handy. All that needed to be done was for the appropriate sum to be filled in and for Dixon to sign them.

No time was then lost. £225,000 of the new temporary stock certificates were pledged to the Equitable Trust Company of New York against a loan of £200,000. The remaining £25,000 went to brokers, Kirkwood Stone & Co., for £20,000.

In both cases the temporary stock certificates were accompanied by a note: 'Our Brokers, Cohen Hoare & Co., will be marketing these shortly, so please don't register them yet, or we shall be faced with double stamp duty.'

The objective here was clear. If the steel combine could be completed quickly and the shares in it disposed of, these loans would be paid off, and the surplus temporary stock certificates recovered and destroyed. What was essential was that the Corporation should not meanwhile receive more temporary stock certificates for registration than the total stock in issue.

Similar tactics with the Gloucester and Wakefield stock produced £219,000 and £350,000 from different banks and finance houses, a total of £789,000, sufficient, had all gone smoothly, to bridge the 'steel gap'. Unfortunately all did not go smoothly. Difficulties began to multiply.

First Mr Page became worried. He agreed to order a similar number of blank temporary stock certificates for the Gloucester stock but approached Dixon more than once to ask when the corresponding number of certificates was going to be surrendered. Dixon put him off with some explanation, but decided to use a different man to procure the necessary Wakefield temporary stock certificates. When he heard this Mr Page's worries must have started to harden into suspicion.

But worse was to come. In spite of the letter urging them not to register their Swindon temporary stock certificates (or conceivably because of it) the Equitable Trust Company of New York did precisely that. There was only one thing to be done. The holders of the genuine temporary stock certificates were informed that registration date, which had previously, for the Swindon stock, been 1 July had now been extended until 31 August. 'An understandable precaution,' as Jowitt was to comment sardonically in his opening, 'since the officials of the Swindon Corporation would have been surprised if they had received more temporary certificates for registration than the whole of the stock in issue.'

Then the rumours began. Through July they grew steadily more widespread. It is never possible to say how these things start. Possibly Mr Page had, in strict confidence, confided his misgivings to a friend who, in equal confidence, had confided them to someone else. Hatry's enemies would have seized on them and fanned the flames. 'When you are engaged on delicate financial operations and the raising of money,' Birkett was to say, 'any breath of rumour against your credit will be disastrous.'

Disaster followed quickly.

Early in August the Council of the Stock Exchange suspended all dealings in the securities of the Austin Friars Trust 'pending a further examination of its affairs'. The Bank of England then stepped in. The well-known City accountant, Sir Gilbert Garnsey, was instructed to make an investigation into the financial background of the Trust.

Then came the final blow. Early in September Hatry and Gialdini had been in Paris on one of their desperate fund-raising journeys. Hatry came back to London. Gialdini made some excuse and stayed behind. When next they heard from him he was in Milan. He and his wife had drawn the bulk of their money from London banks and taken it with them. It was clear that they had no intention of returning.

On Wednesday 18 September, Sir Gilbert Garnsey was telephoned by Hatry who said that he and three of his fellow directors wished to see him and make a statement. He met them, heard what they had to say, asked for a few hours to think about it and consulted the Bank of England. He saw them again late that afternoon and, with their consent, telephoned Sir Archibald Bodkin, the Director of Public Prosecutions. Sir Archibald saw the four men that evening and they made a further detailed statement. They had, at this point, no legal adviser and this statement unfortunately referred, among other matters, to 'fictitious corporation stock'. A source of much misunderstanding later.

Two days afterwards they called on the Director again and surrendered to Inspector Stubbins of the Criminal Investigation Department.

The next four months were occupied by the preliminary proceedings. There were five hearings in front of the Stipendiary at Bow Street where the Crown unrolled its case. The timing was unfortunate since it was on 25 October that the black day dawned on Wall Street and by nightfall American shares had tumbled through the floor. The consequences were immediately felt by the London Stock Exchange.

In a confused way investors began to attribute their losses to Hatry. Had he not shaken international confidence in the integrity of the City of London? Feelings were hardening against him even before he came to trial. Bail, which, subject to suitable sureties and the impounding of passports, would normally have been granted as a matter of course, was refused in the case of all the defendants except Tabor.

Norman Birkett, who had by now been instructed to represent Hatry, protested to the magistrate in vain, and took the matter to the High Court. He pointed out that Hatry had been in Paris a month before and could easily have absconded. Unlike Gialdini he had returned to face the music. The judges, stony-faced, denied the application.

The other three defendants, also, were now very adequately represented: Daniels by Sir Henry Curtis-Bennett, Dixon by Cecil Whitely and Tabor, for whom the buzzer had sounded for the last time, by Roland Oliver. The importance of the matter of the Government was underlined when the prosecution was entrusted to the Attorney-General, Sir William Jowitt.

Jowitt ranked as a careful and painstaking rather than a brilliant lawyer. The worst that could be said of his opening speech, in which he expounded the course of the Corporation dealings, was that, at one point, he was not careful or painstaking enough. When explaining to the jury the steps in which the Corporation Stock was issued he indulged in an uncharacteristic flight of fancy. He likened the process to the birth of a butterfly. The original allotment was the grub; the temporary stock certificate was the chrysalis; the definitive certificate was the butterfly itself. If, in place of this simile from natural history, he had explained to the jury, in the careful words used by Hatry in his 1931 statement, what the steps were and the exact significance of the different documents involved, they might have had a better chance of understanding what it was they had to decide.

For though there were thirty-nine separate charges, they all fell under two heads. Fraud and forgery. Fraud was a common law offence. Forgery was a different matter. It was a felony, a statutory offence under the Forgery Act 1913 and it carried very heavy penalties. There will be more to say of this later.

For four days Jowitt expounded his case and called his witnesses. Accountants, Corporation officials and bank managers. For the most part they were not cross-examined. The exceptions were Hatry's solicitor and friend, Stanley Passmore and Sir Gilbert Garnsey. From both of them Birkett obtained agreement that Hatry had behaved with scrupulous and sometimes uncalled-for honesty and generosity in the past, that he had not himself made a penny piece out of the transactions then in front of the court and that at the critical moment in June 1929 Hatry had been greatly overstrained and was working long hours without any proper breaks for meals or very much sleep.

At this point Avory was impelled to intervene. He said, 'Really, Mr Birkett, are such details material?' To which Birkett replied that he thought that the position at Pinners Hall in 1929 might become most material. Avory made no comment.

'Throughout the trial,' said Hatry, in the account he wrote for the *Sunday Express*, 'I watched the icy features of the judge and wondered what he would have to say at the end.' On the fifth day, when all the defendants had bowed to the inevitable and changed their pleas to 'Guilty', he was to find out.

Although the court was packed with eminent professional men and the cream of the English criminal bar, it was unquestionably dominated by two men, Norman Birkett and Horace Avory. Both men have passed from history into myth.

Birkett, as a defender in criminal cases, might have ranked second in a popular poll to Marshall Hall, but opinion at the Bar would almost certainly have placed him at the top. 'If it had ever been my lot to decide to cut up a lady in small pieces and put her in a suitcase,' said Sir Patrick Hastings, 'I should without hesitation have placed my future in Norman Birkett's hands. He would have satisfied the jury (a) that I was not there; (b) that I had not cut up the lady; and (c) that, if I had, she thoroughly deserved it.' 'His power of persuading juries,' said another of his contemporaries, 'was such as to make him a menace to the administration of justice.'

In 1930 he was at the peak of his powers. Two years before, to the accompaniment of a wild outbreak of cheering from the gallery, he had secured the acquittal of Mrs Pace, the tragic widow of Coleford. Three years later, in circumstances very similar to those suggested by Hastings, he was to win freedom for Tony Mancini, the accused in the Brighton Trunk Murder case.

In his cross-examination of Stanley Passmore and Sir Gilbert Garnsey he extracted every possible admission in favour of Hatry. He was aiming not for an acquittal – in the circumstances this would have been impossible – but for mitigation. It was to this end also that he advised his client to change his plea to one of guilty. Their own admissions had already made the prosecution's task lighter. This step would make it lighter still and the court more conducive to lenience.

It is probable that, with another judge, these tactics would have been successful. On Mr Justice Avory they had no effect at all, as he made clear by his interventions. He said that it 'strained his credulity' to say that, but for their admissions, the evidence against the accused would have been slight. At one point he even descended to levity. Frederick Smith, the manager of Barclays Bank, who was explaining the increase of their loan from £25,000 to £28,000, pointed out that, since the new Wakefield Stock was in denominations of £5,000, they had to have £3,000 of the earlier, genuine, stock. Avory saw no reason for this generosity. 'Surely,' he said, 'it would have been just as easy for them to have printed a certificate for £3,000.'

This produced the tribute of laughter which is always paid to judges' jokes; but, as will be seen, it was a damagingly simplistic misstatement.

Avory has featured before in these pages and this is an appropriate moment to consider his reputation. In common repute he has been called a sadist. If this is taken to imply that he derived some sexual pleasure on the numerous occasions when he donned the black cap, it must almost certainly be wrong. If it simply means that he had a streak of cruelty in his nature, this also needs qualification. He certainly sent a number of men to the gallows whom a more merciful judge might have sent to prison; and he caused a notable number of offenders to be flogged. Traditionally, he did so with an icy lack of emotion which made the terrible sentences he pronounced more terrible still. It is a short step from this to saying that he enjoyed pronouncing them; but it is a step which has to be taken with caution.

'I can understand', says his biographer, Gordon Lang, 'those who believed that the judge had a positive pleasure in passing sentences upon guilty wretches, because he invariably addressed them as if they were themselves the offences to which they had pleaded guilty. He seemed unable to hate the sin without somehow conveying a detestation of the sinner. Yet I question very much if he had pleasure in dealing out justice. Or, for that matter, regret.'

The fictional character who seems to come closest to this real life judge is Inspector Javert in Victor Hugo's *Les Miserables*. Javert was born in a prison. Avory was a child of the Old Bailey, where his father had occupied for many years the post of clerk. Of Javert, Victor Hugo says, 'This man was a compound of two sentiments, very simple and very good in themselves, but he almost made them evil by his exaggeration of them; respect for authority and hatred of rebellion against it; and in his eyes, theft, murder, all crimes, were only forms of rebellion.'

What was reprehensible in Avory, both as counsel and judge, was that he was prepared to exploit every technicality of law and practice to secure appropriate punishment for those whom he, personally, considered as deserving it. In the Adolf Beck case, by a questionable device, he secured the exclusion of evidence which would almost certainly have led to Beck's acquittal. (It needed a public enquiry to whitewash him and the whitewash, when examined closely, seems a little thin.) Even more detestable than this had been his conduct in the Stella Maris case; so called after the name of the bungalow in which Alfonso Austin Smith had, either deliberately or accidentally, shot John Derham. Smith maintained that he had bought the gun to take his own life and that in a struggle to take it from him, it had gone off and killed Derham. Avory patently disbelieved him and said so in his summing up, which was a clear direction to the jury to find Smith guilty; if not of murder, then of manslaughter. The jury refused to do so and acquitted him on both counts. Checking the obvious public enthusiasm Avory pointed out that there was a further charge. Possessing a firearm with criminal intent. Smith had admitted that he intended to take his own life. Suicide was, at that date, a crime. Avory was thus able to satisfy a small part of his evident frustration by sentencing Smith, on this count, to twelve months' imprisonment with hard labour.

This was the judge who, on the fifth day, sentenced Hatry to fifteen years' penal servitude, the maximum possible under the law: Daniels to seven years: Dixon to five: and Tabor to three. Two months later Birkett took the case to the Court of Criminal Appeal in an attempt to have the sentence on Hatry reduced. The Court rejected the appeal. 'Not a day too much,' said Lord Hewart. In fact, by declaring that the sentence should run from the date of the appeal they added two months to it.

In the light of the efforts which Birkett had made, and continued to make afterwards, on Hatry's behalf, it may sound ungrateful to suggest that he was the wrong counsel for this particular case. The points he made were points of sentiment, but arguments based on abstract justice, on previous good conduct, and present helpfulness had no effect on Avory. On the other hand, Avory was a lawyer and would have appreciated arguments of law. What was needed, had one been available, was an advocate of the calibre and background of Rufus Isaacs; a man who understood, from first-hand knowledge, the working and language of the City and could explain tangled financial transactions in a manner comprehensible to the dullest juryman. Might he not have presented a simple proposition? *That Hatry had committed no forgery at all.*

'It is an essential element of the crime of forgery,' said the Attorney-General, 'that there should be intent to defraud.' This is putting the cart before the horse. Certainly there was fraud in this case. But was there, in the sense in which the expression is legally understood, forgery?

The documents which were impugned as forgeries of Corporation Stock were, in fact, temporary stock certificates. (These were receipts of money coupled with an undertaking that they could eventually be exchanged for Corporation Stock.) They were issued by Corporation and General Securities Limited and were signed by the Secretary of that company.

The offence of forgery is dealt with by the Forgery Act of 1913, which defines it as 'the making of a false document' and states that a document is false (a) if it purports to be made by a person who did not make it and (b) if, though made by the person purporting to make it, the time or place of making or the number or any distinguishing mark is falsely stated.

How could the temporary stock certificates be brought within this definition? They were, at the worst, promises made by Hatry's company which he and they knew were not going to be fulfilled. Fraudulent, certainly. But forgery? It is intriguing to consider what the answer would have been if the point had been argued squarely either at the original trial or at the appeal.

To find an answer it is necessary to reintroduce a character who has slipped out of the story.

In his opening, the Attorney-General had mentioned the leading part played by John Gialdini. It seemed from the statements of the other defendants that the steps taken on that fateful Sunday in June had been first proposed by Gialdini; and had not only been proposed by him, but advocated forcefully. 'It appears,' said Jowitt, 'that Gialdini threatened to blow his own brains out if they were not adopted. He has, however, omitted to take this step and is living quietly in Italy.' He pointed out that, unfortunately, no legal step could be taken to bring him back to this country. Under the Extradition Treaty of 1873, it was laid down that neither Italy nor Great Britain would have the right to demand of each other the return of their nationals. This was not confined to those accused of political crimes, but was an absolute bar.

There was a storm of protest. Members of Parliament wrote letters to *The Times*. The *Observer* suggested that a personal appeal might be made to Mussolini, but the Duce was not inclined to intervene. The agitation did have an effect, however. Following a formal application made by the British autorities through their Ambassador, Gialdini was arrested in Milan and removed to the San Vittorio prison.

Evidence was taken at the Guildhall, in camera, before the presiding Alderman, Sir George Truscott, and was transmitted to Italy to assist the prosecution. These steps were concluded by the end of May, but the Italians were in no hurry and Gialdini's trial did not open until June of the following year. This caused no undue hardship to the accused since the ample means at his disposal enabled him to obtain a private apartment in the prison, together with food and attention.

When the matter finally came before the court, Gialdini was represented by two leading Italian lawyers, Doctor Gonzales of Milan and Doctor Marchesano of Rome. The trial occupied the court for eight days. Since the prosecution case rested simply on the evidence from England most of this time must have been occupied by the submissions of defence counsel. On the ninth day, sentence was pronounced. Gialdini was to be imprisoned for five years and ten months, one year, however, being remitted under an amnesty granted to celebrate the wedding of the Prince of Piedmont.

Doctor Gonzales was not satisfied with this. He announced that the accused would appeal on the grounds that the offence committed had been misunderstood in the English proceedings and the decision was bad in law. The appeal was heard in December.

It was here, at last, that the true defence came to be considered by a court of law.

'The scrip,' said Gonzales, 'might be described as a deceiving promise, or as a trick. It could not be considered as a forgery, *just as a cheque drawn on an overdrawn account could not be considered as a forgery.*'

After mature consideration the Court of Appeal accepted this argument. What had taken place would be classed, they decided, under the Italian code, not as forgery, but as falsity in a private document. Gialdini's sentence was accordingly reduced to two years and two months to run from the date of his arrest. He was released in June of the following year. (In *The Times*, up to that point, he had been 'Gialdini'.

He now became 'Signor Gialdini'. He was thus restored not only to liberty, but to respectability.)

Would a defence on these lines have been effective in Hatry's case? It would no doubt have been brushed aside by Avory, but it must have been seriously considered by the Court of Appeal when it reviewed the sentences.

For the statutory offence of forgery the maximum sentence of fourteen years' penal servitude might have been considered tolerable. Had fraud alone been in point the position was more difficult. The courts demanded consistency in their sentencing policy and could only look at precedents. Birkett could have provided them with a number from his own experience.

Terence Hooley, 'the modern Midas', was sentenced to twelve months' imprisonment for what the judge considered a bad fraud; and later, as ring-leader in the Jubilee Cotton Mills swindle, went to penal servitude for three years. A solicitor who had betrayed his position of trust and fraudulently converted large sums of his clients' money was imprisoned for twenty-one months. The notorious Horatio Bottomley, at the culmination of a career of fraud, received what was regarded as the maximum sentence of seven years' penal servitude.

It is a matter of surmise only, but had the legal argument been accepted it is hard to see how the original sentence could have stood.

The last word on the subject of forgery belongs to the postscript for it is one of the oddities of Hatry's case that it was not over when the gates of Maidstone prison closed behind him.

The public rancour subsided very slowly. In 1931 a solicitor, in bankruptcy proceedings, attributed his losses to the Hatry crash. Subsequently convicted of fraudulent conversion, he met Hatry in Maidstone prison and totally withdrew the suggestion. Following his release he wrote to Hatry's son, 'I desire to take this first opportunity to state in the most explicit manner that I have never desired to throw upon your father the blame for my unfortunate position,' and went on to enumerate the numerous kindly and helpful things which Hatry had done for him.

In 1935 a Woking magistrate, Mr Francis Wellesley, was found dead in the river Wey. 'Another Hatry Crash Victim', said the headlines in a national newspaper. Hatry's friends approached Mr Wellesley's executors who confirmed, first, that Mr Wellesley's death was an accident, not suicide, and secondly that he had never had any dealings with any of the Hatry companies.

The national newspaper did not apologise.

The pendulum swung slowly. Hatry's son and his friends worked quietly, talking to witnesses and gathering facts. Appeals were made to successive Home Secretaries for a reduction of the sentence. Among those who made such appeal were both counsel who had appeared for the prosecution in the original case, Sir William Jowitt and G. B. McClure, by that time promoted to be Senior Prosecuting Counsel for the Crown.

Finally, all the evidence was collected and printed as a sixty-four page pamphlet which was signed by eighteen well-known Members of Parliament, academics, professional men, editors and writers. Their efforts secured a remission of eighteen months.

The more substantial benefit to Hatry was that this reaction enabled him to start again. It took a little time for confidence to return, but by 1950 he had established a profitable consortium of bookstores, based on Hatchards of Piccadilly. To it he added publishers, printers and a number of trade papers. It was the old technique of the combine.

He was never entirely well, but people who met him were impressed by his serenity. 'A thin, awkward figure, with generous blue eyes and a bald head fringed with silvery grey hair.'

He died in a London hospital on 10 June 1965.

LEOPOLD HARRIS

War in the City

IN the boardroom of the offices of William Charles Crocker, Solicitors, of Farringdon Street in the City of London there is to be found, on top of a bookcase, the model of a Merryweather Fire Engine, on a heavy slab of polished onyx marble. The plaque on the base reads:

> Presented to William Charles Crocker by the Underwriters of Lloyd's. In recognition of his services in the conduct of the Fire Conspiracy prosecution of 1933.

Like some war memorial, tucked away in the corner of a village square, faded, but still honoured, this trophy in the only visible surviving record of a series of engagements fought out in the streets of London, Manchester and Leeds, between 1931 and 1933. The fascination of the warfare was that at no time until near the end was the outcome certain.

The antagonists were evenly matched.

In one corner of the ring, Leopold Harris.

Leopold had succeeded to, and, with the help of his brother, David, greatly expanded the business of his father – Harris & Co. (Assessors) Ltd. – and was one of the most successful practitioners in the line of damage assessment in the City of London. His photograph suggests the man; the powerful face with the heavy jowl and shaded eyes, the double-breasted melton top-coat, the square, almost military bowler hat. Harold Dearden, writing about him in his book *The Fire Raisers* (Heinemann, 1934) says, 'He was a simple man. All he wanted was money.' His colleagues, more in respect than in mockery, named him 'the Prince'.

These colleagues were a closely knit band. Some were attached to Leopold by ties of blood; as David, his brother, and Harry Gould, his brother-in-law. Some by association in business: Louis Jarvis, Bernard Marks, Felix Bergolz, Harry Priest, Leonard Riley, Simon Wolfe and his brother Ernest and others who will appear in due course.

On the outer fringe was an army of hangers-on; people who might be useful to the Prince and were rewarded with regular donations of turkeys at Christmas and seasonable gifts at other times in the year.

In two particular cases the rewards were more substantial. This was appropriate to the standing of the recipients.

Adam John Loughborough Ball was a professional assessor of fire damage, whose services were used by a number of individual syndicates at Lloyd's and by Tariff and non-Tariff offices. Captain Brynmore Eric Miles, MC, was the Chief Officer of the London Salvage Corps.

In the opposite corner, William Charles Crocker.

He had found his own firm, independently of his father and had, with the help of his brother, considerably expanded it; but at this point any resemblance to Leopold Harris ceases. Crocker was an unflamboyant, hard-working, solicitor.

In his autobiography, *Far from Humdrum*, he gives an account of his unconventional start in the Law:

> Law students in those days came to London from all over England and Wales to the most famous of all law coaches, Gibson and Weldon. Their services were not open to me. I was not merely an articled clerk, but a solicitor's clerk, doing a full-time job. I could not have done it with half my days spent in a Chancery Lane classroom. I had to compromise. Unfortunately I have a freakish memory. It hoards any number of useless facts, but jibs at retaining the uninteresting things which really matter. I found it impossible to learn by rote 'The History of English Law' narrated so tediously in the Preface to Stephen's Commentaries. Warned that at least one question would spring from this dry material I tortured the whole of it into rhymed couplets. The labour of turning Stephen's heavy prose into jingling lines with plausibly musical endings did the trick. My odd mind was now stocked (for the necessary few months) with everything that the

examiners might wish to know on this subject. All that remains to me of the masterpiece itself is the triumphant –

> Hail then the Statute blessed for evermore
> 12 Charles the Second, Chapter Twenty-four.

Now this account reveals more of the author than he may have realised when he wrote it. Crocker was not – and would never have claimed to be – a man to whom the theory of law appealed as an academic discipline. He was a practitioner. From the start of his career he was involved in such matters as road collisions, factory accidents and personal injury claims, the bread and butter of a litigation practice. But, as his account shows, he had been blessed with two special talents. Ingenuity and perseverance. And these were talents of which he was going to have quite exceptional need in his contest with the equally ingenious Mr Harris.

Meanwhile, he went off, like many others of his generation, to the wars. The Solicitors' Book of Service notes, in its unemphatic way, that he 'joined on 9th June 1917 as a private the 28th Battalion of the County of London Regiment (the Artists Rifles); was gazetted 2nd Lieutenant in the 4th Battalion of the Dorsetshire Regiment in June 1918; was attached to the 1st Battalion in October 1918.'

Crocker himself records only the following scrap of information: 'I believe it is the done thing for an officer to say a few words to the men before leading them into battle. I faced this blush-making situation only once when my depleted platoon (about ten all told) was to force its way across the Canal de La Sambre. Before our barrage began I told them that if they would stick close to me they would all be safe because the ruined barn in which we had passed the night had been marked by the enemy with my own lucky number, 33. Not one of them was scratched.'

On this, or some other similar occasion, he was awarded the Military Cross.

When he got back in 1919 he set to work to rebuild his disrupted practice. It lay largely in the field of insurance claims. This was an unhappy period; the start of the second and more serious post-war slump, the years of the Depression, mounting unemployment and the Hunger Marches.

The war was now history, but not forgotten history. It was alive in the thoughts of young men who watched the antics of Hitler and Mussolini and calculated apprehensively the chances of bloodier Sommes and muddier Passchendaeles in which they might be called on to emulate the feats of their fathers.

One of the things which had slumped spectacularly was war surplus stocks. Bought hopefully in the immediate post-war years there was now no market for them and there seemed to be only one way of disposing of them. Insure them for a substantial sum. 'It seemed,' says Crocker, 'that they were no sooner insured (or over-insured) than they burst mysteriously – one might have thought even spontaneously – into flame.'

It was at this moment that an acquaintance of Crocker's, George Mathews ('a shrewd middle-aged cockney'), happened to drop into his office in Bucklersbury, in the City. He brought with him a friend, a Mr Cornock, and he had an intriguing story to tell.

The 'foolish and boastful' Harry Priest had endeavoured to enlist him as an arsonist! The proposal was that Cornock should open a shop with some conveniently combustible stock. Priest would arrange for it to be heavily insured and set on fire; and they would share the profits.

Nine men out of ten would have assumed that Priest was drunk or mad and would, politely or impolitely, have refused his offer. Mathews was the tenth man. It happened that he had worked for some years in the Intelligence Branch at Lloyd's and he knew two things. One was that, in those hard times, arson of shops and warehouses had almost become commonplace. The other was that William Charles Crocker was the best man to talk to about it.

If it be supposed that, immediately he understood what Mathews was telling him, Crocker would have donned his armour and plunged into battle on behalf of his endangered insurance clients, the idea must be dismissed.

There were two good reasons for holding back and proceeding, if at all, very slowly.

Mathews might have reported his conversation with Priest accurately enough, but was Priest himself speaking the truth? An acquaintance had described him as a boastful fool with an over-developed sense of humour and his whole story might easily have been born of beer and the desire to impress saloon bar acquaintances. In any event, Crocker was a solicitor, not a detective. Even if the story were true, was it not something that ought to be reported to the police?

Which led to a second stumbling block.

Priest had asserted that the 'gang' who would be responsible for the fire had powerful allies. In the Fire Brigade, he had said, and the Salvage Corps; among Insurance Officials and Claims Adjusters, and – above all – at Scotland Yard. If this were only marginally true, Crocker saw that he would have to watch his step. The extent of the campaign that he was going to conduct was not, at that point, at all clear, but if he did take things further he was going to need allies, and he was going to need money.

It was here that the organisation of the insurance world became a matter of importance. It was, as Crocker says, 'an amorphous community. Its members, the individual syndicates at Lloyds and the Tariff and non-Tariff offices, continually engaged in competition with each other.' If he were to approach such a powerful, but inchoate body, it must be with something more than a public-house rumour.

After considerable thought, what Crocker said to Mathews was, in effect, this. The City was full of stories of suspicious fires. He had dealt with a number of them himself. He could only take the matter seriously if Mathews was prepared to play his part. He must cultivate Priest, posing as a potentially dishonest, but timid wrong-doer, 'letting I dare not wait upon I would,' needing constant encouragement if he was to take the plunge.

Priest responded to this treatment enthusiastically.

He mentioned four fires to Mathews. He was a little vague as to details, but three of them were later located by Crocker as having taken place at Deansgate, Manchester, in November 1927 ('a sixty thousand pounder,' said Priest as though recording the taking of a gigantic salmon), at Goswell Road, EC, in November 1929 and at Staining Lane, also in the City of London, in December 1930.

Mathews pretended to be unconvinced. All those fires, as he pointed out, had been widely reported in the press, particularly the last one, since Staining Lane, like many City thoroughfares, was so narrow that fire engines had had great difficulty in approaching the blaze (a fact which was to become uncomfortably apparent in the Blitz of 1940). There was an easy way of convincing him, said Mathews. Tell him about the *next* fire.

It seems incredible that even a man as stupid as Priest should have fallen for this, but it has to be remembered that, to him, Mathews represented a valuable proposition. He and his friend Cornock were the owners of businesses which had, from the insurance point of view, a considerable advantage. They had never had a fire. In this respect they compared favourably with, for instance, 26 Blackfriars Street, which had already had three fires and was shortly to suffer a fourth. Such readily inflammable properties soon found it difficult to get any insurance at all.

So Priest obliged.

The next fire, he said, would take place in an antique shop at 25 Poland Street, off Oxford Street. It belonged to a man called Felix Bergholz and his wife Dagmar and it represented their maiden effort in the field of arson. With their clear record they had been able to obtain cover for £6,000. This was approximately seven times the highest valuation of their stock, but would be supported by a number of carefully doctored invoices.

When Crocker heard this he acted like a true solicitor. He prepared a full and careful account of everything that Mathews had told him and sent it, by registered post, to himself, at his bankers. No one could now deny that he had advance notice of the Poland Street fire.

On the night of 1 June 1931, no. 25 Poland Street duly went up in flames.

What followed was partly coincidental. The Lloyd's Underwriters, who were not in the secret, happened to employ Crocker, as they had on many similar occasions, to act for them. A claim was duly presented by L. H. Harris & Co. It amounted to £5,863 – a nice touch, this, with insurance cover for £6,000. Who could doubt that the damage had been meticulously assessed?

Unfortunately for the Bergholzes and their backers, Crocker, armed with the knowledge that the supporting invoices were falsified, did question it. He went further. He rejected the claim as fraudulent.

It was dropped.

At this point an important decision had to be made.

It should not be supposed that Crocker was altogether ignorant of the machinations of Leopold Harris. He knew that he was unscrupulous, suspected that a number of the fires in which he had acted for the insured owner were the result of deliberate arson, and knew, as a fact, that the claims which were presented were often ridiculously inflated.

But to move from suspicion of dubious activities to proof of criminality which would stand up in a court of law was a long and difficult step.

To start with, this type of arson was almost unprovable. The arsonist had free access to the premises, could legitimately be there at any hour of the day or night and, if he proceeded with reasonable caution, the apparatus of fire-raising would be destroyed in the fire itself.

Where fraudulent claims were concerned the investigation was not quite so difficult. Forgery is a more sophisticated pursuit than arson. On one occasion, in Crocker's experience, a claim had been supported by production of the (somewhat hastily) doctored books of the firm that had suffered the fire. The assessors retained the books for a short time and then, having apparently no further use for them, returned them to the owner, who was delighted to be afforded the chance to make even more skilful and convincing adjustments to his book. The end result, said Crocker, was a masterpiece of the forger's art. Unfortunately Crocker had retained photographs of the books as originally presented.

This was another claim that was not pursued.

Now the Poland Street fire offered the first convincing proof of an act of arson. If properly handled it would almost certainly result in criminal charges against Priest, and possibly against the Bergholzes as well.

But was this sufficient? It cut off one of the limbs of the hydra, without getting near to the heart and the head. Or, to vary the metaphor, Crocker had now in his hand a small fish which, used as a bait, might trap the king of all the fishes.

After what must have been very careful consideration he took his story to two other men. A Mr Otter-Barry, general manager of the oldest fire office in London, the Sun Insurance Office, and a Colonel Robert Roylance, a Lloyd's broker and a personal friend.

Here again coincidence played its part. Both men were sitting at that time on a committee which had been formed to sort out differences between the Tariff Companies and Lloyd's. They were thus well placed to speak for the insurance market as a whole. They knew and trusted Crocker and from them he received his mandate: to investigate all suspicious fires, past and future, and establish the common links between them. It was a mandate backed with adequate funds and (even more important in view of Harry Priest's statement) with a promise of secrecy.

Where past fires were concerned the important documents would be on the relevant insurance files. If Crocker applied for these files himself it was probable that some word of his activities would get out. The solution was to bring in no more than three or four of the top men in the offices which handled most of the claims. They could ask their subordinates for the files without arousing any suspicion and would forward them personally to Crocker.

Practical investigation was another matter. The only clear lead into the tangle was Priest. For a start it occurred to Crocker that it would be a good idea to have him photographed. He tells the story in his own book: 'When Priest left his printing works one day he was startled to see a camera levelled straight at him. With a look of surprise, he stopped dead. "Would you mind moving on guv'ner," said the photographer mildly. "They want a picture of the empty street." Priest then realised that "they" were a couple of young men measuring the roadway, presumably in connection with an accident case. For a moment Priest had thought his own picture was being taken. It was an excellent portrait and well worth the trouble.'

As well as being photographed, Priest could be followed. This was done by one of Crocker's men in a car owned and driven by his own daughter; and it led to precisely nothing at all.

As a P. G. Wodehouse character once remarked, in the matter of investigation the average man is a Watson, not a Holmes. He needs a lot of luck if he is to get started.

'The luck', Crocker records, 'turned up in the form of a young and prepossessing Scotswoman.'

She introduced herself, cautiously, as Mrs Brown, but quickly abandoned this alias on the grounds that she could see, from his face, what a reliable man Mr Crocker was. He closely resembled their old family doctor. Her real name, she admitted, was Mrs Capsoni. Her husband, Camillo Capsoni, could almost have been described as a founder member of the Harris gang. He was prepared to tell Crocker everything he knew. Fetched from a nearby tea shop in which he had been lurking, Capsoni confirmed his wife's statement.

Crocker was not to know then, although he discovered later, that there was an intriguing background to Mrs Capsoni's arrival and the subsequent involvement of her husband. Her own explanation was that she was tired of the life of degradation and uncertainty which was the inseparable drawback to any criminal enterprise and had decided to disclose a limited amount of the truth to the Scottish Union and National Insurance Company. In fact her main objective was to get a certain Mr Jarvis, whom she had personal reasons to dislike, into trouble. Jarvis had been involved in one of the four previous fires mentioned by Harry Priest – the 'sixty thousand pounder' at Deansgate, Manchester – and also in an earlier one, which Priest had not mentioned, at Margaret Street in London.

The assistant secretary of the company, to whom this confession was made, had passed her on to the Chief of the Salvage Corps, Captain Brynmore Eric Miles, MC, who must now be properly introduced.

When Crocker eventually learned the truth about Captain Miles it afforded him no satisfaction at all. His story seemed to him a sad example of the Rake's Progress. Having obtained the chief post in the Salvage Corps, which carried with it not only a substantial salary, but free quarters and other benefits, Miles had decided to supplement his finances by gambling on the Stock Exchange. The late Twenties were not an easy time for an amateur to indulge in such activities and the Captain was soon in trouble and ended up in the hands of the moneylenders. Knowing that if this got out it would lead to the loss of his job he had, in desperation, contrived a meeting with Leopold Harris and had made him an offer.

In return for regular cash payments he would not only undertake to give Harris immediate notification of any fire in the metropolis (valuable information since the first claims assessor on the spot usually got the job), but he would, in addition, use his influence to quash any unfortunate implications that a fire had not been the result of natural causes.

The enormity of this second offer only strikes home when one appreciates that the London Salvage Corps was not a government-sponsored body. *It had been set up and was paid for by the insurance companies themselves to protect them from fraudulent claims.*

It will now be appreciated that the involvement of the Scottish Union put Captain Miles in a very difficult position. If Mrs Capsoni had come to him directly there would, no doubt, have been ways in which he could have fobbed her off, or at least ensured that her story went no further. Now it was much more difficult. He had to do something. In the end he decided to hand the matter over to Mr Otter-Barry of the Sun Fire Office. In view of their existing arrangements Otter-Barry, of course, sent her straight over to see Crocker.

With perfect propriety Crocker warned the Capsonis that he could make them no promises. He could, however, do his best to see that they would feature, in any proceedings, as Crown witnesses and might expect the usual indemnity which such witnesses received.

Satisfied with this assurance, Capsoni started to talk. It was soon clear that he was going beyond his wife's original intention of incriminating Louis Jarvis. He was prepared to disclose everything that he knew.

Crocker listening, fascinated, heard the true inside story of the Deansgate fire.

The moving spirit was Louis Jarvis. He had already had a profitable fire in his premises in Margaret Street. This gave him experience and confidence, but meant that his appearance in other premises would be a red light to the insurance world. He had therefore decided to mount his next venture through a limited company, which he formed using his earlier name of Jacobs. He had persuaded Mr and Mrs Capsoni to join him in the project and all three of them became directors of the Fabriques de Soieries Ltd., with a modest capital of £300. Leasehold premises were secured at 196 Deansgate, Manchester, and stock was laid in. Part of it was damaged stock from Margaret Street, at knockdown prices. Part was new stock, bought on credit terms, dates of payment being carefully negotiated so that they occurred after the date contemplated for the fire.

The next step was to obtain some more than adequate insurance cover. The stock itself, which was never worth more than £4,000, was insured for £40,000, with further insurance of £20,000 for 'consequential loss'. In genuine cases, this type of insurance is an important extra, covering the trading loss which a business would be bound to suffer in the event of fire. In this case the consequential loss policy was even more outrageous than the stock cover, since the Fabriques de Soieries Ltd., having been established only in order to be incinerated, had hardly troubled to do any business at all. The sales for the four and a half months of its existence amounted to less than £1,000.

Next Capsoni came to the fire itself. Crocker listened with close attention whilst he described the method which had been employed in at least eight previous fires and was to be employed in five more in the future.

The basis of it was a pair of the sort of trays used by photographers for the development of negatives. These particular trays were of German manufacture and were highly inflammable. One was placed inside the other and a wax taper was 'nipped' between the two trays and held upright. The whole contraption was then placed in a bucket.

Before the taper was lit there were other preparations to make. The bucket was surrounded with piles of crêpe de Chine. 'Beautiful, delicate and deliciously inflammable.' Then the interior of the showroom had to be rearranged. Further lengths of material were draped round the wooden stands and suspended from shelves. So important was this aspect of the matter, said Capsoni, that a photograph of the room when rearranged was taken and sent to Mr Harris for his approval. He considered this aspect of the matter with critical care, pointing out the stupidity of placing dresses on metal hangers when wooden ones were available.

All being ready, at a quarter past six on 7 November, Capsoni lit the taper, which was timed to burn for thirty minutes, and walked round to the Midland Hotel where the secretary of the company, a Mrs Bing ('so intimate a friend of Mr Capsoni's as to be as nearly as possible his wife'), was awaiting him. Mr Harris was there also, ready to handle the insurance claim.

Capsoni and Jarvis sat up all one night forging invoices, but in this case they were not needed. The insurance company's assessor was an old friend of Mr Harris. He had passed the claims, not for the full amount, but in the quite handsome sums of £19,650 for material and £9,726 for consequential damage.

Finally there was the pleasurable task of dividing the spoils. Either Leopold Harris or his wife got £7,800. His company, Harris & Co., took £650. Capsoni got £948.18.0. and David Harris, who seems to have supplied some of the stock or guaranteed loans for its purchase, was awarded £1,000. The way in which this particular sum was paid seems to have attracted the author of *The Fire Raisers* (a book which is singularly free from any moral judgment on the events it records).

'One thousand pounds was paid to Mr Harris's brother, David, for he also had modestly assisted in the financing of this lucrative enterprise. It seems, however, to have been feared by the other parties in the venture that the receipt of this large sum all at once might have an adverse effect on Mr David Harris, for a good deal of delicacy and tact was used in the transference to him of the sum in question. A cheque was first sent to him for nine hundred and ninety-two pounds six shillings and eightpence, the balance being withheld for a day or two, presumably to allow him to recover. Then – a charming touch – Mrs Jarvis sent him her own little cheque for seven pounds thirteen shillings and fourpence. With regard to Mrs Bing, one hopes she received at least the cordial thanks of the Board. She certainly appears to have received nothing else.'

The assistance provided by Capsoni's confession will be readily appreciated. It did not, of itself, lead immediately to a point where Leopold and his assistants could be charged with arson and conspiracy. The courts are notably reluctant to accept the testimony of an accomplice in crime unless it is backed by credible supporting evidence.

What it did do was to enable Crocker to put his evidence into proper shape. Up to this point his investigations into the files of previous fires had necessarily been piecemeal. He did not even know, for certain, which of them were accidental and which had been contrived. Now he had a limited, but specific, number of fires to concentrate on. His list started with Margaret Street, in April 1926, and continued with Deansgate, Manchester, in 1927. Three fires in 1929 (Basinghall Street; Lever Street, Manchester; and Goswell Road). Two, both in London, in 1930 (Oxford Street and Staining Lane) and finally the predicted fire in Poland Street in June 1931, which had set the whole investigation in train.

Each of these fires could now be considered and classified under different headings. The occupiers of the property. The source of the cash. The origin of the stock. The arrangements for insurance. The organisation of the fire. The distribution of the profits.

The paperwork grew and proliferated.

In view of the fact that fires could be organised in offices as well as in shops, certain precautions had been taken. The original of any important document lived by day in Crocker's office, but was moved to a safe deposit each night. Three prints were made of each document, each set of prints being sent for safe custody to a different building in the City.

It has been calculated that, at the height of Crocker's investigations, around two thousand prints were being produced daily and that, by the end of the day, they numbered close on a million. This demonstrated immense industry, but also underlined an inherent danger. The reason for the failure of many prosecutions for fraud has been that the complexity of the evidence has first puzzled, then frustrated and finally overwhelmed the juries trying the case. They are ordinary citizens, not financiers or accountants; and they are mindful that before they bring in a verdict of guilty they must be clearly convinced of guilt. Such convictions can be obscured rather than helped by a mass of documentary evidence.

This aspect of the matter caused Crocker a lot of thought. In the end, in the spirit in which he had reduced Stephen's Commentaries to rhymed couplets, he produced 'Willesden Junction'.

This was a large piece of paper, round the edges of which were written the names of the fires, each in a small circle with an identifying number. In the centre of the paper were four large circles. One was entitled 'Harris Finance' and related to all those occasions on which it could be shown that money had come from him to assist in setting up the business concerned. Two similar circles were marked 'Harris Relatives' and 'Harris Colleagues' and served the same purpose. A fourth was entitled 'H. Gould and Co.' and its inclusion was one of the chief fruits of Capsoni's story.

It transpired that some of the stock which had been used in setting up the business at Deansgate had come from a firm called H. Gould & Co., who were in business as purchasers of salvage. It also appeared – a more significant fact – that the leading light in this firm was a certain Harry Gould who had married Leopold Harris's sister. This clarified a whole aspect of the business. Clearly Gould was in a position to serve a number of useful purposes. He could buy up any goods which had escaped in one fire, re-wrap them carefully if they chanced to be singed and then sell them to stock the next shop destined to go up in flames. Finally, regardless of what he might actually be paid for them, he could invoice them to the new business at any prices he fancied. The invoices were never destined to be met, but they were useful evidence of the value of the goods when the insurance claim came to be made.

There existed, in connection with the Deansgate fire, a record which seems to have come into existence solely owing to Jarvis's love of beauty. Capsoni had, at his request, compiled an album into which he had pasted a snippet of every roll of silk dealt with by the Fabriques de Soieries Ltd. Against each snippet Capsoni had recorded the name of the vendor and the money actually paid. When completed, it was such a work of art that Jarvis, when destroying all the other records of the company, could not bring himself to let it go.

It was a mistake he was to regret when accountants Cook Mahoney & Co. got hold of the album and used it to reconstitute the accounts of the company on a rather more realistic basis.

Whilst these matters were occupying Crocker it must not be supposed that Leopold Harris and his friends were idle. They had no reason, at the moment, to suspect that anything was wrong and in the short period of not much more than three months between 8 September and 18 December they achieved three fires, one in Manchester and two in London.

The Manchester fire at 27 York Street was in many ways the most interesting, being what came to be described as a 'twin' fire. On previous occasions the gang had run into trouble with co-tenants of the building they had decided to work on. There had been the shop in the Regent Arcade which they had taken, only to find, after they had signed the lease, that the ceilings were all equipped with 'sprinklers'. Worse than this, there was a large fanlight in their own stockroom which gave on to the communal staircase. Bearing in mind that it was in this room that the taper must eventually be lit, Capsoni had had this fanlight blocked; to be met with concerted protests from the other tenants about the darkening of the staircase, which had forced him to unblock the window.

All these difficulties, it occurred to Harris, could be overcome if the building concerned were entirely or chiefly under the control of businesses sponsored by him.

The York Street story starts with the formation of a modest limited company, Acevose Silks Limited, which set up shop in Victoria Street, Manchester. The shareholders and directors were William Herivel, who had been concerned in the Staining Lane fire mentioned above, and a new character, James Cross. Cross being an undischarged bankrupt, his Acevose shares had to be held in the name of his wife who, it should be made clear, was unconnected with any of the skulduggery that followed.

When Leopold Harris agreed with Herivel and Cross to finance their company, it was time for them to leave their modest premises in Victoria Street and look for something more spacious. An ideal site was found at 27 York Street where the first and second floors were both to let. Acevose was duly installed on the second floor, and another company, Richard Glen & Co., was incorporated and given possession of the floor below. It was here that the fire was planned to start.

The importance of this was explained to his co-director by Herivel. Since he had been involved in a fire at Staining Lane, a second fire, actually starting on his premises, would arouse the worst suspicions of the insurers. Hence Richard Glen & Co.

This was a curious company.

Looking round for somebody to head it Harris found the Wolfe brothers. Simon Wolfe, a furrier, had already been involved in his activities and unfortunately, as Dr Dearden unkindly points out, 'It was essential to have a man with an unblemished reputation; and, of course, that automatically ruled out most of Mr Harris's personal friends.' However, Simon had a brother, Ernest. He was not an obvious choice for running a silk merchant's business, being a fishmonger operating in Billingsgate Market. There was no slur on his reputation, apart from a tendency, when irritated or bored, to use the language traditionally associated with that part of London. He was accordingly put in charge, at a salary of £10 a week, to give Richard Glen & Co. a simulacrum of business.

There was not much in the way of business to transact and as time went on Ernest became bored and his language more lurid. But his release was at hand. It was clear to him that something was going to happen. Van after van arrived at their doors with bales and cartons of goods for both concerns. Roland Oliver's brief identifies 'moth-eaten furs, short lengths of taffeta with their burnt edges clipped away, silk linings which had suffered water damage and a huge consignment of woollens which filled the Acevose stock room to the roof.' These all arrived on 7 September.

This seemed to Ernest to be significant, and he was right, for on the night of 8 September a fire broke out in the Richard Glen premises and spread upstairs (with satisfactory results in both cases) to the premises of Acevose Silks Ltd. Thereafter, though partners in disaster, their fortunes did not then follow the same path.

Acevose obtained £26,751 in respect of material loss, which must have been very satisfactory to them in the light of what they had paid for their stock. Their claim was dealt with by the same assessor as had been so helpful in the Lever Street fire, a Mr Satterthwaite. Roland Oliver's brief says, 'There is no direct evidence available of Satterthwaite having been bribed, as he undoubtedly must have been.' As will be seen later, Mr Satterthwaite's guilt did not fall to be decided by a court of law.

In other respects the claimants were less fortunate. William Owen, an obstinate Yorkshire assessor, rejected the 'consequential loss' claim as ridiculous. Mr Burkinshaw, who was dealing with the Richard Glen claim, having had the benefit of Crocker's advice, rejected that also.

Neither claim was pressed.

In the light of these portents it appears curious that Harris should have pursued his course of planned arson.

Rumours must already have reached him of Crocker's activities. He had already made a great deal of money. How much it is difficult to say, since the fires which were to bring him to court may have represented less than a third of the ones he had a hand in. Though not imputing all of them to Harris, *The Times* was to refer later to 'frauds of £500,000 a year'. Surely it was time for a prudent man to stop.

However, as will be seen from other cases under consideration in this book, stopping appears to be a very difficult thing for a swindler to do. The reasons may be psychological. If one has got away with something twenty times, why not twenty-one? None of the fires which followed could have been regarded as really satisfactory. Metro Radio Ltd., another of Harry Priest's efforts, went up in flames in October. The stock was valued at £10,000 and most of it was destroyed, but the assessor, Mr Arber, made a number of enquiries, as a result of which he advised the insurers not to pay. Harris was indignant and threatened legal proceedings. He did not initiate them.

The fire which took place a week before Christmas at 37 Barbican was even more unfortunate. It almost seemed as though the stars were fighting against the fire-raisers. This, also, was to be a 'twin' effort. The ground floor was occupied by the 'United Cigar and Tobacco Company' nominally belonging to Bernard Marks, but, in fact, owned by Leopold Harris and Harry Gould. The basement was occupied by one of Marks's old friends, one Walter Ernest Westwood, who was set up in business by Harris as a dealer in second-hand radio sets and gramophones. He seems to have made no sales and expressed no curiosity as to what he was meant to be doing. A promising fire, based on the inflammable property of old-fashioned gramophone cases, was duly lit in the basement. It made an excellent blaze; in a way too excellent. The heat which it produced melted a lead water pipe which ran across the ceiling and the resultant downpour was more effective than any sprinkler system. It is true that this added to the damage suffered by Mr Westwood, but it prevented any damage at all to the much more valuable stock of Mr Marks upstairs. Result, a paltry £2,500 for Westwood and nothing for the United Cigar and Tobacco Company.

There were two fires to come before the curtain fell, both involving Priest's partner, Leonard Riley. One was in Church Street, Manchester, the other at 26 Blackfriars Street in London (the fourth which that unfortunate business had sustained in five years), but since neither of them produced a penny for the gang they hardly deserve detailed description.

By now Harris must have suspected that his course was run, but it is possible that he was sustained by one thought. There might be ample evidence that some of the fires with which he had been concerned had been deliberately lit by the owners, but was there any evidence – hard evidence of the type to stand up in a court of law – that he had any hand in them? His official position, in each case, had been as assessor presenting a claim to the insurance company. Some of the claims may have been inflated, but the figures came from the owners, not from him. He was merely passing them on. The worst that might transpire was that, in some of the cases, he had received sums of money, although even this would not be easy to prove since the payments had normally been made in cash, and if they were proved, was he not entitled to a handsome commission for the excellent settlements that he organised?

These thoughts must have been in his adversary's mind too, and before bringing down the curtain Crocker decided to make one last effort to obtain direct evidence of Harris's connection with the raisers of the fires. He selected, as his tool, Capsoni, who was by now in the position almost of an employee of the opposition. His debts had been discharged and he was receiving a subsistence allowance every week, which he supplemented from time to time with small sums extracted from Harris by the covert threat of betraying him to Crocker.

Capsoni expressed himself as willing to help in any way.

The plot was based on the supposition that Harris, who was already suspicious of Capsoni's treachery, might be contemplating having him put out of the way. If Capsoni could be involved in a car accident (the damage, he was assured, would be more apparent than real) he could summon Harris to his bedside with great indignation, coupled with threats of immediate exposure. He would be provided with a private room, suitably wired for sound, and the ensuing conversation would surely be conclusive evidence that Harris was, in truth, the Prince of this Kingdom of arson and fraud.

Reverting to his army experiences, Crocker drew up an operation order in nine numbered paragraphs, starting:

'1. On Sunday, 8th January 1933 R.C.W. [this was one of Crocker's partners, Bobbie Whiting] will call in a car driven by S [an obliging client] at the surgery of Doctor B [who was dubious of the ethics of the whole affair and desired to remain anonymous].

2. S will proceed along Berkeley Street and enter Manchester Square arriving at precisely 6 p.m. (watches having been synchronized with railway time) . . . '

What was to happen then was that the car was to drive close to the kerb, Capsoni was to step off with his right foot and fall back on to the pavement, the doctor (so providentially on hand with his car) was to pick up Capzoni, dazed and moaning, and whisk him off to a selected nursing home and install him in the prepared bedroom.

After one false alarm the plan operated with admirable precision. An intermediary informed Harris that an indignant Capsoni was stretched on his back in pain, uttering threats of what he would do unless Leopold turned up with explanations and apologies. The trap had been set.

Whether the wily Mr Harris would, in the event, have walked into the trap must remain for ever a matter of conjecture. Crocker had made one of his rare mistakes. He had explained the plan to the head of the London Salvage Corps, Captain Miles. Needless to say, the many sympathetic friends who visited Capsoni with flowers and grapes in those January days did not include the Prince.

By the beginning of February, Crocker decided that they had waited long enough. Harris knew now that Crocker was heading the opposition. He had had his office watched, to the indignation of a newspaper seller who had his pitch outside. He had noticed the watcher and, being a friend of Crocker's, had offered 'to knock his block off'. A kindly offer, but one which Crocker thought it wise to refuse.

Other people were getting nervous, too. Captain Miles came to see

Crocker and told him, in a spirit of soldierly frankness, that he thought Crocker ought to know that Harris had once guaranteed his overdraft at the bank to the tune of a thousand pounds. If, said the Captain disingenuously, any proceedings were, perhaps, contemplated against Mr Harris, he would not want this fact to be sprung on the prosecution.

Crocker now understood only too well why his Manchester Square scheme had misfired, but beyond cutting off Miles from all further information he did nothing about it for the moment. His hands were more than full.

When it comes to the point of arresting a number of members of a gang it is important that all should be arrested simultaneously and without any chance of communicating with each other. The usual reason is that the members who are forewarned may go into hiding or leave the country. Here there was an additional, and even stronger, reason. The individuals concerned might destroy the vital documentary evidence which was going to link them with the Prince's organisation.

The first step was to secure the co-operation of the Director of Public Prosecutions (at that time Sir Edward Tindal Atkinson). In a case of this importance the prosecution would normally have been handled by the Director, but in this instance he agreed that Crocker should conduct the Crown case as his agent. This demonstrated either singular breadth of mind (since such an honour had never been accorded to a solicitor before), or understandable prudence when he was told that at the preliminary hearing alone it would be necessary to call over 150 witnesses and to put in over 500 exhibits.

The next step was to obtain eighteen warrants, a proceeding which, had it been conducted in the routine way at Bow Street, would certainly have alerted the Press. With the authority of the Director behind him matters were suitably arranged. The magistrate agreed to sit, during the lunch hour, in the Treasurer's Office at Gray's Inn.

The final move was to organise the actual arrests. These were entrusted to Chief Inspector Yandell.

There were minor hitches. The elusive Mr Gilbert, Simon Wolfe's father-in-law, who had been concerned in the York Street fire, disappeared overseas and was heard of no more, but all in all, as Harold Dearden puts it, 'had the arrest of the gang been a society wedding with all the advantages of a full dress rehearsal, it could not have proceeded with more decorous and overwhelming smoothness and precision.'

The simile is an apt one because, for Crocker and his assistants, the police court proceedings *were* a rehearsal. A rehearsal for what was to follow at the Old Bailey. They were able to organise their squad of witnesses so that each could be produced, armed with the appropriate documents, without delay or confusion.

One arrangement was typical of Crocker's pragmatic approach to the law. He realised the danger of confusing the magistrate and, later, the jury with the multiplicity of the minor witnesses, bank managers and officials, necessary to prove the passage of money from crook to crook, much of it in bank notes. He therefore arranged that they should simply speak of the facts in each case, without attempting to explain their significance. Once this had been done the accountant, Joseph Cook, producing the careful schedules he had prepared, linked and clarified all that had gone before.

The Bow Street proceedings occupied thirty days. One of the prisoners was released to give evidence for the prosecution. The other seventeen were duly committed for trial at the Old Bailey.

All observers in court were struck by the odd combination of old and new; the historic trappings imposed by tradition and the instruments of modern efficiency imported (with the somewhat reluctant consent of Mr Justice Humphreys) by Crocker.

'Posies of sweet smelling herbs,' said the *Daily Mirror*, 'microphones, the silk and lace ruffles of the City Sheriffs and flashing telephone indicators', and the *Daily Express* commented that the famous No. 1 Court at the Old Bailey 'looked not unlike an American court'.

In fact, the instruments of modernity were kept under very strict control. The clerk to the court had allotted Crocker what he described as 'a spacious and well furnished apartment in the basement, where I could lodge our battery of filing cabinets with a small staff to look after them.'

This raised the question of communications. The preliminary proceedings had indicated roughly which of the thousands of documents the different witnesses would wish to refer to and these could be available at the appropriate moment in the court room. Unfortunately judges have a habit of suddenly demanding the production of a document referred to by the last witness but three. In the ordinary way this would produce a hiatus in the proceedings, whilst counsel kicked their feet and the jury lost the thread of what was going on.

Determined to prevent this, Crocker had asked permission to have a special telephone installed at the solicitors' table. It was described as a whispering telephone. Incoming calls made no noise. They were indicated by a red light. Outgoing calls could be whispered since an amplifier at the other end increased their volume to normal pitch. Crocker pointed out to the clerk the manifold advantages of this. Since he had available a complete list of documents, each identified by a number and a letter, a whispered 'D. 135' would produce the right document in the time it took one of his assistants to sprint up from the basement.

The clerk said he would ask the judge whether such an arrangement would be allowed. His personal feeling may have been that since most of the things done in No. 1 Court were governed by centuries-old ritual, any innovation would be frowned on. Mr Justice Humphreys said, 'Let the 'phone be put in, but if it creates the slightest nuisance it will be removed instantly.'

In his autobiography, which was published in 1967, Crocker appends a footnote: 'It is still there.'

The case opened on 4 July 1933, one of the hottest days of that hot summer. The heat in the court was stifling and the men in the public gallery were, as the *Daily Mail* noted, mostly in tennis shirts. Compared with a sensational murder trial the attendance was sparse, since everyone who had read of the preliminary hearing must have realised two things clearly. It was going to be a very long trial and most of the evidence was going to be very dull. However, it did have a certain atmosphere of its own, as Roland Oliver, counsel leading for the prosecution, opened the Crown case.

'Hour after hour,' said the *Daily Mail*, 'Mr Oliver continued his fascinating recital and as he spoke, in a slow melodious voice, there came a vision of roaring flames in the heart of big cities, the crash of falling buildings, the swift dash of fire brigades and the zeal of salvage corps.'

After this colourful opening, the action dragged. Roland Oliver must sometimes have considered with feelings akin to suffocation the massive array of exhibits which he had to produce. His brief alone was a document of more than three hundred pages, four inches thick and weighing nearly a stone. He ploughed on nobly, but public interest flagged. The case fell out of the popular press. A pilot-officer had been manhandled by the police. Amy and Jim Mollison had made a forced landing on their non-stop flight to New York. Even more enthralling, Fred Perry and Bunny Austin had, at long last, succeeded in winning the Davis Cup for England.

It was only when one or other of the accused threw up the sponge and agreed to plead guilty that the case crept back into the headlines. Gould and Bergholz gave in at the start. Cross joined them on 12 July and Harris himself acknowledged his participation in all but four of the fires. The rest soldiered on.

Travers Humphreys, one of the finest criminal judges of his generation, interrupted very little. Once he was provoked into doing so. Ernest Wolfe, the fishmonger, who remained cheerful throughout, had made a statement implicating Harris. His counsel, Mr Elam, attempted to soften its effect by saying, 'I imagine, Mr Wolfe, that when you made this statement you thought you might be in the witness box, not the dock.' Upon which Humphreys said, 'Substitute "hoped" for "thought" and he'll agree with you.' And added, in heartfelt tones, 'We can all hope. We can hope this case will soon end.'

Crocker, who had to sit through every minute of it, clearly regarded the conclusion as certain in most instances, but knew that one defendant was in with a fighting chance. This was the assessor, Adam Loughborough Ball, who was being defended by Norman Birkett. He was in a different category to the others. There was no charge of arson or conspiracy against him. Only one of fraud: that he had taken bribes to influence his reports in favour of Harris's clients. This was not easy to prove, since the money was paid in cash. The fires concerned were the ones at Margaret Street, Staining Lane and Oxford Street. In the end, wisely perhaps, the prosecution decided to concentrate on the last of these.

It was known from Capsoni and confirmed by Gould (when, having pleaded guilty, he went into the witness box to give evidence for the Crown) that on this occasion £400 in one pound notes had been placed in a box, tied and sealed, and sent to Loughborough Ball by Gould's own firm. This was proved by a remarkable piece of perseverance on the part of Detective Sergeant Hatherill, an officer who was subsequently to rise to the top of the tree, as a Commander and Chief of Staff at Scotland Yard. He enquired at Gould's office where registered package receipts were kept, to be told by the director concerned, 'Nowhere. I just stuff 'em in my pocket.' 'And when your pocket gets full?' Hatherill persisted. 'Oh, I tip the lot into a drawer in my bedroom.' 'Then let's have a look at the drawer.' The drawer was crammed with papers. These were all turned out and the registered package receipt which covered the £400 glove box was found.

'The last nail in Ball's coffin,' says Crocker; but admits, too, that 'Monotony vanished when Birkett was on his feet. I shall never forget either his golden voice or the gallant battle he waged in the forlorn hope of saving Ball from gaol.'

The longest trials come finally to an end and it fell, at last, to the judge to sum up, which he did on day 33, with his usual fairness. On the one hand he leaned over backward to see that no injustice was done to Ball. 'If the jury took the view that a reasonable answer was forthcoming to the charge that he received money, they would not be satisfied to convict him merely on the evidence of his alleged negligence. *No amount of negligence and carelessness could amount to fraud.*'

On the other hand he let Capsoni have it with both barrels: 'In my opinion he is a highly dangerous criminal. He is a man of great ability and of very persuasive manner. He has all the charm which we associate with natives of his country, allied to a wickedness which is entirely his own. He is that most dangerous and detestable type of criminal, a blackmailer. You should pay no attention to his evidence unless you are satisfied that there is a prima facie case against the person about whom he has spoken.'

He concluded, 'I am sorry to be unable to give him the sentence he so richly deserves.'

It did not take the jury long to make up its collective mind, and they returned a verdict of 'guilty' in the case of all the men in the dock. Sentences followed, each one accompanied by some winged words from the judge.

'Leopold Harris, you were the head and front of this conspiracy and I have no doubt that you made, at the time, enormous sums of money out of it. You are also responsible for the presence in the dock of many of your fellow defendants and you have pleaded guilty to no less than ten cases of arson. The sentence of the court upon you is that you be kept in penal servitude for fourteen years.'

Other sentences followed, some of which appear, in the light of the sort of example set by Mr Justice Avory, to be surprisingly mild.

Gould was sent to prison for six years. David Harris for five. Marks for three and a half years. Riley, Priest, Ball and Jarvis for three years each. Cope for twenty-one months. Bowman, Herivel and Simon Wolfe for eighteen months. Ernest Wolfe for fifteen months. Bergholz for twelve, Cross for nine and Westwood for four months.

As may be imagined, the sentence which was received with the least composure by its recipient was the three years imposed on Loughborough Ball. With full remission he was released in a little over two years and seems to have spent most of his time brooding on the injustice of his sentence. As soon as he was released he put pen to paper and produced *Trial and Error – The Fire Conspiracy and After*. It is not a convincing book, consisting of all the points made in his favour by his excellent Counsel and ignoring the points made against him. There is, for instance, no mention of the £400 in notes and the box in which they were posted to him, so carefully tracked down by Sergeant Hatherill.

As minor ripples follow the crash of a wave on the beach, so did a number of lesser characters reap their deserts. In his summing up the judge said, 'I am going to say nothing as to any persons other than those who have been proved to be involved. But it is perfectly obvious to anyone who has heard this case that . . . a great many people occupying different positions were in fact involved and might have been put in the dock along with the rest of you.'

It will never be known how many apparently respectable citizens shuddered at this remark. Even before the trial one of them had gone. Inspector Yandell had gone to Manchester to take a statement from Mr Satterthwaite, assessor in the Lever Street and York Street fires in that city. After making a long statement, Mr Satterthwaite went into his garage, closing the doors behind him, but failing to switch off the engine of his car. The coroner's jury brought in a verdict of 'Accidental Death'.

One man who might have been prosecuted dived in front of a tube train, first depositing his watch on the platform. Two other fire claimants and two assessors subsequently went to gaol. The information in all these cases came from Leopold who, with nothing to lose, was becoming daily more communicative.

Which brings us to Captain Miles. He must have known, long before the end of the trial, that the hand of Nemesis was on his shoulder. The result of his trial before Mr Justice Hawke was a foregone conclusion.

The judge spoke the epitaph which might serve for all the conspirators and their families.

'I bear in mind the punishment which you have brought upon yourself and which you have inflicted upon others; but I feel I must do my duty.'

He sentenced him to penal servitude for four years.

Leopold Harris survived his sentence and emerged from it a fitter man. He was a sufferer from a form of pernicious anaemia and it is doubtful whether he would, at liberty, have had the strength of mind to endure the nauseating diet of raw liver which the prison doctor prescribed and enforced. At the end of his sentence he was a fit man once again.

He resumed his business with some success. His clients may well have assumed that he knew more about the cause and effect of fires than most men.

JOHN STONEHOUSE

Death of an Idealist

In a review of one of his books, the *Times Literary Supplement* described John Thomson Stonehouse as 'a solid, labour, grammar-school lad, bred in the co-operative movement, handsome, eloquent and the terror of Africa's white settlers.' It adds, 'the story of his life, which is now in all the newspapers, reads like a fantasy. Where did it begin?'

It began on 28 July 1925 in a council house in Southampton. In the years before John's birth his father had worked in the Portsmouth dockyard. He had lost his job in the economy cuts which followed the end of the First World War, had bicycled the thirty miles to Southampton and had been fortunate enough to find work, almost at once, as a post office engineer. No doubt the pay was not munificent, but it was sufficient. The background to John's childhood was strict economy, but not poverty.

It was a background of striving, of integrity and of thought for others. His father became secretary of his trade union. His mother, a local councillor, worked her way up to become President of the Southampton Branch of the Co-operative Society.

One can visualise the table in that living room, covered with papers, notices of Branch Meetings, agenda, minutes. As soon as he could write John would have been roped in to address envelopes and help in their distribution. Naturally he was brought up as a Socialist. 'Socialism,' he was to say later, 'is not just concerned with legislation and state ownership. It is a way of life.' From the start it was *his* way of life.

At the age of eight he went as a day boy to Tauntons Grammar School on the outskirts of Southampton. Here he encountered a remarkable teacher. The head of English at Tauntons between 1930 and 1947 was Horace King, an enthusiast for Macaulay, Homer and Sherlock Holmes. He, like his pupil, was to leave teaching and enter politics. Better known by the name he adopted later of Maybray-King, he became MP for one of the Southampton divisions, in the first socialist parliament after the war, was elevated to the peerage and held the post of Speaker in the House of Commons from 1965 to 1970.

By that time, as will be seen, his erstwhile pupil had taken a number of steps in the same direction.

It would have been agreeable to record that when John left school, Maybray-King recognised his potential and pointed him towards his destiny. In fact his only comment was that the boy had limited ability and should be apprenticed to a butcher – a fate which, as Stonehouse records, he narrowly escaped. His first job was an assistant to the Senior Probation Officer in Southampton. It was a post which, in normal times, would have been filled by someone considerably older, but it was 1941 and there was a dearth of young men. So this boy in his teens found himself not only supervising delinquents on probation, but even offering advice to married couples.

The war changed his life for him, as it did for most people that it touched. In 1944 he joined the RAF, went to America, where he was taught to fly and found a niche as Education Officer. When he was demobilised he qualified for an ex-serviceman's grant which took him to the London School of Economics. An important step.

This was the post-war heyday of that institution; a wonderful place and a wonderful time for left-wing youth. 'We sat', he says, 'at the feet of Harold Laski, that great teacher and political philosopher, and took his lessons to heart.'

At Westminster the Labour Party had swept into power and was initiating a round of social legislation which rivalled the great Liberal reforms at the start of the century.

Stonehouse read the signs. He threw himself into political work. He joined and ultimately became chairman of the Labour Party at the LSE and stood, in his second year at the School, as candidate for Norwood in the London County Council election.

But before he could board the political ship the tide had begun to turn. When the parties went to the polls in the spring of 1950 the substantial Labour majority of four years previously had dwindled to ten. The omens were clear. The Government would tack and veer for a brief period, hoping for a favourable wind, but as successive by-elections went against it, a new mandate would be needed. By the exercise of strict party discipline Labour managed to survive until the following autumn. Then it was the turn of the Conservatives, the beginning of thirteen years of right-wing government, first under the old lion, Winston Churchill – by now a battered and war-worn lion – then successively under Eden, Macmillan and Douglas-Home.

Stonehouse contested both the 1950 and the 1951 elections: the first at Twickenham, the second, more successfully, at Burton, where he lost by only 700 votes. It was at this point that he received a shrewd piece of advice. His mentor was Fenner Brockway, a veteran of the party. In the same spirit as American grey-beards counselled youth, 'Go West, young man,' Brockway said to Stonehouse, 'Go to Africa. It is the seed-bed of the future. Make a name for yourself there. Then come back to politics with something behind you.'

It was advice well calculated to appeal to the young Stonehouse. In Africa there was no shortage of people in trouble, people being oppressed, people to be helped. There were infant states struggling out of their swaddling clothes. There were entrenched commercial interests supported by right-wing governments whose actions seemed to be almost fascist in their oppression of the black majority by a white minority. In short, a land of opportunity.

Yet it must have demanded courage to take the first step. He was no longer on his own. He had married in 1949 and already had a daughter and a second child on the way. His wife Barbara, however, supported him fully. In 1950 the family landed at Mombasa and took the long, dusty train journey across the south of Kenya, through Nairobi and on into Uganda. Their house in Kampala ('mud and wattle and corrugated iron sheets') faced the old palace of the Baganda King. Stonehouse does not seem to have spent much time in it. He was working as a manager for the African Co-operative Movement and it was not long before the whole-hearted way in which he threw himself into the interests of the black farmers aroused the suspicions of the white settlers. At this point, for the first time, his name begins to emerge from the great mass of nonentities and to appear in the British press. It was not yet in the headlines or on the front page. Just a short paragraph, on a back page of *The Times* on 25 February 1953: 'John Thomson Stonehouse, a former student at the London School of Economics, an official in an organisation known as The Federation of Uganda African Farmers Limited gave evidence on behalf of Achieng Onieko, of the Luo tribe. He had impressed him, he said, as anxious to use all available constitutional means for the progress of his people.'

This was the well-publicised trial of Jomo Kenyatta and other leaders of the Mau-mau rising. Whether or not as a result of Stonehouse's intervention Onieko was the only one of the accused to be acquitted. (We have to look ahead to *The Times* of 1958 for the sequel. At question time in Parliament Mr John Stonehouse, MP, was to raise the matter of the detention of Achieng Onieko, who had been charged with being a Mau-mau organiser in 1954 and acquitted. In spite of this, how could the Secretary of State for the Colonies justify the fact that he had been kept in detention under order of the government for four years?)

But we are ahead of chronology. In 1954 Stonehouse was not yet an MP. He had come home from Africa, his desire to help his fellow men as strong as ever, seeking only the best way of doing so combined with the necessity to earn a living. His solution of the problem was logical. In Uganda he had been working for the African Co-operative Movement. Now he turned to the English organisation. He found in it what he described as 'two convenient and flexible part-time jobs'. They seem to have been concerned with propaganda, travelling and speaking. He soon made his mark. By 1956 he was on the Board of Management of the London Society.

In dealing with Stonehouse's experiences in the Co-operative Movement one has to exercise caution. There are two discrepant accounts of the matter, one in his own book, the other in the writings of his critics. It is possible that they were only two sides of the same coin.

To Stonehouse, the enemy was the Communist Party. Their hostility increased as he rose in position and influence. It became extreme when, after a bitterly contested fight, he was elected President. He says, without qualification, 'the communists hated me and determined to destroy me'. Their philosophy was that the end justified the means. It also justified every weapon short of physical assassination.

When the Board appointed an American firm, Batten, Barton, Durstine and Osborne (BBDO) to provide some professional expertise in their sales campaign, this opened a promising field. What easier than to hint that Stonehouse had secret financial links with BBDO and was receiving payments under the counter from them? As a crowning effort it was suggested that they had bought him a large estate in the country. This proved difficult to swallow, since Stonehouse was demonstrably living in a small house at Potters Bar, which he had bought on mortgage. Never mind. If one piece of mud fails to stick, throw another – so a homosexual relationship was suggested, between Stonehouse and one (unspecified) executive of BBDO.

It was the Goebbels technique. Go for the big lie. There was, needless to say, no truth at all in any of these suggestions, which were rejected both by Stonehouse himself and by BBDO.

Matters came to a head when Stonehouse, as President, supported by two other Board members, refused to sign the report and accounts which had been adopted by the majority. He did so on the grounds that they were not only erroneous, but libellous, and he and his supporters prepared a minority report. The knives were out now. The majority sought an injunction to restrain its publication. The court refused to grant it and the report was duly published. It showed, among other matters, that the Movement had lost £800,000 of its members' money.

In this version Stonehouse was the knight in armour, standing up for the right amid the slings and arrows of the unrighteous.

In an article published in the Sunday *Observer* its authors, Laurence Marks and Peter Gallagher, saw the matter from a different angle. They did not accuse Stonehouse of dishonesty, but of incompetence. His simplistic view of finance and his arbitrary actions had contributed to the difficulties of the Movement. The real trouble, as they saw it, was that 'he had used autocratic methods without having the power to enforce them'.

Stonehouse as an autocrat? It was a novel conception. But there is more than one indication in his own writings that there may have been an element of truth in it.

The idea of rule by committee was splendidly egalitarian in theory, but apt to break down in practice.

'It reminded me', Stonehouse wrote, 'of a meeting I attended in a remote area of Uganda, where the tribe was so democratic that no decision was possible and no action taken unless every single adult male had said his piece and agreed with the proposal. The meeting went on for three days and still reached no conclusion. The local District

Officer, an Englishman, was so exasperated that he suddenly jumped into his Land Rover and drove at high speed into the crowd, scattering them in all directions.'

It is important to bear in mind this underlying streak of authoritarianism in Stonehouse's character. At moments of crisis, he was apt to leap, metaphorically, into the nearest Land Rover and drive away.

The power struggle in the Co-operative did not come to any final conclusion. Stonehouse successfully retained the presidency until 1964 and then resigned in order to pursue his political career which had suddenly reached a vital point.

Once again we have gone ahead of chronology. In dealing with Stonehouse's career in the late fifties and early sixties this is inevitable. He was leading two other lives besides his Co-operative one – his political life and his African life. Indeed these latter two became increasingly entangled and can only be dealt with side by side.

To turn to politics first.

In 1957 a vacancy had occurred in the Staffordshire constituency of Wednesbury, on the retirement of the sitting member, Stanley Evans (known to the press as 'Featherbed Evans' on account of a notorious comment he had made about British farmers.) By now the Conservatives had been in power for seven years and the natural swing of the tide was beginning, very slowly, to assert itself. Stonehouse fought a vigorous campaign, supported by, among others, George Wigg and gained a handsome victory, increasing the Labour majority.

The press now began to take some notice of the new member. Photographs appeared and from them it is possible to see that John Stonehouse had one of the attributes which assist a rising politician, though it may not have had the paramount importance that it does in this television age.

He was a very good-looking young man.

His maiden speech presented, from a party standpoint, an uncontroversial view of the pending Suez crisis. The only real solution was to work through the United Nations for an International Convention which would supervise the oil companies, ban monopoly and ensure that part of their profits was ploughed back into local welfare.

The opposition had a simpler solution. Use the navy. They did not go as far as to suggest 'use the army'. When this was tried it was not a success. However, the Suez fiasco did not result in a change of government. Its outcome was the departure of Anthony Eden and his replacement by a much tougher character, Harold Macmillan.

As the years went by glimpses can be caught of the young socialist MP. He wrote letters to the papers, which they seemed happy to publish, treating him as an acknowledged expert in African affairs. When he spoke, his speeches were reported with gratifying regularity. He was opposed to subliminal advertising on television, was against arming the Germans with nuclear weapons, deplored the increase in unemployment and advocated the unilateral discontinuance of hydrogen bomb tests.

There was nothing very original in any of this and certainly nothing offensive to party doctrine. It was when he spoke on African matters that people really listened. And these were the occasions on which the leading figures in the party increasingly supported him. When he asked the Secretary of State for the Colonies if an assurance could be given that no constitutional changes in Northern Rhodesia would be imposed before the House had a chance of debating them the member for Cardiff SE, Mr Callaghan, followed him, characterising the conduct of the Secretary of State as morally and criminally wrong, a charge which seemed to worry Mr Lennox-Boyd very little.

In February 1960, when he turned his attention to the conduct of the Monckton Commission in Rhodesia and Nyasaland and crossed swords with Mr Butler, no less a figure than Hugh Gaitskell came in on his side. In April of the same year he raised the prickly question of Mr Segal and Mr Tambo. These two men, after arousing the hostility of the South African government by their speeches, had evaded capture by the police and escaped across the border into Bechuanaland (as Botswana was then called). The South Africans sought to have them extradicted and they had appealed to the authorities of Bechuanaland for political asylum. Here was a case calculated to arouse the sympathy of all liberal-minded people. Stonehouse made an impassioned plea on their behalf and on this occasion it is recorded that he gained 'the cheers of the opposition'. He also received once more the support of Mr Gaitskell. He was on the way up.

Meanwhile, in his character of 'the terror of the white settlers', Stonehouse had paid visits to Africa which were to have important results.

In 1959 he was selected as a member of an all-party mission of enquiry to the Central African Federation. This was an impermanent structure which had been cobbled together for administrative purposes in 1953 by uniting Northern Rhodesia, Southern Rhodesia and Nyasaland. Stonehouse made a number of speeches to the Southern Rhodesian National Congress. Their tone annoyed Sir Edgar Whitehead, the Southern Rhodesian Prime Minister, so much that, somewhat unwisely, he advised Sir Roy Welensky, the Federal Prime Minister, that any further visit by Stonehouse was inopportune. Steps were taken accordingly, he was declared a 'prohibited immigrant' and refused admission to Nyasaland. The immediate result was massive publicity in the press, most of it in Stonehouse's favour.

Nor was it the end of the matter. It will be remembered that at about this time the new Conservative Prime Minister, Harold Macmillan, paid a visit to Africa, during which he made his celebrated speech about 'the wind of change'. One of the functions he attended was in Lusaka. At luncheon there the Mayor of Lusaka was moved to make an attack on certain 'foreign pests'. In particular he named John Stonehouse and Barbara Castle. 'They come here to make money, to create trouble, to write sensational articles without regard to the truth. The more sensational the articles are and the more they slam the white man in Africa, the larger the size of the type in the headlines and, no doubt, the size of the fee.'

To accuse two Members of Parliament of telling lies, in print, for money, was unwise. It was unwiser still of the *Daily Mail* to report the speech. A libel action ensued and resulted in apologies, coupled with the payment of costs and damages.

The second escapade was of a more barnstorming type. It involved long flights by air, intervention of the authorities, sudden changes of plan, the adoption of a pseudonym and other improvisations. Almost it might be regarded as a dress rehearsal for a later and even more dramatic foray in another continent. Stonehouse tells the story in his book.

It started in Dar-es-Salaam, on the sea-board of Tanganyika. His plan was to fly to Blantyre, near the southern tip of Nyasaland, from there to Salisbury, the capital of Southern Rhodesia and thence by train to Bechuanaland. If he realised that he was giving hostages to fortune by entering two of the component states of the Central African Federation, whose head had already declared him to be *persona non grata*, he did not allow it to deter him.

At Ndola the Rhodesian police took over. They knew that an enthusiastic crowd of Africans was waiting at Salisbury to welcome the man who had become one of their foremost champions. It was a demonstration the authorities were determined to prevent. At Salisbury he was hurried out of the civilian plane, put aboard a Rhodesian Air Force plane and flown to Francistown on the border of Bechuanaland and, quite simply, dumped.

'I was left holding my case with nobody about. It was lonely and desolate to be left like that in the middle of Africa.'

He was not to be deterred. He hitched a lift with a Dutchman to Serowe where he stayed with Seretse Khama and his wife before taking the train for South Africa, accompanied by warnings, at every stop, that he would be arrested as soon as he got there; which he was, at the frontier, by two stalwart policemen who bundled him into a car and drove him to Johannesburg. During the drive he scribbled a fifteen-hundred-word article for *Reynolds News*, who were financing the trip, and succeeded in dispatching it.

He discovered that being escorted by the police conferred advantages. The paramount objective of the authorities was to get rid of him and he found himself, with no delay, on the inaugural flight of South African Airways to Brazzaville, in the Congo. It was on this flight, whilst the celebratory champagne corks were popping, that he realised what a celebrity he had become. The man sitting next to him discoursed at some length about 'the antics of that fellow Stonehouse' – and remained friendly when he found that he was talking to him.

After further adventures in Brazzaville and, across the river, in Leopoldville where he posed for three days as Mr Smith, a journalist, he flew back to England via Ghana. It was, he says, 'an interesting visit'. It was also one which set the seal on his reputation as an expert on African affairs. And the wind of change was indeed blowing. Northern Rhodesia, shaking free of the Federation, lifted its ban on him. He was invited to attend the Kenya Independence celebrations. The prediction of Fenner Brockway was being fulfilled.

This could not have happened at a more opportune moment. At the Labour Party Conference in the autumn of 1961 George Brown had spoken of 'a responsible party, looking forward to the responsibilities of power'. And Stonehouse had been selected to open the debate on the Common Market. It was a clear sign of favour and his speech had been well received. Nevertheless when the ballot for the Labour shadow cabinet took place in November he had not pressed his claims. This was sensible. Time was on his side.

At the end of 1962 Labour was calling loudly for a General Election. 'Next autumn at the very latest.' *The Times* agreed. The last election had been in 1959. Under the Quinquennial Act, Parliament would have to be dissolved in the autumn of 1964. 'Support for the government had been seriously eroded over the past six months,' they said.

By that time Sir Alec Douglas-Home had taken over from Harold Macmillan. He was a cricketer. His philosophy was that the game was not decided until the final ball had been bowled.

It was generally recognised by now that the Labour party would return to power. The only question in people's minds was the size of their majority. Would it be substantial enough to guarantee them a comfortable spell of office? Was it to be a repetition of the triumph of 1946? Or would they just scrape home? When the votes were counted the answer appeared. Harold Wilson and his party were in power. Their overall majority was five.

Stonehouse retained his seat at Wednesbury without difficulty and awaited his reward. To start with, he realised, it would be a small one. Harold Wilson offered him the post of Parliamentary Secretary to the Minister of Aviation. ('You were a pilot, weren't you?') He accepted willingly, particularly since it would mean working under Roy Jenkins, a man he had always respected. At their first official meeting Roy made a sensible suggestion. Instead of their treading on each other's toes the work would be divided. Stonehouse's main job was to be the export of aircraft and everything connected with them, including the increasingly sophisticated control and early warning systems.

This suited him well. He was a good organiser and a persuasive salesman. Monthly meetings were arranged with the sales managers of the main aircraft companies. The objective was to cut out internal competition and get the orders for the company best fitted to carry them out. Many of his efforts were directed to selling the VC10 and the Super VC10, the opposition coming not, primarily, from competing salesmen, but from BOAC who preferred the American Boeing aircraft on the grounds of economy of operation. One man who assisted him in his efforts was Freddie Laker.

In one field Stonehouse chalked up an unquestioned success. Operating with Group Captain Geoffrey Edwards he negotiated a £300 million sale to Saudi Arabia of Lightning fighter aircraft and radar equipment. This was in direct competition with America. At a moment when the sale seemed to be faltering, Stonehouse remembered the old tag, 'If you can't beat them, join them'. He flew across to the Pentagon and talked to their head salesman, Henry Kuss. It was a fortunate moment. Macnamara, the Defense Secretary, was prepared to do something for Britain in return for getting sales for his own swing-wing aircraft. Once it was clear that the Americans were prepared to be benevolently neutral the Saudi objections were smoothed over and the deal went through.

This transaction becomes significant in the light of after events. Like Ivar Kreuger, Stonehouse had demonstrated the ability to talk to technical people in their own language, to visit them, to negotiate with them face to face and to carry those negotiations through to success.

His success as a salesman was recognised by the Prime Minister of an administration perennially short of cash and in the first governmental reshuffle which took place after the inconclusive election of 1966 (Labour majority five) he was promoted to junior ministerial rank as Under Secretary of State for the Colonies. 'Younger men given their Chances' was the predictable *Times* headline.

When in London he divided his time between his own office in Great Smith Street and the ministerial offices in Marlborough and Lancaster House where, with Fred Lee, his political master, he 'engaged in the task of dismantling the residue of the British Empire'.

There were compensations. The residue was widely spread around the globe and this gave him unlimited opportunities for his favourite occupation of long distance air travel. One of the additional sweets of his new position was that he was now able to visit Africa in a very different guise. As an honoured guest he attended the celebrations when Bechuanaland transformed itself into Botswana, under his old friend Seretse Khama, and when the tiny South African enclave Basutoland emerged to a not entirely happy independence as Lesotho. 'It would be difficult for even the South Africans to arrest me this time.'

In January 1967 there was a further Cabinet reshuffle. The Colonial

Office ceased to be an independent organisation. Both it and the Commonwealth Relations Office were drawn in under the wing of an enlarged Foreign Office.

Stonehouse was moved sideways and upwards. He now became Minister of State for Aviation, a post which was re-styled, one month later, as Minister of State for Technology. This was an exciting position and one particularly suited to his talents. There was the air-bus, on the question of which, in view of previous promises to America, he had to bat defensively; there was the start of the space programme and overshadowing everything else there was Concorde.

He was not in at the birth of this remarkable Anglo-French aircraft – credit for that had to be given to Julian Amery, the Conservative Minister for Aviation – but it fell to Stonehouse to preside over its childhood. And it was a troubled childhood. The majority of the cabinet were either luke-warm about it or actively opposed. Why should scarce resources, needed for a multitude of social schemes, be squandered on something from which, in the outcome, only the very rich could benefit? Then there was the vexed question of the sonic boom. The Americans naturally made the most of this phenomenon in their bitter opposition to what they recognised as a serious competitor in the fight for transatlantic traffic, but there was also a strong opposition on genuine amenity grounds in the South of England too. Stonehouse was convinced that the threat was being exaggerated. He initiated a series of tests. The first one, unannounced, was over Dorchester. There were no complaints. For later tests warnings were given. This was asking for trouble and the complaints duly rolled in. But they did not halt the programme. Concorde was a step from which there was no turning back.

One feels that if Stonehouse could have stayed with aviation his career might have been very different. He was happy in it and he was successful. There was foreign travel, to Russia and America. Harold Wilson clearly approved of this forthright young man who came from much the same sort of social background as himself. Had he not signalled his support by recommending elevation to the Privy Council? The sun was shining warmly.

What came next was a step up and a big one. He was to be Postmaster-General. At this particular moment it was a challenging position. The Post Office was ceasing to be a department of state, with a minister at its head, and was being converted into a trading corporation. As a start a considerable segment of history had to be rewritten. There was a 244 page Bill, a document repealing or amending some 500 Acts of Parliament. The new corporation employed close on half a million people and had an annual investment programme of two billion pounds. Its head would have extensive powers, subject only to the ultimate control of the Minister of Posts and Telecommunications. There was widespread belief that Stonehouse might step out of politics and assume the chairmanship himself.

It would be a logical step, as *The Times* pointed out. Who better equipped for the job than the man who had been such a success as Minister of Technology? It added, not quite accurately, that his father had spent his entire working life in the Post Office. Again, if Stonehouse had accepted this advice much might have transpired differently.

It seems to be a rule of life that misfortunes tread on each other's heels. Stonehouse had enemies. It was not now a question of Communist hostility. In many cases the knives were in the hands of political colleagues. They distrusted his comparatively rapid rise to power, which was in part the result of backing the right horse. As long ago as 1960 he had made his position plain. Gaitskell had been wrong to defy the Party Conference. Harold Wilson was the man who was 'eminently fitted to lead the party, being endowed with quite exceptional abilities to make an excellent Prime Minister'. He was on record as having repeated this view a number of times since. One of the men who disliked him most was the clever, unscrupulous Wykehamist, Richard Crossman. In 1969 Stonehouse made two mistakes.

The first was when, speaking impromptu at a luncheon given by the Electronics Engineering Association, he had said that devaluation had not been a success when the country was fighting for economic survival. He had also made a number of suggestions as to how the financial situation might be improved. There does not seem to be anything very blameworthy in this and he was surprised, next day, to read the severe criticisms in certain sections of the press. 'It was the height of irresponsibility', said one of his colleagues, speaking at a meeting of the Parliamentary Party, 'to voice such opinions on the eve of an important by-election'. And in any case, what right had he to speak on matters outside his own ministry?

The second set-back was a matter of more substance. In the *Observer* article already referred to, the authors, speaking of Stonehouse's 'increasingly autocratic methods' gave as an example his settling of the Post Office Workers' strike. Anxious, as he well might be, to clear this matter up he had authorised a settlement of the strikers' claims which had not only been premature, but, in the general view, over generous. This was a point on which a Labour Minister was particularly vulnerable.

If the two matters mentioned above could, to a greater or lesser degree, be accounted Stonehouse's fault, the next one certainly could not. One day in 1968 he was staggered to receive a summons to No. 10 Downing Street and to be faced, at a meeting attended only by the Prime Minister, his Principal Private Secretary, and Elwell of counter-intelligence, with an accusation from a defector that he had been guilty of passing information to the Czech secret service.

As has recently been seen, such accusations are easy to make and impossible conclusively to disprove. They need not be true. They need only the smallest measure of plausibility for them to take root. Now Stonehouse had had a long, if spasmodic, association with Czechoslovakia. In 1957, the year of his election to parliament, he had, with other members of the Board of the London Co-operative Society, paid visits to Vienna and Prague. They had been well received and on the last day in Prague, before catching the plane home, had lunched perhaps more well than wisely. The slivovitz had flowed freely both at the lunch and at the airport. Their host, the veteran communist Zabotnik, had been particularly friendly. Stonehouse, in his book, records the moment when he boarded the aircraft with some difficulty and raised his right arm in a clenched fist salute. Zabotnik raised his in reply. The cameras were, no doubt, clicking busily.

The contact, having been established, was maintained. Stonehouse records a number of lunches in London with the Czech diplomat Vlado Koudelka, whom he met again when, on his way to the Leipzig Trade Fair, he broke the journey at Prague. From his point of view there was nothing exceptional about any of this. As a member of the Council of Europe and the European Assembly his contacts with European politicians and diplomats were frequent and widespread. 'During the two years I served on these bodies I visited every western European country from Turkey to Norway, sometimes two or three times in a year.' He noted, however, that the Czechs were particularly persistent in their attentions.

One thing which weighed heavily in Stonehouse's favour was the fact that after all these meetings, even after informal lunches, he made careful notes of what had been said and passed copies to British security. Gradually the incident was relegated to the obscurity from which it should never have emerged.

Stonehouse says, 'The Prime Minister never discussed the spy issue with me again.'

But did it leave a small cloud behind? It is possible that it did. But in view of the much darker clouds that were gathering in 1970 it ceased to be significant.

The Labour government, which had survived for six years with low single-figure majorities, went once more to the polls and suffered a decisive defeat. Confounding the prophets, the Conservatives, under Edward Heath, obtained a majority of forty-three. A month later the Labour Party, licking its wounds, overhauled its own internal organisation. Stonehouse was one of six former senior ministers who failed to be elected to the shadow cabinet.

Was this the writing on the wall? It may have seemed so to him. Certainly it called for a re-thinking of his position. The salient factor was money. If he continued as a back bench MP he would have to subsist on his salary, augmented by occasional fees from broadcasts and from the writing of articles and books. He had three children now. The youngest, a boy, was at the expensive age of eleven. No doubt it could be managed – he had learned the lessons of economy in his youth – but was it justifiable?

If he counted up his assets they were not inconsiderable. There was his position, as a successful Member of Parliament (his own majority at the last election had been 15,885, an increase where others were slipping) and his prestige as an ex-Minister and Privy Councillor. Add to this his proven powers as a negotiator and, most important of all, his multiple contacts in Europe and on the other side of the Atlantic. If he could make a success of a business career, when his party came back to power – as assuredly they would – he would be in a very strong position.

In the event, Stonehouse involved himself in two separate enterprises, thus ignoring the advice given by Lord Beaverbrook to Clarence

Hatry; that a man who tries to do too many things will succeed in none of them.

First there was the setting up of a financial mini-empire, with its headquarters in Dover Street. Here Stonehouse had the help of his nephew, Michael Hayes, who in March 1970 (three months *before* Labour lost the election) incorporated for him three companies. The first and most important was Export Promotion and Consultancy Services Limited (EPACS). Its name expresses the scope of its operations. It was Stonehouse acting in corporate form. It soon secured a number of prestige accounts, among others BAC, the Dowty Group and International Computers. The second company, operating on the same lines, was Systems and Consultancy Services. The third, which seemed to have little logical connection with the other two, was Connoisseurs of Claret, a mail order wine club.

These three were wholly owned Stonehouse concerns. As EPACS expanded, obtaining orders for customers overseas, a fourth company was incorporated, Global Imex. In this there were outside directors, one of whom was Jim Charlton, but Stonehouse retained control through his majority shareholding.

These, with the later addition of Ronval Properties, constituted the commercial group, simply and avowedly designed to make as much money as possible. But there was a second enterprise which reflected the idealistic side of Stonehouse's character. To understand it we have to turn, briefly, to the unhappy history of the Indian sub-continent in the years which followed the end of the British Raj and the division into 'India' and 'Pakistan', a division based on the age-long bitter hostility between Hindus and Mohammedans. This had involved the creation of not one, but two sub-states: West Pakistan, usually referred to simply as Pakistan, and East Pakistan or, as it came to be called, Bangladesh.

Bangladesh was the poor relation. The massacres and natural disasters which followed its bid for independence have become part of a bloodstained page of history. Stonehouse became emotionally involved in its troubles. Never a man to take things at second hand, he paid a number of visits to Calcutta and from there, at considerable personal risk, penetrated into Bangladesh itself. It was a journey which few outsiders were prepared to undertake until the Indian Army had, belatedly, intervened and restored order. After that some attempt had to be made to clear up the devastation. As Stonehouse records: 'Ten million refugees to return to shattered homes, crops destroyed and cattle lost. Communications to be restored . . . and the need for supplies of all descriptions, food, clothing, medicines – the list was endless.'

It could only be done with outside help and help was forthcoming. The Bangladesh Fund had been set up in London, under the trusteeship of Abu Sayeed Choudhury (later to be President of Bangladesh) and Donald Chesworth, the Chairman of War on Want. Stonehouse, who had been rewarded for his efforts with honorary citizenship of Bangladesh, became a third trustee. In 1971 the fund raised and transmitted more than £300,000 in cash as well as help in kind for the unhappy infant state.

Which brings us to the British Bangladesh Trust and a turning point in the story.

The idea originated in the mind of K. B. Ahmed, who came, one day in 1972, to talk to Stonehouse at the House of Commons. It was to create a British Bangladesh Bank. It could not, initially, adopt that specific title since no institution can style itself a bank until its status and objects have been approved by the Bank of England. The reaction from Threadneedle Street was, in principle, favourable. Stonehouse explained that his object was two-fold. To bring into the British banking system a large number of Bengali immigrants and to set up a bridge between Great Britain and Bangladesh. Commerce and Idealism lay down together. They were to prove uneasy bedfellows.

The issued capital of the new bank, modest by modern standards, was to be one million pounds. Promises of investment came from a number of well-known companies and institutions – Guest Keen and Nettlefold, the Plessey Group and the Crown Agents among others – who saw that shares in this bank would give them a useful toe-hold in Bangladesh. The financial press started to take an interest in the project.

This was encouraging, as far as it went. But for Stonehouse it did not go far enough. The subscribers he wanted – maybe for only a few shares each – were the Bengali immigrants. This was the other side of the scheme: the formation of a bridge between them and their fellow countrymen. A difficulty became apparent. Very few of these immigrants read the *Financial Times* or studied the financial pages of

The Times and the *Telegraph*. What happened next must be closely examined, since it is the key to much that followed.

As part of the promotion campaign for the new bank, the editor of the Bengali newspaper *Janomot* published a special news sheet, for distribution to its readers, describing the origin and purpose of the bank. It was here that Stonehouse needed to tread with the utmost caution, for he was entering a minefield.

That formidably named piece of legislation, the Prevention of Fraud (Investments) Act, had been enacted with the praiseworthy object of driving out of business the bucket-shop owners and other unscrupulous operators who pocketed the savings of the innocent and unwary by offering them shares in worthless companies. In summary, it prohibited the issue of any circular inviting investment unless that circular was in the approved form of a prospectus. But what was and what was not a circular the Act did not attempt to define, leaving this to the decision of the judicature. It was not an easy question. One judge, with memories of his schooldays, said that since any circle could be constructed if three points on it were known, he supposed that a document sent to three or more people could be described as 'circular'. But this judicial flippancy evaded the real issue. When did such a document *actually make an offer of shares*?

This nice legal point became of great importance when, five days before the subscription list for the new bank closed, the *Sunday Times* splashed, in its business section, a half-page, four-column article entitled 'Five questions on the British Bangladesh Trust'. The tone of the article can be judged from its opening: 'John Stonehouse, as Chairman of the British Bangladesh Trust has spent most weekends over the past few months talking money to Bengali groups. "Help Bangladesh, help yourself" advertisements have appeared in the Bengali Newsweek Janomot. But in the course of this £25,000 promotion campaign John Stonehouse and his colleagues have adopted somewhat unorthodox methods of soliciting investment.'

Of these methods five examples were given. Three were trivial and hardly unorthodox, but there was a sting in two of them. Publishing, in *Janomot*, what amounted to a draft prospectus; and claiming that the Bank of England would give permission for the name to be changed to the British Bangladesh Bank after twelve to eighteen months' working.

In his answer to these two points, Stonehouse pointed out that the

Janomot publication was a news sheet, not a prospectus. And that a proper translation of what had been said about the Bank of England was not that permission *would* be granted, but that it *might* be granted. It depended on the translation of a Bengali word.

Who was right about these nice points is unimportant and they were never tested in court. What was important was the predictable result of such an article appearing at such a moment. The expected flood of applications dried up to a trickle. Only £651,160 was subscribed and even this figure would not have been reached if Stonehouse had not thrown in all the available resources of his companies and of himself.

This rings a number of bells. Whitaker Wright fighting for Lake View Consols by pouring in money from the Globe; Ivar Kreuger despoiling his match companies to finance his climactic loan to the Germans; more closely still, Clarence Hatry spending the money put by for his United Steel venture to keep up the price of the shares in his other companies. In the middle of Stonehouse's struggles to keep his bank afloat it was attacked from another quarter. The dragon's teeth sown by the *Sunday Times*'s article now sprang up in the form of Mr Newman, an investigating officer from the Department of Trade and Industry, followed, even more menacingly, by Inspector Grant from the Fraud Squad.

An investigation of this sort is the direst example of the fallacy that there's no smoke without fire. In the end it was decided that there was no case against the bank and its proprietors. But irreparable damage had been done. Inspector Wright had carried out his investigation with ponderous rectitude. Individual Bengali investors, small men and easily frightened, had all been questioned.

'Did you see the news sheet in *Janomot*?'
'Yes.'
'Did you subscribe to the British Bangladesh Trust?'
'Yes. I bought two shares.'
'*After* you saw the news sheet?'
'Yes.'

Post hoc or *propter hoc*? Who could say? What was certain was that the bad news would spread. There was something wrong with the bank. It was expected to be founded firmly on the savings and support of the Bengali community. These foundations had been eroded by this article.

Stonehouse switched his attention to the part of his commercial empire which seemed to be flourishing. Global Imex was going ahead. EPACS had valuable consultancy agreements in America. In November 1974 Stonehouse and his fellow director, Jim Charlton, flew to Florida to follow up a contact which had been made with the Bank of Miami. They stayed at the Fontainebleu Hotel on Miami Beach, said to have some connection with Mafia operations. It was on 20 November that the news hit London.

'John Stonehouse, Labour and Co-operative MP for Walsall North and a former Minister is missing, feared drowned in waters off Miami. He was last seen going swimming. His clothes left in a beach-hut changing room had not been claimed.'

Jim Charlton said that he had warned Stonehouse against swimming out too far. Had the tide caught him? Or might his death be suicide, as the Miami police speculated? Stonehouse's secretary, Mrs Buckley, told reporters that she thought he was being blackmailed.

Mr Molloy, the Labour member for Ealing North, put forward a different theory. Stonehouse had shown himself to be a tough and uncompromising negotiator. It was common knowledge that he had made enemies throughout the world. In May the car which he had left at Heathrow had been wrecked by a hundred-pound bomb. Was it not possible that he had been destroyed by the Mafia? This idea gained credence when the Miami police unearthed a blood-stained concrete 'coffin' from the sandhills behind the beach.

Whether accident, suicide or murder this development caused consternation in two quarters. The executives left behind in the Dover Street headquarters started a frantic examination of the records and accounts of the group to see whether they offered any explanation for the theory of suicide. At the same time five major insurance companies were considering the position. In the period between the beginning of May and the middle of July that year policies had been effected on Stonehouse's life, in favour of his wife, with the Yorkshire General, Canada Life, the Phoenix, the Norwich Union and the Royal Insurance Company. The total sum insured was £125,000.

All these policies had come into force, the last of them, the Royal, on 18 September and Michael Hayes had already made a formal approach on behalf of the widow. It was very much in their interest to discover what exactly *had* taken place in Miami.

On Christmas Eve all questions were answered. The Melbourne

police reported that, following a raid in a Melbourne suburb, they had detained a man believed to be John Stonehouse. Three days later the identification was confirmed. Stonehouse was being held in custody so that a deportation order could be considered.

So far we have been following events as they appeared to the public at large. It is now time to turn to the other side of the story and to consider the facts which emerged in the next sixteen months and culminated at the Old Bailey in March 1976.

A clue had been offered, but overlooked. On one of his plane journeys it had been observed that Stonehouse was reading, with close attention, Frederick Forsyth's book *The Day of the Jackal*. From that apparently unimportant detail, Sherlock Holmes might have remarked, it should have been possible to construct the whole story.

In the Forsyth book the 'Jackal' demonstrated the ease with which a false passport could be obtained. All that was necessary was to find a person who had died, but who, had he lived, would have been roughly the same age as the applicant. The next step was to obtain a copy of the birth certificate of the deceased, a matter of paying a small fee at the Registry. The application form could then be filled in. The final step was to obtain the confirmation of some respectable witness that the photograph of the applicant affixed to the form was that of the dead man whose name he was adopting. With these simple instructions in mind ('Forsyth is clear and yet dramatic,' says Stonehouse, 'a brilliant writer with a tang of authenticity') he had set about obtaining one new passport and two new identities.

He contacted a hospital in his constituency and learned the names of two men, either dying or recently dead. These were Joseph Arthur Markham and Donald Clive Mildoon. By the third week in July he had collected both birth certificates and on 1 August the application for a passport in the name of Markham went in. As the signature to verify the photograph he selected Neil McBride, MP, who died at about that time.

The next step was to construct some background for his *alter ego*. This he did by booking a room in Markham's name at the Astoria Hotel in St Georges Drive and by employing Management Business Services as a forwarding agent, with instructions to send any mail received in Markham's name to the Bank of New South Wales.

It is clear that by this time the idea was already fixed in Stonehouse's mind. He would start life afresh in Australia; though whether it was to be as Markham or Mildoon does not seem to have been finally decided. This was a point which was to prove of unexpected importance later.

The next step was to transfer to Australia sufficient funds to support him when he arrived. Most of the money would have to come from his companies. It was the point of departure, the definitive switch from the legal to the criminal.

Stonehouse achieved his objective in two steps.

The first was to prime EPACS with ready money. This was not too difficult. A bank lending money to a limited company normally requires a personal guarantee from one or more of its directors. In this case the Chairman was an ex-Minister of the Crown and a Privy Councillor. They were prepared to lend generously. Between May 1972 and October 1974 Stonehouse gave his personal guarantees in support of bank loans to his companies totalling £729,500. And he topped this off with a final loan, shortly before his departure, of another £10,000 from Lloyds Bank.

At a later period an article in the *Sunday Times* had its own explanation for the generosity of the banks. 'Banks do not as a rule lend money to an individual without security. But National and Grindlays received a special request from a third party to accommodate Mr Stonehouse. It granted the overdraft facility.' The article described this helpful character as a 'Mystery MP' and a 'Senior Member of Parliament'. It did not name him.

The next step was to transfer a substantial portion of this money to Australia. Here we are in a maze of confused transactions, involving twenty-four accounts in seventeen different banks.

Some of the passages of the money have been clearly plotted. For instance, there was an account in the name of Markham in the Midland Bank in Vauxhall Bridge Road. This reached a total of over £14,000. On 3 September, Stonehouse, as Markham, called on the manager of the Bank of New South Wales in Threadneedle Street where he opened an account with a transfer of £12,000 from the Vauxhall Bridge Road bank. He explained that he was contemplating emigration to Australia and would need an account in their Melbourne branch. He was assured that this could be arranged without difficulty.

The next step was to arrange for the the transfer of money from the

EPACS account to Stonehouse's personal account at Lloyds Bank, St James's. Two such transfers were subsequently noted. One of £16,000 and another, on 1 November, of £29,000. There were other transactions on which the curtain was subsequently lifted. A consultancy fee was to be paid to EPACS by the Garrett Corporation of America. It was $25,000, payable half on signature of the agreement and half when the services were complete. The initial cheque for $12,500 was paid into Stonehouse's personal account and not passed on to the company. There would, no doubt, have been other more regular credits in this personal account such as remuneration and expenses due to the Chairman. The final total must have been substantial. Where did the money go to? For it certainly went somewhere. At Stonehouse's departure only £147 was left.

'It goes all the way to Switzerland,' Michael Corkery was to say, 'and gets lost in Swiss banking secrecy'. So all was now ready. The alternative personalities had been created. Money was either in Australia or on its way there. The next step was to disappear and this Stonehouse achieved very simply, by leaving one lot of his clothes in a beach hut at Miami, dressing in a second set which had been left handy and catching a plane that evening for San Francisco. For this journey he was Markham, using his passport and financing it with money from his American Express Card. On 24 November, again using Markham's credit card, he purchased a ticket to Honolulu and onward to Sydney.

He had business to transact in Honolulu. He was carrying with him a large sum in English and American currency. Introducing himself to the Bank of Hawaii as a Mr Lewis Jones he got them to exchange this for a bank draft for $13,177 in the name of Markham.

This piece of business done, he flew on to Sydney and, by 27 November, was in Melbourne. Here he immediately opened an account in the Bank of New South Wales. This had already been adumbrated in London. Into it would go his balance from the Threadneedle Street branch and the Honolulu bank draft of $13,177.

A fortnight later he opened further accounts. A current account in the Bank of New Zealand in the name of Mildoon; and current and deposit accounts in the Australian and New Zealand Bank in the name of Markham. Two days later he opened current and deposit accounts in the name of Mildoon in the Commonwealth Banking Corporation.

The reason for the multiplicity of these accounts is not clear. It seems likely, as Stonehouse himself was to admit, that he was, by this time, in a state of 'personality confusion'. Whatever the reason, it had dire consequences. A stranger who had been in the Australian and New Zealand Bank had noted the Englishman opening accounts in the name of Markham. Happening to be in the Commonwealth Bank two days later he had been surprised to find the same man opening accounts under the name of Mildoon. He felt it to be his duty to inform the police.

From that moment Stonehouse was under observation. The Victoria State Police became interested in this Englishman with a lot of money, many bank accounts and more than one name. Their first idea was that he might be Lord Lucan. When Stonehouse was mentioned as a possibility, a description was obtained from Interpol and certainly seemed to fit. By Christmas Eve they felt certain enough to accuse him. After a very brief prevarication Stonehouse admitted the truth. He seemed almost relieved to do so.

On the day that the information reached England, the Scotland Yard Fraud Squad was called in and a week later Detective Chief Superintendent Etheridge was on his way to Australia. He was back by 25 January. One must assume that the information he had unearthed was far from straightforward since nearly two months went by before a warrant could be obtained from Bow Street Magistrates' Court for Stonehouse's arrest; and a further six weeks before extradition proceedings began in Melbourne on 5 May.

That these proceedings should have dragged on for a further three months was due to a number of reasons, not the least of them being the determination of the Australian authorities (strongly demonstrated recently in the so-called 'M.I.5 affair') not to be dictated to by England. On one occasion when the vexed question of the grant or refusal of bail was before the Melbourne Court, the prosecuting counsel made the tactical mistake of stating that the Chief Metropolitan Magistrate had advised against it. He was sharply reminded that Australia was no longer a colony and that its courts were independent of direction from Bow Street or anywhere else.

Another difficulty was the fact that Stonehouse was a member of the British Parliament. Initially this proved favourable for him. At that time the only charge available was that he was an illegal immigrant. Under the Parliamentary Conventions, Australia admits any member of a Commonwealth Parliament without restrictions. The Minister of Labour and Immigration decided that he should be accepted as an MP with the right to stay. Particularly as he had not committed any offence against Australian laws.

This concentrated the minds of the British authorities on the relevant point: *what offences had he committed?* And were they offences for which, under the Extradition (Commonwealth Countries) Act 1966, he could be extradited? For this Act had a sting in its tail. If extraditable charges were now preferred and Stonehouse was taken back to England for trial, those charges *could not be added to* without the consent of Australia.

The English investigators had therefore to be careful to include no charge which could not be substantiated in an English court. The care which they exercised can be judged from a report which appeared in *The Times*. £750,000, it seems, had been spent by eight police officers investigating the Stonehouse affair in Britain, Switzerland, Denmark, Liechtenstein, Hawaii and the United States.

Initially fifteen charges were preferred against Stonehouse and his secretary Mrs Buckley; others were added as the efforts of the investigating team found their way through the financial maze that Stonehouse had constructed. Stonehouse was allowed bail. He took advantage of his freedom of action to apply to seven countries for sanctuary. Gradually some replies came back. Sweden and Mauritius, favourable in principle, but not definite. Botswana formal and negative. From Zambia, Tanzania, Kenya and Bangladesh no reply.

In the end Stonehouse took the same decision as Whitaker Wright. He would travel back to England voluntarily to face the music. But, like Wright, he went under escort.

As statements were gathered in from a hundred and fifty witnesses, the Director of Public Prosecutions built up his case. There was every reason for care. Stonehouse still had friends and a following. The National Council for Civil Liberties, polling its members for an outstanding Parliamentary figure in the cause of freedom, recorded that the jailed MP John Stonehouse showed up strongly despite, as they delicately expressed it, 'problems of managing a full attendance in the House'.

That eminent polemicist, Bernard Levin, was even more outspoken: 'The sheer indecency of the Labour Party's behaviour in assuming the worst of a colleague, in presuming him guilty of crimes with which he has not even been charged, in ignoring the obvious and tragic fact that, on all the evidence, he is clearly suffering from a severe breakdown and in making such unseemly haste to rid themselves of possible embarrassment and to restore their tiny majority in the House should not pass without censure.'

Clearly the trial was going to be closely watched, by enemies and friends.

It opened, at the Central Criminal Court, before Mr Justice Eveleigh on 24 April 1976. Senior Treasury Counsel, Michael Corkery, led for the Crown. Lord Wigoder, QC, appeared for Mrs Buckley. Stonehouse decided, after some hesitation, to represent himself.

The most rational way of viewing the trial is to see it as through a stereoscope; 'An instrument,' says the dictionary, 'by which the images of two pictures differing slightly in point of view are seen one by each eye and so give an effect of solidity'.

First, then, the general outline as viewed by the Crown. 'This is a story', said Michael Corkery, 'of a crime where a very able man, over a period of four months, covers up his disappearance and spins a web of deception in which almost every strand is fashioned with ingenuity and great ability.'

To put the matter shortly, Stonehouse had transferred abroad, into his own accounts in Australia, sums of money which belonged to his companies and not to him, thus incidentally defrauding the creditors of those companies. He had procured this money, for his companies and for himself, by pretending that he intended to repay it. He had insured his life heavily, so that his widow should benefit by his supposed death. He had procured bank cards and drawn money by means of them – again with no intention of repaying it. He had adopted two 'cover personalities' and in doing so had been guilty of a number of incidental offences.

Such was the outline of the Crown case. It could not rest there. Under the rules of English law it had to be expressed as a number of specific charges, each demonstrating a breach of the criminal code. Twenty-one such charges were, ultimately, put forward. The easiest method of following them will be to set them out in the order adopted in the previous paragraph.

First, and most important, were five charges of theft of money from his own companies. The total was £22,811, to which was added the conversion of the Garrett Corporation cheque for $12,500 to his own account.

The obtaining of loans was covered by two charges of 'obtaining a pecuniary advantage' and the general monetary charges were rounded off with one of a conspiracy to defraud the creditors of EPACS.

The next batch of five charges were of attempting to obtain money by deception from the five insurance companies.

The remaining seven charges were of a more procedural nature. Three of obtaining the Markham and Mildoon birth certificates and the Markham passport by means of forged applications and four for misuse of different bank cards to obtain services and airline tickets.

Such were the charges. It was necessary to produce witnesses to prove them. As has been mentioned, statements had been taken by the prosecution from more than a hundred and fifty people. It was not intended that all of them should be called. The many abortive attempts to convict Horatio Bottomley had taught the Crown that it was fatally easy to confuse the jury with a superabundance of testimony. They had therefore made a tentative arrangement with the defence that only the forty more important ones should appear in the witness box. Agreed summaries of the evidence of others should be read out.

Stonehouse, perhaps with reason, objected to this and withdrew his consent. He may have seen in the length of the trial a chance of salvation. However, in three instances he did concede, on humanitarian grounds, that witnesses should be spared the ordeal of a personal appearance. It had been intended to call the three widows, Mrs Jean Markham, Mrs Elsie Mildoon and Mrs Bridget McBride. He agreed that their evidence should be taken as read.

Most of the Crown witnesses were, necessarily, bank managers and officials and others concerned with the passage of money from England, via Hawaii, Zurich and Liechtenstein to bank accounts in Australia. An important witness was the solicitor Michael Hayes. His appearance produced one of the 'scenes in Court' with which the hearing was liberally punctuated. Unfortunately there is a dearth of detailed daily reports. As the trial wound its weary way along, most of the reporters had given up and confined themselves to very brief paragraphs. It is therefore difficult to reconstruct exactly what the argument was about. It seems to have arisen on Hayes being asked why he had agreed to the winding up of the companies without consulting Stonehouse. To which he replied, 'Well, he wasn't there to be asked, was he?' This produced an outburst which led to the Court's being adjourned for the day.

Alan Lefort, who had been accountant both to EPACS and Global Imex, gave evidence which supported, in turn, both the prosecution and the defence. He agreed that he had been uneasy about some of the manoeuvres of the Chairman; such as the bank guarantees which he was giving so freely and the movement of cash from one company to another in order to maintain the liquidity of each (a device for which, it will be remembered, Whitaker Wright was criticised). He also pointed out that loans to directors should comply with the provisions of the Companies Acts and that when a fee of £10,000 had been voted to Stonehouse he should have been debited PAYE of £3,300 before the balance was handed over. 'Pay me the lot,' Stonehouse had said. 'I'll deal with the tax later.'

On the other hand, and this is important when we come to consider the defence to the charges, he agreed that Stonehouse had worked hard to earn the large consultancy fees and had from time to time drawn money from his own account to reduce his loan account with EPACS and to bolster up the finances of the British Bangladesh Trust.

Another accountant, a Mr Stokes, had been worried by some of the loans which the Trust had made and by the fact that in a number of cases, where the repayment date had gone by, the period was simply extended, unpaid interest being added to the loan. As an example of this Mr Hastings, a friend from Stonehouse's RAF days, told the Court that he had wished to purchase £12,000 worth of shares in the Trust, but lacked the money to do so. He had been granted a loan of a like amount. To date, he had not been asked to repay it. All this was evidence of an improvident way to run a business, but contained no element of defalcation or dishonesty. Mr Hastings added an interesting rider. Stonehouse had told him that he hoped, ultimately, to be leader of the Labour Party. Mr Hastings had considered this to be quite possible.

So far we have applied the right, or prosecution, eye to the stereoscope. Let us now use the other eye.

Stonehouse's defence, which started on 1 July, can be considered under two main headings. A general defence, based on his state of mind at the time of his disappearance and a specific defence to each of the charges.

To consider, first, the specific points; and in doing so it will be convenient to take them in the same order as before. There was no question of theft of money from EPACs, or from any other company, said Stonehouse. Legally, no doubt, they were incorporated bodies, but in fact he was what might have been described as a sole trader. The contacts were his, the visits to conclude deals were made by him, the only third party with any claim to his profits was the Inspector of Taxes and he would call evidence to show that all tax due had been paid. The money could either be regarded as fees, or, if the prosecution preferred, as loans to him. In neither case was he stealing it. Had not the Crown's own witness, Alan Lefort, confirmed this? The one case in which this defence seemed to fail was in regard to the Garrett Corporation $12,500. A point to bear in mind when considering the verdicts.

The question of the very substantial loans which Stonehouse had negotiated in the months prior to his disappearance was a difficult one. Had the banks been deceived? Yes, said the Crown. They had been offered a personal guarantee which Stonehouse must have known to be valueless, since he intended to disappear. There seemed to be an element of *ex post facto* in this reasoning; and at the committal proceedings Stonehouse had obtained one valuable admission from Alfred Gundry, the manager of Lloyds Bank, St James's. In examination by Tudor Price the following exchanges had occurred.

> *Tudor Price*: If you had known he was planning to depart, would you have authorised the overdraft?
>
> *Mr Gundry*: (choosing his words carefully): If it was the fact that he was planning to disappear *and* I had known of the fact, then of course I should not have authorised the overdraft.
>
> *Tudor Price*: Did you believe his personal guarantee to be a guarantee of value?
>
> *Mr Gundry*: I believed it to be a guarantee of value and I still believe it to be of value.
>
> *The Magistrate* (intervening): You still think it of value?
>
> *Mr Gundry*: Yes. I still believe it to be of value.
>
> *The Magistrate*: Why?
>
> *Mr Gundry*: Because I think Mr Stonehouse has a good life ahead of

him. He has a potential force for good. If, in the event, I have to rely on the personal guarantee, I do not consider it bad in the long term.

If all the bank managers who granted loans had followed Mr Gundry the charges of 'obtaining a pecuniary advantage' would have looked very thin.

The five insurance company charges raised complex points of law which had to be further considered when the matter came before the Court of Criminal Appeal and, ultimately, before the House of Lords. Consideration of them is best reserved until then.

The 'catch-all' charge of conspiracy was ultimately to be dismissed, both against Stonehouse and Mrs Buckley. It is not popular with judges and is usually taken as a sign that the prosecution is not sure of its case.

The seven 'procedural' charges were easy to prove, but in two cases were elusive when the Crown attempted to pin criminal sanctions on to them. This was particularly so with regard to the Mildoon and Markham birth certificates, alleged to have been 'obtained by a forged application'. The defence solicitor was able to demonstrate (by himself making an application) that such certificates could be obtained *without the applicant signing the form at all*. This defence did not, of course, cover the passport application, which has to be both signed and certified. The two birth certificate charges were dismissed.

The arguments about the misuse of the various credit cards were inconclusive. On the one hand Lefort confirmed that sums due had invariably been paid monthly up to the time of Stonehouse's disappearance. To which the answer of the prosecution was that the charges related to sums drawn after his disappearance, which he had never had any intention of repaying.

Having considered the specific charges from two points of view it is now necessary to look at the more generalised line of defence. 'I do not propose', said Stonehouse, 'to pursue Mr Corkery up every cul-de-sac. The Jury should judge me as a human being, in the general context of my life and what I was doing at the time.' He then gave, in a remarkable passage, his own explanation of the 'Markham' and 'Mildoon' characters.

They began, he said, as fantasies only, providing relief for the pressurised and overburdened public figure of John Stonehouse, Privy

Councillor and Company Chairman. By the middle of 1974 'Mr Stonehouse' has become an intolerable burden to him. He was the front man. He was putting on a façade, an image, where the real person behind it was different. In 1974 Mr Stonehouse was a humbug and a fraud. Not in the sense that the prosecution had alleged, but in his political and his business life. At first 'Markham' was only five per cent of his life. Ninety-five per cent was 'Stonehouse'. Gradually the Markham factor grew. Finally, 'Stonehouse' disappeared while swimming. He recalled the great elation and freedom of never having to live as Stonehouse again. In Australia 'Stonehouse' reappeared and the conflict between 'Markham' and 'Stonehouse' was renewed. For this reason he felt it would be better to live as a third person. Clive Mildoon.

His principal witnesses supported this version.

Dr Gerard Gibney, a psychiatrist from Victoria, said that the adoption of a parallel personality was the typical symptom of a depressive. It was a suicidal equivalent, an effort to escape the public figure. He was followed by Dr Lionel Hayward, a consultant psychologist. He produced six paintings by Stonehouse which demonstrated, in his view, that Stonehouse was a hysteroid personality. It was common, he said, for such people to begin with bright colours, yellows and greens, to recapture some of the pleasures the world had formerly given them. But gradually the pictures would be overlaid by dark and sombre colours, usually dark brown, sometimes black. All these signs he had found in Stonehouse's paintings.

Michael Corkery cross-examined him at length on this interesting theory. But whilst the man in the street can be relied on to laugh at the performance of psychiatrists in the witness box, it is important not to lose sight of the objective of this evidence. Stonehouse was *not* trying to prove that he was mad.

The matter was clearly expressed in an exchange which he had with the prison doctor, who suggested to him that he could plead diminished responsibility. Stonehouse explained that this was not his intention. In the prosecution's view, he said, only criminality could explain his disappearance. The medical evidence was simply to explain that it was due to a breakdown. It was designed to rebut the suggestion that it showed criminality.

After the closing speeches and the Judge's summing-up the eleven members of the jury retired to consider their verdict. They were out for more than nine hours. To start with, they could only reach unanimity on four of the charges. The Garrett cheque, the Markham application for two of the credit cards and the insurance policy taken with the Royal Insurance. Why this should have been differentiated from the other four insurance companies' charges is far from clear. The conspiracy charge was dismissed unanimously. When the Judge indicated that he was prepared to accept a majority verdict, the vote was ten to one of 'guilty' on fourteen of the remaining charges, the two which related to obtaining the birth certificates having already been dismissed.

The sentences followed. Six years concurrently on the major charges and a further year for uttering a forged application for a passport; seven years' imprisonment. Mrs Buckley, for whom the Judge expressed sympathy, was sentenced to two years' imprisonment, suspended for two years, so that she went free immediately.

For lawyers the most interesting part of the sequel was the appeal which went through the Court of Criminal Appeal to the House of Lords. It concerned, principally, the five insurance charges. Two grounds were argued for the invalidity of the conviction on these courts. The first was a question of fact. Had any claim in fact been made? Was a letter, written by Michael Hayes, a claim; or was it a notification that a claim might exist? Even if it was a claim, there was a further point of law. Could a criminal charge be brought in England where the decisive act in a series of acts (the pretended drowning) took place abroad? There was little precedent, but finding some analogy in Scottish law, the noble Lords decided that it could.

There was considerable sympathy for Stonehouse. Possibly people agreed with Bernard Levin and the National Council for Civil Liberties that a man's actions should not be too carefully scrutinised when the pressures on him have become intolerable. Possibly they were reacting to Stonehouse's own plea: 'I make only one request of the reader. Please just read this book out of interest in a real life adventure story.'

The pressure for clemency mounted when it became known that Stonehouse had been operated on for heart trouble. In August 1979 he was released after serving only three years of his sentence. A year later the bankruptcy order which had been made against him was discharged. Gradually normal life was resumed.

He remained a character in the public eye. In a feature article in *The Times* last year John Stapleton asked a number of well-known men what was the biggest regret in their lives. He was surprised when Stonehouse made no mention of the criminal offences which had wrecked his political career.

'I think,' said Stonehouse, 'that the biggest regret I have is that, from my earliest years, I was brought up as an idealist, a believer in a new society. For all those years I was pursuing false hopes. And when you have false hopes, you get your life wrong.'

Not a bad summary.

SOURCES

WHITAKER WRIGHT
Memoirs of a Public Prosecutor, S Felstead and Lady Muir, The Bodley Head, 1927
Sir George Lewis, Juxon, Collins, 1983
Rufus Isaacs Vol 1, The Marquis of Reading, Hutchinson, 1942
Wealth and Wild Cats, Raymond Radcliffe, Downey & Co, 1898

HORATIO BOTTOMLEY
Horatio Bottomley, Julian Symons, Cresset Press, 1955
Horatio Bottomley, Alan Hyman, Cassell, 1972
Criminal Days, Travers Humphreys, Hodders, 1946
A Lance for Liberty, J O Caswell Q C, Harrap, 1961

IVAR KREUGER
The Financier, George Soloveytchik, Peter Davies, 1933
Kreuger, Paul Bjerre, Kurt Lindberg, Stockholm, 1932
The Incredible Ivar Kreuger, Allen Churchill, Weidenfeld and Nicolson, 1957

CLARENCE HATRY
The Millionaire Mentality, Michael Pearson, 1961
Horace Avory, Gordon Lang, Herbert Jenkins, 1935

LEOPOLD HARRIS
The Fire Raisers, Dr Harold Dearden, Heinemann, 1934

Far from Humdrum, William Charles Crocker, Hutchinson Publishing Ltd, 1967

JOHN STONEHOUSE
Death of an Idealist, John Stonehouse, W H Allen, 1975
My Trial, John Stonehouse, Wyndham Publications Ltd, 1976

INDEX

Acevose Silks Ltd, 148–50
Africa, and John Stonehouse, 162–3, 164–5, 166–8, 170
African Co-operative Movement, 162, 163
Ahmed, K. B., 176
Allied Ironfounders, 118, 120–1
Amery, Julian, 171
Amsterdam, 95, 96
Anglo-Egyptian Bank, 116
Annan, Mr, official receiver, 57
Arber, Mr, insurance assessor, 150
arson (fire-raising), 135, 138–59
Asquith, Herbert, 21, 65
Astbury, Mr, KC, 36
Athenaeum Printing Works, Redhill, 53, 54, 60–1
Atkinson, Sir Edward Tindal, DPP, 153
Austin Friars, Hatry's office in, 109, 113
Austin Friars Trust, 114–15, 116, 121, 122, 124, 125–6
Australia, Stonehouse in, 180–4, 185, 190
Australian and New Zealand Bank, 182, 183
Austrian Immigrants Insurance Association, 109
Auxiliary Associated Gold Mines, 21
Avory, Horace (Mr Justice Avory), 12, 14, 38, 47, 62, 63, 106, 127, 128–30, 133, 157

Baker Street and Waterloo Railway, 30
Balfour, Arthur, 21, 35

Ball, Adam John Loughborough, fire assessor, 136, 156–7, 158; *Trial and Error – The Fire Conspiracy and After*, 158
Bangladesh, 175–8
Bangladesh Fund, 176; *see also* British Bangladesh Trust
Bank of England, 119, 122, 126, 176, 177, 178
Bank of Hawaii, 182
Bank of New South Wales, 180, 181, 182
Bank of New Zealand, 182
Barbican 'twin' fire, 150–1
Barclays Bank, 123, 129
Barnato, Barney, 22
Barnes, Mr, official liquidator, 32–4
Barrow, Frederick, solicitor, 57
Basinghall Street fire (1929), 146
Batten, Barton, Durstine and Osborne (BBDO), 163–4
Beavan, Gerald Lee, 110, 114
Beaverbrook, Lord, 118, 174–5
Beck, Adolf, case of, 130
Bechuanaland (later: Botswana: Lesotho), 166, 167, 168, 170
Behn, Sosthenes, 102
Belgian match industry, 89
Bergholz, Dagmar, 140, 141
Bergholz, Felix, 136, 140, 141, 156, 158
Bering Sea Commission, 58
Betjeman, John, 21, 25
Bigham, Mr Justice, 13–14, 38, 41, 42–3, 44

Bigland, Reuben, 71–2, 74; *The Downfall of Horatio Bottomley*, 72
Bing, Mrs, 145, 146
Birkett, Norman, 10, 48, 62, 117, 125, 126, 127–8, 130, 133, 156, 157
Birt, Mr, Hansard General Manager, 60
Bjerre, Dr Poul, 11, 78, 94
Blackfriars Street fire, 151
Bobby's store, 116
Bodkin, Sir Archibald, DPP, 126
Boliden mine, Sweden, 100–1
Bottomley, Horatio, 9, 10, 11, 13, 15, 22, 46–77, 95, 110, 133, 186
Bowden, Mr, clerk, 62
Bow Street Magistrates Court, 72, 73, 126, 153, 154, 183
Bradlaugh, Charles, 49
Brazzaville (Congo), 168
Bredberg, Broro, 94–5
Briand, Aristide, 104
Bridge Papermills, Cullompton, 53, 54–61
Brighton Trunk Murder case, 128
Brigstocke, Mr, 37
Brit-Am (British American Corporation), 22, 32
British Bangladesh Trust, 12, 176–8, 187
British Glass Industries, 111
British Goodrich Rubber, 116
Brockway, Fenner, 162, 168
Brown, George, 168
Brown, Sir Raymond and Lady, 15
Bruce, John, 111
Buckley, Mr Justice, 36–7, 39, 41; *Buckley on the Companies Act*, 36
Buckley, Mrs (Stonehouse's secretary), 179, 184, 185, 189, 191
Burkinshaw, insurance assessor, 150
Burton Son and Sanders, 111
Butler, R. A., 166

Caledonia Copper company, 22
Callaghan, James, 166
Canada Life insurance company, 179
Capsoni, Camillo and Mrs, 142–6, 147–8, 151–2, 156, 157
Carson, Edward, 48, 68, 69
Carter and Bell, solicitors, 71
Cassalt, A. J., 19

Casswell, J. O., *A Lance for Liberty*, 70
Castle, Barbara, 167
Cederschiold, Gunnar, 89
Central African Federation, 167–8
Chapman, Clarke, & Company, 111
Charlton, Jim, 175, 179
Charterhouse Investment Group, 111
Chesworth, Donald, 176
Choudhury, Abu Sayeed, 176
Churchill, Alan, 85, 100; *The Incredible Ivar Kreuger*, 91
Churchill, Winston, 162
Church Street (Manchester) fire, 151
City Equitable, 110
City of London, 12, 20, 22, 24, 32, 112, 116, 119, 121, 122, 126, 135
Clarke, Sir Edward, 48, 56, 60
Clement Smith & Company, 52
Cohen, Mr, solicitor, 74
Cohen Laming and Hoare, brokers, 123, 124
Connoisseurs of Claret, 175
Collins, Arthur, 119
Colombia Kootenay company, 22
Colorado Coal and Iron Company, 19
Commercial Bank of London, 113–14, 115
Committee of Inspection, 37
Commonwealth Banking Corporation, 182, 183
Communist Party, British, 163
Companies Act (1901), 32, 187
Concorde aircraft, 171
Consolidated Engineering Company, 83
Cook, Joseph, accountant, 154
Cook Mahoney & Company, 148
Co-operative Movement, 163–4, 165
Corkery, Michael, 182, 185, 189, 190
Cornock, Mr, 138, 140
Corporation and General Securities Ltd, 115, 116, 119–20, 123, 131
Corporation Loans (Corporation Stock Certificates), Hatry's, 101, 107, 118–20, 121, 123–33
Court of Appeal, 73, 132, 133
Court of Criminal Appeal, 130, 189, 191
Cox, Tommy, 52
Crippen, Dr, 9
The Critic, 64, 66–7

INDEX

Crocker, J. W. T., 15
Crocker, William Charles, 135, 136–57; *Far from Humdrum*, 136–7, 142, 155
Cross, James, 148, 156, 158
Crossman, Richard, 172
Crown Agents, 176
Curtis-Bennett, Sir Henry, 127
Czechs, Stonehouse's association with, 173–4

Daily Mail, 155, 167
Daily Mirror, 154
Danckwerts, Otto, 34
Daniels, Edmund, 115–16, 122, 123, 127, 130
Darling, Mr Justice, 68, 70–1
Davies, Sir Horatio, 62–3
Dawes Loan, 98
Day, Ernest, clerk, 57
Deansgate fire (1927), 139, 143, 144–6, 147–8
Dearden, Harold, *The Fire Raisers*, 135–6, 145, 149, 153
Debenture Corporation, 53, 57, 59
Derham, John, 130
Devlin, Lord Chief Justice, 14
Diamond Match Company, 93
Dictionary of National Biography, 18, 19, 47, 108
Dixon, John Graham, 116, 123, 124, 125, 127, 130
Dollman, Charles, 52–3, 54, 55, 60
Donoughmore, Lord, 23
Douglas-Home, Alec, 162, 169
Drapery Trust, 116–17
Dufferin and Ava, Frederick Hamilton-Temple, first Marquess of, 23, 29, 32, 33–4
Dundee Trust, 115, 116
Duveen, Sir Joseph, 112
Duveen, Louis, 112
Dyer, Mrs, baby farmer, 10

'East and West Leroy' companies, 22, 32
Easum, Dalton, accountant, 53
Eden, Sir Anthony (Lord Avon), 162, 166
Edward VII, King, 22, 25
Edwards, Group-Captain Geoffrey, 170

Elam, Mr, barrister, 156
Ellis & Co., brokers, 114
Equitable Trust Company of New York, 124, 125
Ericcson Telephone Company, L. M., 100, 102
Estonia, 91, 98
Etheridge, Detective Chief Superintendent, 183
Evans, Stanley, 165
Export Promotion and Consultancy Services Limited (EPACS), 175, 179, 181–2, 186, 187, 188
Extradition (Commonwealth Countries) Act 1966, 184
Extradition Treaty (1873), 131–2

Fabriques de Soieries Ltd, 144–5, 147–8
Farman, Mr, solicitor, 59
Federation of Uganda African Farmers Ltd, 163
Ferguson, Charles, 108
Ferguson, Violet *see* Hatry
Fielden, Rev. Randle, 15, 29–30
The Financial News, 33
Financial Times, 20–1, 176; 'Men of Millions' pictorial supplement (1897), 22
Finanz Gesellschaft fur die Industrie, Switzerland, 94, 95, 97
Finlay, Robert Bannatyne, Attorney-General, 35, 37
Fire Brigade, 139
Fire Conspiracy case (R. vs. Leopold Harris and Others), 15, 135, 138–59
First World War, 87–8, 109, 110, 111, 137–8
Flower, John, broker, 35–6
Flowers, Edward, 40–1
Forgery Act (1913), 127, 131
Forsyth, Frederick, *The Day of the Jackal*, 180
France, and Ivar Kreuger, 90, 91, 97–8, 99, 100, 103, 104, 105
Frederic, Harold, *The Market Place*, 19
Freyberg, Bernard, 110
Fuller Construction Company, 83

Gaitskell, Hugh, 166, 172

Galbraith, John Kenneth, 93
Gallagher, Peter, 164
Garanta *see* N. V. Financeaelle Maatschapp Garanta
Garnsey, Sir Gilbert, 126, 127, 128
Garolfo, Theresa, 15
Garrett Corporation of America, 182, 186, 188, 191
Garvin, James Louis, 107, 115
General Omnibus Company, 117
The Gentle Art of Exploiting Gullibility, 47, 76
Germany, and Kreuger, 86, 90, 91, 92, 98–9, 100, 102
Gialdini, John, 116, 122, 123, 126, 131, 132–3
Gibney, Dr Gerard, 190
Gilbert, Mr (Simon Wolfe's father-in-law), 153
Gill, Mr, barrister, 54, 59, 60
Glendyne, Robert Nivison, first Baron, 119
Global Imex, 175, 179, 187
Gloucester Corporation Loan, 120, 123, 124, 125
Glowacki, Dr, 91
Goddard, Lord Chief Justice, 14
Gonzales, Doctor, of Milan, 132
Gore-Brown, Mr, 34
Goswell Road fire (1929), 139, 146
Gough-Calthorpe, Lieutenant-General the Hon. S. J., 23, 24, 34
Gould, Harry (H. Gould & Co.), 136, 147, 150, 156, 158
Grant, Inspector, Fraud Squad, 178
Grantham, Mr Justice, 64, 65
Grantly, Lord, 122
Greece, 91
Guest Keen and Nettlefold, 176
Guggenheim, Untermeyer and Marshall, 38
Guildhall, 62
Gundry, Alfred, 188–9
Gunnison Iron and Coal Company, 19

Haigh, John George, 9
Hall, Marshall, 48, 49, 72, 128
Hall, Mr (owner of Cullompton Mill), 54, 56–7

Halsbury, Hardinge Giffard, Lord, 49
Hamilton & Hansell, 88
Hansard Publishing and Printing Union, 52–61, 62, 64, 65, 66
Harris, David, 135, 136, 145–6, 158
Harris, Leopold, 9, 10, 13, 15, 135–59
Harris & Co., L. H., 135, 140, 145
Harrison, John, 52
Harrods, 111
Hastings, Sir Patrick, 48, 128
Hatchards of Piccadilly, 134
Hatherill, Detective Sergeant, 156–7, 158
Hatry, Clarence Charles, 9, 11, 12, 13, 14, 15, 89, 98, 101, 106–34, 174–5, 178
Hatry, Mrs Clarence (*née* Violet Ferguson: 1st wife), 108
Hatry, Julius, 107, 108
Hawke, Mr Justice, 158–9
Hawkins, Mr Justice, 47, 54, 55–7, 58, 60, 61
Hayes, Michael, 175, 179, 186–7, 191
Hayward, Dr Lionel, 190
Heath, Edward, 174
Heath, Neville George, 9
Hemmerde, Mr, KC, 68
Henie, Sonja, 103
Henning, Sigmund, 104
Herivel, William, 148–9, 158
Hess, Henry (Hess case: 1902), 49, 64–8
Hewart, Lord Chief Justice, 14, 130
Hooley, Ernest Terah, 10, 22, 115, 133
Houston, Henry, 47
Hoover, President Herbert, 103
Howard, Mr, stockbroker, 74
Hugo, Victor, *Les Misérables*, 129
Humphreys, Travers (Mr Justice Humphreys), 55–6, 73–5, 76, 155, 156, 157, 158
Hungary, 91
Hyman, Alan, 47, 48, 51, 52

India, 89–90, 175
International Match Corporation (IMCO), 93–4, 96
insurance: fire, 137, 138–59; life, 179, 185, 189, 191

INDEX

International Nickel transaction, 39
International Telephone and Telegraph (IT & T), 102
Inveresk Paper Company, 116
Isaacs, Sir Henry, 52, 53, 54, 56, 59, 60
Isaacs, Joseph, 52, 53, 54, 55, 57, 59–60
Isaacs, Rufus, 24, 31, 34, 38–42, 48, 49, 130; son of, 22, 28, 41
Italian Bonds, Kreuger's forgery of, 101–2, 103–4

Janomot (Bengali newspaper), 177–8
Jarvis, Louis, 136, 143, 144, 145, 147–8, 158
Jarvis, Mrs, 146
Jeffreys, Judge, 14
Jelama, Mr, wine merchant, 74
Jenkins, Roy, 169
Jesse, Tennyson, 9
Joel, Woolf, 22
John Bull, 46, 73; libel case (1911), 68–71
John Bull Investment Trust, 74
Joint Stock Trust and Finance Corporation, 51, 61–4
Jonkoping-Vulcan combine, 87, 88, 89
Jordahl, Anders, 83, 86, 93
Jowitt, Sir William, Attorney-General, 125, 127, 131, 134
Jubilee Cotton Mills swindle, 10, 133
Jute Trust, 111–12, 113, 118

Kahn, Julius, 84
Kalmar Trust (United Swedish Match Factories), 87–8, 89, 92, 99–100
Katz, Richard, 91–2
Katzenstein, Henriette (Mrs Julius Hatry), 107
Kegan Paul, C., 52, 60
Kennard, Coleridge, 52, 53
Kenya, 162, 163, 168
Kenyatta, Jomo, 163
King, Horace *see* Maybray-King
Kirkwood Stone & Company, 124
Kleinworts, merchant bankers, 115
Klondyke Gold Fields, 21
Koudelka, Vlado, 173
Kreuger, Ernst August, 80, 84

Kreuger, Ivar, 9, 11, 12, 78–105, 170, 178
Kreuger, Peter Edvard ('Consul Kreuger'), 79–80
Kreuger, Torsten, 87
Kreuger & Jennings, shipping firm, 79
Kreuger and Toll, 84–7, 96, 101, 105; US subsidiary, 93
Kreuger and Toll Building, 86–7
Kuss, Henry, 170
Kylsant, Lord, 10

Labour Party *see* Stonehouse, John
Labour Party Conference (1961), 168–9
Lagerman, Alexander, 80
Laker, Freddie, 170
Lake View Consols, 21, 22, 23, 30, 39, 40, 178
Lake View Mines, 10–11, 33
Lambert, George, 35
Landru, Desiré, 9
Lang, Gordon, 129
Lange, Karl, 95, 96
Larceny Act (1861), 36, 37
Laski, Harold, 161
Latvia, 91, 98
Law Trust and Guarantee Society, 68
Leadville mining boom, 18
Lee, Fred, 170
Lefort, Alan, 187, 188, 189
Lehmann, E. G., 95
Lennox-Boyd, 166
Lethbridge, Sir Roper, 52
Lever, John, architect, 63
Lever Street fire (1929), 146, 150, 158
Levie, Leonard, 51–2, 62, 63
Levin, Bernard, 184–5, 191
Lewis, Sir George, 20, 38, 39, 42, 43
Leyland Motors, 110
Liechtenstein, 94–5, 97, 184
Littorin, Krister, 104
Lloyd-George, David, 21
Lloyds Bank, 123, 181, 182, 188
Lloyds Underwriters, 135, 136, 138, 139, 140, 141
Lock, Lord, 23
'Loddon Valley' company, 22–3, 33
London and Globe Finance Corporation ('Old Globe'), 22, 28

London Assurance, 112
London Co-operative Society, 163–4, 165, 173
London Public Omnibus Company, 111
London Salvage Corps, 136, 139, 143, 152
London School of Economics, 161
Lothbury, Wright's office in, 22, 24, 26, 30
Luther, Herr, German Finance Minister, 99

McBride, Mrs Bridget, 186
McBride, Neil, 180
McCall, Mr, KC, 64, 66–7
McClure, G. B., 134
Machiavelli, *Il Principe*, 88
Maclery, Mr, company director, 23
Macmillan, Harold (Lord Stockton), 162, 166, 167, 169
Macnamara, Robert, 170
McRae Curtice & Co., 52
Maidstone prison, 133
Mancini, Tony, 128
March, Lord (later Duke of Richmond), 110
Marchesano, Doctor, 132
Margaret Street fire (1926), 143, 144, 146, 156
Markham, Mrs Jean, 186
Markham, Joseph Arthur *see* Stonehouse, John
Marks, Bernard, 136, 150, 151, 158
Marks, Laurence, 164
Mason, Sir Josiah, Orphanage of, 46
match industry, Kreuger's, 80, 86, 87–92, 93, 97, 98
Mathews, George, 138, 139–40
Matthews, Charles, 54, 58
Mau-Mau rising, 163
Maybray-King, Horace, 161
Maybrick, Mrs, murderer, 10
Melbourne, Stonehouse in, 179–80, 182, 183
Metro Radio Ltd fire, 150
Miami, Stonehouse goes missing in, 178
Mildoon, Donald Clive *see* Stonehouse, John
Mildoon, Mrs Elsie, 186

Miles, Captain Brynmore Eric, 136, 143–4, 152–3, 158–9
Molloy, Mr, MP, 179
Monckton Commission (1960), 166
More, Sir George, 25
Morgan, J. P., 97–8, 99, 102
Muir, Sir Richard, 38, 47, 62, 73; *Memoirs*, 18–19
Mullens & Company, brokers, 119
Mussolini, Benito, 101, 132, 138
Myrstedt & Stern building Stockholm, 84–5

National Council for Civil Liberties, 184, 191
National News, 74
New Globe Company, 22, 23, 29–42, 87, 178
Newman, Mr, of Department of Trade and Industry, 178
New Orleans, Kreuger in, 82
New York Times, 17, 19, 37
News of the World, 106
Nickel Corporation, 23
Nivison and Company, 119
Norman, Montague, 98, 119, 122
North, Colonel, 22
Northern Rhodesia, 166, 167, 168
Norwich Union insurance, 179
N. V. Financeaelle Maatschapp Garanta (Amsterdam), 95–6

Oak Investment Corporation, 115, 116
Observer, Sunday, 107, 117, 124, 132, 164, 173
Odhams Press, 68
O'Hagan, Osborne, 71, 73–4
Old Bailey (Central Criminal Court), 9, 38, 43, 72, 154; Bottomley's trial at, 73–6; Fire Conspiracy trial (1933), 154–9; Hatry's trial at (1930), 106, 126–31; Stonehouse's trial at (1976), 180, 185–91
Oliver, Roland, 15, 116, 127, 149, 150, 155
Onieko, Achieng, trial of, 163
Orton, Arthur *see* Tichborne claimant
Otter-Barry, Mr, of Sun Insurance, 141, 144

INDEX

Owen, William, insurance assessor, 150
Oxford Street fire (1930), 146, 156

Pace, Mrs, acquittal of, 128
Page, Mr, of Austin Friars Trust, 124, 125
Pasch, Gustav, 80
Passmore, Stanley, 127, 128
Patmore, Deighton, 109
Pearson, Michael, 15; *The Millionaire Mentality*, 107, 109, 111–12, 123
Pelham-Clinton, Lord Henry Edward, 23
Peru, 91–2
Pettifer, Dr, 57
Philadelphia (USA), Wright in, 18–19
Philadelphia Mining Exchange, 19
Phillips, John, 52, 54
Phoenix Insurance Company, 179
Photomaton Ltd, 122
Pinners Hall, 116, 128
Pirrie, Lord, 43–4
Planet Insurance Company, 110
Plessey Group, 176
Poincaré, Henri, 97–8
Poland, 91, 95–6
Poland Street fire (1931), 140, 141, 146
Post Office Workers' strike, 173
Prevention of Fraud (Investments) Act (1958), 12, 177
Price, Tudor, 188
Priest, Harry, 136, 138–40, 141, 142, 143, 150, 158
Punch, 21
Purdy and Henderson, 83

Radclyfte, Raymond, *Wealth and Wildcats*, 28
Redhill-Cullompton transaction, 53, 54–61
Retail Trade Securities Ltd, 115
Reynolds News, 168
Rhodesia/Southern Rhodesia (later Zimbabwe), 166, 167, 168
Ribblesdale, Lord, 110
Richard Glen & Co., 149, 150
Rigby, Sir John, Solicitor-General, 47, 54, 58
Riksbank, 100–1

Riley, Leonard, 136, 151, 158
Robertson, Sir William, 23
Ronald, Francis Joseph, 68–70
Ronval Properties, 175
Roome, H. D., 73
Rossland Great Western company, 22
Royal Courts of Justice (Civil Law Courts), Strand, 9, 38, 43, 44
Royal Insurance Company, 179, 191
Roylance, Colonel Robert, 141
Russell, Sir Charles, Attorney-General, 47, 54, 55, 57, 58
Russia, 86, 98
Rydbeck, Oskar, 87, 99, 104, 105

Salter, Mr Justice ('Dry Salter'), 13, 73
Satterthwaite, Mr, insurance assessor, 150, 158
Saturday Evening Post, 103
Saudi Arabia, sale of Lightning fighters to, 170
Scandanaviska (Swedish Credit Bank), 87, 99, 101
Schacht, Dr, 99
Schwab, Charles M., 19
Scotland Yard, 139, 156; Fraud Squad, 178, 183
Scottish Drapery Corporation, 116
Scottish Union & National Insurance Company, 143
Scrimgeour, Messrs J. and A., 119
Secretarial Services Ltd, 115, 116
Seddon, Frederick, 9
Seretse Khama, 168, 170
Shaplen, Robert, 93
Sierra Grande Mine Company, 19
'Silence Room', Kreuger's, 89, 90
Simon, John, 71
Smallman, Sir George, 62
Smith, Alfonso Austin, 130
Smith, F. E., KC, 68–9, 70
Smith, Frederick, 129
Smith, George Joseph, 9
Smith, Harold, barrister, 68, 70
Smith, Madeleine, murderer, 10
Snake River, Wright's trip to, 18, 82
Soloveytchik, George, 78, 80, 85, 92, 102–3
South Africa, 166, 168

Spensley, Mr, company director, 23
Staining Lane fire (1930), 139, 146, 148, 149, 156
Standard Exploration Company, 23, 32, 39, 40
Stanhope Gate, London house of Hatry at, 118, 123, 124
Stapleton, John, 191
state monopoly loan agreements, Kreuger's, 90–2, 95, 97, 98–100
Steel Industries of Great Britain Ltd, 120–1, 122, 123, 124
Stella Maris case, 130
Stewart, C. J., official receiver, 53, 58–9, 60, 61
Stock Exchange, London, 13, 20, 23, 122, 125, 126, 143
Stockholm *see* Kreuger, Ivar
Stockholm Civic Hall, 85
Stockholm Exhibition, sliding track, 85–6
Stockholm Technical High School, 81
Stonehouse, Barbara, 162
Stonehouse, John Thomson, 9, 10, 11, 12, 160–92; *My Trial*, 15
Stubbins, Inspector, 126
Suez crisis, 165–6
The Sun, 65, 67
Sunday Evening Telegraph, 74
Sunday Express, 106, 128
Sunday Times, 177, 178, 181
Sun Insurance Office, 141, 144
Swan and Edgar, 111, 116
Sweden *see* Kreuger, Ivar
Swedish Match company, 88–90, 93, 96
Swindon Corporation Loan, 120, 123, 124–5
Switzerland, 94, 97
Sybarita, Wright's yacht, 25
Sydar, Amelia von (Peter Kreuger's wife), 80
Symons, Julian, 15, 47
Syracuse University (USA), 83–4
Systems and Consultancy Services, 175

Tabor, Albert, 116, 123, 126, 127, 130
Tanganyika (Tanzania), 167
Taunton Grammar School, 160–1
Tichborne Claimant (Arthur Orton), 9, 48
The Times, 30, 32, 44, 66–7, 72, 99, 105, 132, 150, 162–3, 169, 170, 172, 177, 183, 191–2
Times Literary Supplement, 160
Toll, Paul, 84, 86
Treasury Counsel group, 73
Truscott, Sir George, 132
Turner, Sir Charles, 65, 66

Uganda, 162–3
Union Industrie A. G. (Liechtenstein), 95, 97
United Cigar and Tobacco Company, 150–1
United States, 116; and Ivar Kreuger, 82–4, 90, 92–4, 96, 97, 98–9, 102–3, 105; Wall Street crash (1929), 116, 126; Whitaker Wright in, 17–19, 37–8
United Steel Companies Ltd, 121, 123, 178
United Swedish Match Factories *see* The Kalmar Trust
Untermeyer, Samuel, 37–8
Upper Brook Street, London house of Hatry in, 112

Vanoni & Company, 52
Vera Cruz, Kreuger's trip to, 82–3
Vickers, Henry, 52
Victoria, Queen, 22
Victoria State Police, 183
Victory Bond Club case, 73, 74–6

Wakefield Corporation Loan, 120, 123, 124, 125, 129
Wall Street crash (1929), 116, 126
Walpole's, shorthand writers, 48
Walton, Lawson, Attorney-General, 38, 41, 42, 44
Waring & Gillow, 87
War Stock Combination case, 73–6
Webster, Kate, 10
Wednesbury, Stonehouse elected Labour MP for, 165, 169
Welensky, Sir Roy, 167
Wellesley, Francis, 133–4
Wendler, Anton, 101–2

INDEX

West Australian Exploration and Finance Corporation, 22
Westminster Bank, 123
Westralians, 21, 22
Westwood, Walter Ernest, 150–1, 158
White, Arnold, 37
Whitehead, Sir Edgar, 167
Whitely, Cecil, 127
Whiting, R. C. (Bobbie), 152
Wigg, George, 165
Wigoder, Lord, 185
Williams, Owen Wyatt, 75
Wilson, Harold, 169, 170, 171, 172, 173
Windt, Harry de, 21
Witley Park (formerly Lea Park), Surrey, Wright's estate, 15, 25–8, 43–4; underwater apartment, 15, 27–8, 29
Wolfe, Ernest, 136, 149, 156, 158
Wolfe, Simon, 136, 149, 153, 158
Wood-Milne Rubber Tyre Company, 116
Worters, Mr, auditor, 24
Wright, Inspector, 178
Wright, Whitaker, 9, 10–11, 13–14, 15, 17–45, 87, 178, 184
Wyman & Sons, 52

Yandell, Chief Inspector, 153, 158
Yorkshire General, insurance company, 179
York Street 'twin' fire, 148–50, 153, 158
Young Loan, 98–9
Yugoslavia, 91

Zabotnik, Czech, 173